ACTING for Life
A textbook on acting

Jack Frakes

MERIWETHER PUBLISHING
A division of Pioneer Drama Service, Inc.
Denver, Colorado

Meriwether Publishing
A division of Pioneer Drama Service, Inc.
PO Box 4267
Englewood, CO 80155

www.pioneerdrama.com

Editor: Arthur L. Zapel
Assistant editor: Audrey Scheck
Cover design: Jan Melvin
Interior photos: Jack Frakes

Library of Congress Cataloging-in-Publication Data

Frakes, Jack.
  Acting for life : a textbook on acting / Jack Frakes.-- 1st ed.
    p. cm.
  ISBN 978-1-56608-107-8 (pbk.)
1. Acting. I. Title.
  PN2061.F68 2005
  792.02'8--dc22

                                                    2005009006

        7   8   9   20   21   22

*This textbook is dedicated
to my wife, Janet,
and the pleasant memories
of the countless movies
and plays we have
shared together.*

Acknowledgments

There have been so many people who have been valuable influences; it's hard to remember them all. While some are now deceased, each in his or her own way gave me something that is part of this textbook. In particular, I wish to note and thank the following people.

From grades six through nine, Mary MacMurtrie and her Tucson Children's Theatre, which was one of the few in the nation at that time, guided me in key roles for stage and radio and famous stories from the past.

In college, Dr. Klonda Lynn, head of the Speech Department at the University of Arizona, generously spent hours of her personal time teaching me to understand the value of images and honesty in delivering lines. These experiences are amplified all throughout this text, and I'm extremely grateful.

Professor Hubert Heffner of Stanford University gave scholarly lectures and thoughtful analysis to Aristotle's *Poetics* on the structure of drama. Much of that material is sifted into this text's material on elements and structure of drama.

As an associate teacher with Lloyd Roberts at Tucson High School, I learned the practical side of operating a busy high school drama program. I learned from the knowledge and skills he had developed in his army theatre experiences and his many years of teaching in educational theatre.

Rosemary Gipson, of the University of Arizona Drama Department, gave me an overview of curriculum offerings that are needed for a high school drama teacher. Although she was a scholar, her creative drama and theatre games played a large part in her teachings. Her influence is found in many areas of this textbook.

In appreciation of the fellow high school teachers and friends in Tucson, Arizona who, when I became drama coordinator for the district, were willing to field test many of my creative drama exercises, use ideas on directing and produce many of my original plays. Those with whom I worked most frequently and still think of fondly as friends are: Bill Burgess, LoRetta Cona, Karen Husted, Robin (Robert L.) Lee, and James N. (Nick) Livieratos.

To one and all … Thank you.

UTRGV MSA

Mathematics & Science

Academy

302017

Contents

Illustrations:

Preface
For the Educator: The View Inside

I suppose it all began in Miss Bannon's fifth grade class. For some reason unknown even today, the school district of Tucson, Arizona decided to have every fifth grade class in town put on an improvised production of *Hansel and Gretel*. The plan for Sam Hughes Elementary was to have 5A present Act I, 5B Act II and 5C, Miss Bannon's fifth grade class, to present Act III. After everyone in the class improvised Hansel, I tried out. Acting was easy because I had been acting out movies for years by myself in my living room. I was cast as Hansel for Act III, the scenes where Hansel and Gretel are captured by the witch, held in a cage and fattened, and finally push her into the oven.

After practicing a whole semester for this twenty-minute improvisation we eventually presented the production for appreciative and doting parents at our own elementary school. It went well for this type of event and would have been fine if it had ended right there.

But no. The school district decided to take Act I from Carrillo Elementary, Act II from Roskruge and Act III from Sam Hughes and perform this improvised production of *Hansel and Gretel* in the Tucson High School football stadium on a warm night in mid-May! It was outdoors with microphones and the audience at least 50 yards away. And we never once rehearsed together!

Well, at this point in time I can only imagine how awful it must have been. I can also understand why the school district decided to abandon the whole project the following year and many years thereafter.

However, it didn't end there for me. I was very fortunate to live in the same town with Mary MacMurtrie, a well-known teacher of children's theatre. Since I had enjoyed playing Hansel, my parents signed me up for summer classes with Mary MacMurtrie's Children's Theatre. For three years I did poems and monologs in back yards and living rooms, radio dramas on Saturday mornings, one-act plays at local churches and full-length productions once a year in the spring at the Temple of Music and Art. It was a great experience and a wonderful way to spend grades six through nine.

After acting in more plays in high school, and then college, while I was majoring in psychology with a philosophy and history minor, I became serious about teaching drama as a lifetime career. This led to studying speech, drama and theatre at the University of Arizona, San Diego State College and Stanford University.

Upon earning my education degree, I had the opportunity to teach high school drama — only drama — in my own studio theatre for fourteen years. During this time I created countless acting exercises, directed many, many productions, wrote original scripts and published four short plays with Samuel French. Two of these, *Final Dress Rehearsal* and *Once Upon A Playground*, continue to be performed by numerous high schools and junior highs. Even more importantly, I had some wonderful students who have become lifelong friends.

When Tucson Unified School District expanded its arts programs, I had the privilege to serve as drama coordinator for the whole district for eight years. During this time I was able to develop curriculum materials and conduct workshops for teachers from kindergarten through twelfth grade. This also gave me the special opportunity to work with some excellent, highly qualified drama teachers in the nine high schools and sixteen junior highs in the district to create new exercises and activities for their classes.

Once, at a Thespian conference, when I was serving as moderator, some teacher asked about a particular subject on acting. I said, "I have four pages on that subject, and I will send them to you." At that point another teacher, with whom I had worked frequently, spoke up and said, "He has four pages on everything." As I smiled I realized that I perhaps had the makings of a whole drama textbook.

Moving to California, I served as artistic director of a community theatre in South San Francisco for six years. This allowed me to work with adult actors in the community, which was a slightly different, but an equally valuable and rewarding theatre experience. During this period I became a member of Dramatists Guild and the Screen Actors Guild.

Over the years, I've continued writing new exercises and activities for the classroom, and my collection of these materials has grown ever larger until they have presented somewhat of a storage problem. Since I almost never throw any of these away, I now have stacks and shelves and boxes and file cabinets full of games, activities, explanations and exercises on acting. I have written and collected these for years and years in the thought that I would someday take time out to actually write this textbook.

I feel truly fortunate to have had a variety of theatre and drama experiences. I just needed to decide which were the best of all these materials, then organize and unify everything into a cohesive textbook on acting for students in high school and college. The hardest part has been deciding on the optimum sequence and what *not* to include.

But now I've done it. This is the result. So, here 'tis. I hope it's helpful.

Introduction

Acting for Life: A textbook on acting is aimed at high school and college level drama students. It is designed in scope for both advanced students who want to improve their techniques and beginning students who want to explore the experience of acting and develop basic skills for the first time.

It is also for the English teacher who is assigned (or chooses) to teach drama and needs a variety of materials for acting, as well as for the experienced drama teacher with extensive training.

Through a chapter-by-chapter planned sequence of explanations, exercises and activities, the student can learn a variety of skills and techniques for acting and gain knowledge of related drama subjects. These step-by-step approaches offer the student a full range of experiences that should not only enhance acting abilities but also increase self-awareness and cooperation among classmates.

Beginning subject areas include: sense awareness, use of body and voice, Hamlet's advice to the players, improvisation, listening and relating to other actors, memorizing and rehearsing, basic blocking and character relations. Advanced chapters include character development with emphasis on character traits and emotions, images, establishing objectives and intentions, script analysis and acting for film.

Just as students take music classes in order to sing or learn to play an instrument, or take art classes in order to learn to draw or paint or sculpt, so too, students take drama classes in order to learn to act and play a wide range of characters.

Through the experience of playing characters in a variety of scenes, these exercises also offer drama's relation to life experiences that not only guide students into better understanding of some processes of acting, but also offer greater self-awareness and better understanding of others in a rapidly changing and ethnically diverse society.

While a great deal of thought has gone into the best sequence in which to present the material in this acting textbook, it is not necessarily an optimum approach for all classes on all levels of drama at all times. It was approached in terms of a natural progression of needed skills and a hierarchy of difficulty. But it is so interrelated that there are references in many chapters to other areas that expand current ideas or are reminders to the actor of former material that reinforces the current activities.

Most of the material is highly accessible for all drama students. Some of the early explanations and exercises may seem too simple for older or advanced students while some later chapters may seem too difficult for younger students who are experiencing classroom acting for the first time. In all cases, the teacher needs to use discretion as to what is appropriate for a particular group and the order in which the material is presented.

There is no way to fully anticipate all the possible situations or variations of valid approaches in advance. Astute teachers will no doubt be able to find an optimum approach for their students to learn the joy of acting and self-discovery. *In acting, as in life,* the interaction of human relations experiences can offer enlightening insights for never-ending personal growth.

Part A
Basic Acting Skills

Chapter 1
Welcome to Drama

"One of my teachers wrote about me:
'This boy shows great originality ... which must be curbed at all costs.'"
— Peter Ustinov, actor and playwright

"A person learns significantly only those things which he perceives as being
involved in the maintenance of, or enhancement of, the structure of self."
— *Being a Person*, by Carl Rogers, psychologist

Why are you interested in drama?

- Someone talked you into "taking drama." A counselor or teacher or parent suggested it. Or, your friends are in a class, and you were curious.
- You like to act. Acting is why most students take drama. Acting is a natural activity. Acting can be fun! There is something special about playing a character that is not you.
- You want to meet interesting people and expand your social life. This is a very good reason.
- You need to express yourself creatively. Drama is a form of self-expression and communication.
- You want to be a part of a group of people who have the same interest. Working with other people for a common goal can help you feel the satisfaction of belonging to a group.
- You are shy. And certainly many people are. Perhaps you have a difficult time being assertive and expressing yourself. In drama you can play another person, assume the personality of your character and feel what it is like to act like another person in a safe environment.
- You need to gain attention, or be noticed by others. Performing publicly can give you this satisfaction. Some students start with this need and later find deeper values in pursuit of drama.
- You admire some actor or character played by an actor.
- And/or, perhaps ... well, who knows why? It could be some combination of the above or none of the above. But you're in a drama class learning something about acting, something about other people and life and hopefully something about yourself.

7

Discussion: Why are you taking drama? Who are some of your favorite actors and actresses? Are they on TV, in the movies or on stage? What is it about these people that you like? Do you like them for the roles they play or the people they appear to be behind the roles? Can you separate the people from the characters in the plays?

For whatever reason, you are here. You should be able to develop personal values and life skills through drama that are not always obvious to many outside the field of drama. In addition, the value to each person developing skills in interpersonal relationships is immeasurable. Both males and females may receive these skills equally and learn to work together cooperatively. Because many of these valuable skills involve personal growth, they are not measurable by some standardized test.

Life Values in Drama, Sports and World of Work

Many of the claims made for the value of sports in school and the skills they develop through participation also apply to participation in a drama program. Also, many of the skills asked for by employers and needed in the world of work are personal and people skills that are taught or are inherent by participation in a drama program.

There are many similarities between participation in drama and participation in sports and workplace employment.

- All are aimed at being democratic in giving opportunities to skilled people who are chosen for their knowledge or talent.
- All have a structure in which there is someone in charge from whom there is guidance: coach, director / teacher or manager / supervisor.
- All are assigned to a position or a place in the structure such as:
    — a guard, forward, center or pitcher, etc.
    — a character or role in a play
    — a job in a department with duties
- All need to work cooperatively as team members, interact and be supportive to other team members.
- All need to assume leadership when called for.
- All need to learn to define and sometimes defend territory and the team or institution that is your area of concern.

- All need to learn the rules and regulations for your position.
- All call for establishing goals and meeting timelines and deadlines.
- All perform in front of people: sports fans, audience, customers and staff.
- All call for a high level of performance in the face of stress and tension and need to improvise creatively when necessary.
- All call for and can develop: a sense of self-worth, poise, confidence, self-discipline, responsibility, commitment, dedication, perseverance, communication, respect for authority and peers and acceptance of both success and disappointment.

An education in drama can offer many real skills and real values so urgently needed in our society. The very nature of drama can offer the most meaningful and relevant personal growth experiences in today's educational curriculum. So, where do you start to learn these valuable acting and life skills? You have already begun!

Who are you?

You are a product of your heredity and your environment. You are a composite of many people. Most of your physical, vocal and character traits originated with your family and were perhaps later modified and developed by a variety of different influences and experiences with friends and community.

Who you are — your basic personality, your character traits, emotions and values — is expressed through your body (posture, movement, facial expressions and gestures) and your voice (qualities, speech patterns, accents and diction). At the same time that you may be similar to your family and friends, you are also a very unique and ever changing individual.

In a sense, *you are already an actor*, because in life, everyone is an actor. Everyone plays roles. You play different roles — act or relate differently — to different people in different situations at different times. When you talk to people, you improvise dialog based on your personality, the other person's personality, and your relation to the person to whom you are talking. By taking a course in drama you will be able to try out a number of different roles in the safety of the classroom.

What is acting for stage?

"Acting is living truthfully under an imaginary set of circumstances."
— Sanford Meisner, teacher

*" ... the purpose of playing, whose end, both at first and now, was
and is, to hold, as 'twere, the mirror up to nature ... "*
— *Hamlet*, by William Shakespeare

In acting, as in life, characters are defined through their physical description and their character traits and emotions. Playing a character other than yourself may involve learning and developing new and different uses of your body and voice to show these different character traits and emotions to an audience.

An actor's primary function is to communicate with an audience. This communication involves an actor listening, thinking the thoughts and feeling the emotions and motivations of another person or character. This character is communicated to an audience through the use of the actor's two basic tools: the body and the voice, which are enhanced by thoughts and emotions. The playing of a character other than yourself can not only be an exciting emotional experience, but should offer you greater understanding of yourself and others. And, it is one of the most important reasons for drama education.

Through explanations, exercises and playing different characters in scenes, you will have the opportunity to experience a variety of acting theories and techniques and develop your own skillful approaches to playing a variety of characters.

Studying and testing these many techniques in order to experience how it feels to play different types of characters is the principal activity of this textbook.

What skills, theories and techniques are needed?

There is no one formula, no one magic way to act. No one technique can make you an actor. In fact, generally speaking, no *one* technique fits *all* actors in *all* situations. And, no one technique or method fits even *one* actor in *all* situations. And, in fact, no one technique or method or approach fits *one* actor in all parts of even *one* situation. This is because, *in acting, as in life*, people are all different, and they react differently in different situations at different times. You will need a variety of different techniques to solve different problems. This textbook is dedicated to exploring a variety of skills and techniques. (Unlike tube socks, one size does not fit all.)

What is your relation to drama?

Of all the arts, drama is closest to everyday life, because drama is concerned with the study of the human personality, of people and relationships, wants, needs, hopes, fears, values, emotions, problems, conflicts and what happens to people. To analyze characters in plays is to better understand other people and yourself in life.

Studying acting and playing diverse characters should give you a greater awareness of the feelings of others, more acceptance of diverse personalities in a diverse world and, hopefully, make you a better person. A really good actor doesn't separate life experiences from acting experiences. Ultimately, drama is not just about acting and working on a play; it's really a whole way of seeing your world and living your life.

> *"All the world's a stage,*
> *And all the men and women merely players:*
> *They have their exits and their entrances;*
> *And one man in his time plays many parts ... "*
> — *As You Like It,* by William Shakespeare

So, whoever you are, or whatever your reasons are for participating in drama, this textbook should help you to achieve your goals. And, here 'tis. Break a leg! In "theater-speak," this means *good luck!*

Chapter 2
Orientation: Body, Voice and the Senses

Warm-up Exercises

A leader performs some of these movements and the group follows. These should take about five minutes at the beginning.

Stretching

Slowly stretch your leg muscles, arms and back, sideways and up. Then, slowly stretch your neck sideways, forward, back and up. Then, slowly reach your whole body out and up. Then, gently shake all the tension out of the arms and hands, then legs and feet.

Shaking and Moving

Shake all over, bend the arms, wiggle your fingers, wave. Bounce an imaginary ball in as many different ways as possible: slow, fast, high, low, etc. Shake all over, bend the legs, climb a ladder, walk on slippery sidewalk, in sticky mud, on stilts. Jog in place. Skate on ice or on roller skates. Pedal a bicycle. Flap the arms, bend the body, flop and relax. Can you look like a crane, turtle, giraffe, or monkey? Chop wood, jump a rope, box with a shadow.

Personal Feelings Involving Body, Emotions and Images

Below are phrases that are in people's everyday vocabulary. As each phrase is read, experience the feeling as best you can. Close your eyes and take each phrase slowly, allowing time to feel and react to the following expressions:

lose your head	no backbone
blood curdling	sorehead
my aching back	save face
spine tingling	keep in touch
shoulder a burden	tight fisted
shrug it off	no guts
give me a hand	itching to do it
two-faced	knuckle down

get a kick out of it

elbow your way

pain in the neck

brokenhearted

stiff upper lip

nosey

hard-nosed

yellow belly

stand on your own two feet

grit your teeth

sweat of your brow

get a leg up

nose out of joint

bleeding heart

gets under your skin

thin-skinned

butterflies in the stomach

Exercise: Emotional Response

React freely to character traits, emotions or moods. You are happy, shy, timid, grouchy, sad, proud, bored, etc. (See Chapter 13 for a longer list.)

Relaxation

You've barely started and we're already talking about relaxing. But, *in acting, as in life,* it is an important factor in performing well.

Whether we're talking about sports, taking a test or performing as an actor on-stage, you coordinate better and think better and perform better if you are fully prepared, physically relaxed and mentally alert.

To begin the class with a warm-up exercise helps everyone relax, unifies the group and focuses on the activities to follow. Warm-up activities are determined by the needs of the group. Different leaders can be chosen on different days to lead the warm-up.

Warm-up: Relaxation Through Breathing

Breathe in through your nose slowly and deeply while imagining you are inhaling positive emotions of oxygen, energy and power. Then, exhale slowly through your mouth and imagine you are getting rid of tension, fatigue, toxins, and negative emotions. Continue this and feel yourself begin to relax and reduce stress.

Warm-up: Yawning

It's possible your breathing exercises will relax you so much you will naturally begin to yawn. Even if it's not natural, yawn three or four times and notice how this also can help you relax.

The Senses

These are activities in experiencing: *seeing, hearing, smelling, tasting, touching* or *feeling.*

Exercise: Topsy-Turvy

Lean back and look up at the ceiling. Imagine what your world would be like for you if everything were turned "topsy-turvy" and the floor was the ceiling and the ceiling was the floor. Imagine what it would be like just going through or over the top of doors and walking around light fixtures. Then, look at, and focus on, one wall becoming the floor and the other wall the ceiling. Take time to get the full image of the experience. What would that be like?

Exercise: Observing and Counting Things

Members of the class go on-stage and are asked to count tiles in the floor or ceiling or count chairs in the room.

Exercise: Observing Colors and Patterns

Count the people in your class who have a touch of red in their clothing. Blue. Green. Yellow. What other interesting colors or patterns do you see?

Exercise: Camera Focus

With your hand coiled or a sheet of paper rolled up so that you can look through either one as if they were telescopes, explore the world around you. This will be like a camera's eye view of things. But you should search for an interesting subject and focus on it, getting it at "just the right angle to make it interesting." This might be particularly interesting where there are a lot of little items to focus on, such as the shop, the library or the classroom. You also might focus on other people in the class such as someone's face, hands or a pattern in their clothing. Then, you can make imaginary photographs of people, their faces as seen looking down, straight on, up or with a change of lighting.

Exercise: Observing People's Eyes

Count the people in your class who have blue eyes, brown eyes, green, hazel, black, etc. Try to remember how many of each, and who had them. Compare with other members of the class.

Discussion: In the previous activities, were you counting, looking, listening as yourself, or as a character? Were these natural activities or tasks, or was it acting?

Since you were focusing on the objective, you were probably doing these tasks as yourself. Therefore, it was natural and truthful and believable. Being involved in an activity or stage business when you are playing a character can help you alleviate self-consciousness. (See "Stage Business" in Chapter 4.)

Remember this as you do the exercises in this book and strive toward being natural and truthful. Acting shouldn't look like acting.

Listening to Sounds

Exercise: The Environment
Close your eyes and listen. Listen for people breathing, sounds from other classrooms, shuffling feet and voices in the hallway or distance, cars going by, planes overhead, etc.; whatever your environment offers.

Exercise: Knock, Knock
Close your eyes. One person knocks in a particular way to indicate character or emotional state: happy, shy, brash, confident, aggressive, hesitant, old friend, first date, sinister, in danger, etc., and the group listens. This may be repeated several times. The person doing the knocking can add to the situation by having an arm full of groceries and having to knock awkwardly or with a foot. After the knocking is complete, discuss what you heard in terms of type of character, the emotions or the situation.

Exercise: Footsteps
Close your eyes. One person moves across the floor, using his/her feet to tell something about the type of person: old, young, a very small person, a very tall person, or the person's physical or emotional state: the person has a wooden leg or is on crutches, happy, hesitant, aggressive, angry, a person in a hurry, tiptoeing, sneaking, shuffling, walking with heavy packages or something else that is heavy. Discuss what you heard in the footsteps.

Exercise: Play The Room
Explore and discover sounds made by different objects in the room. For example, tap a pencil eraser on a desk, a chair, glass, paper or Venetian blinds. By tapping various parts of the room, you can hear different sounds and textures of sounds. These could be used to supplement a scene. Using these sounds is also an excellent way to create a background for stories or plays. For example, a mystery might be enhanced by the use of the sound of a stick tapping or running down a Venetian blind.

Exercise: Finding Your Own Sounds

Bring to class or find in the drama shop items that can produce interesting sounds. For example, tin cans and bottles of various sizes can produce many sounds. Chunks of wood snapped on the floor or hit together for a gunshot, chains, keys, cellophane for a crackling fire, humming into paper on a comb, fingernails on the blackboard or some wood surface, etc.

Exercise: Create Your Own Sound Story

Make up a story using only sounds. This may be done alone or with a group of two to five people with each person contributing something in the way of sound. You may use any combination of the sounds that you have already used such as "Knock, Knock," "Footsteps" and/or "Playing the Room."

Or, in addition to the sounds already listed above, you can create vocal sounds that imitate nature, such as wind, creaking doors or window shutters, metronome sounds with the tongue, cork popping sounds, throaty and nasal sounds for special effects or by coughing, clearing your throat or laughing to establish a character and story. Or, you can create "hands and body sounds" such as slapping or clapping.

Exercise: Finding and Recording Your Own Real Sounds

Many people have radios with a built-in microphone to record audiotapes. With a radio that has recording capabilities, record two to four minutes of sounds. Record sounds from your surroundings and/or the environment: home, work, school, nature, restaurants or streets. Record sounds that are unusual sounds in unusual places. Then, bring the audiotapes to class. Class members can close their eyes, listen and describe what they hear.

(Note: Please be mature enough to keep this a healthy class activity and not record sounds that offend people in an attempt "to be funny.")

Discussion: What emotional response, mood or character is suggested by each sound?

"Remembering the Senses" or Sense Memory

Sense Memory Exercise

You can have a memory of a sense experience, which is called *sense memory*. You can also have a memory of an emotional experience that is an *emotional memory*. (These are defined and explored further in Chapter 13.) You can also use remembered images (further explored in Chapter 14). A leader says the word or words that should conjure up the memory of the remembered sense. Take your time on each.

See: Close your eyes and picture the following: blue sky, rain, hot desert, night, thunderclouds, etc. What are some other images?

Hear: Close your eyes and remember the following sounds: a clock in the next room, distant music, faraway rumble of thunder, distant train whistle at night, a sudden gunshot, country sounds, shopping center, dance, city crew drilling, traffic, ocean waves, etc.

Touch: Feel a soft fur coat, velvet, chewed bubble gum sticky on your fingers, an ice cube, an egg, a soft wind in your face, the sun on the beach, sand between your toes, tickling the nose with a feather, etc.

Smell: Smell a rose, a garbage can, apple pie cooking in oven, tar, gas being put into car, buttered toast, sour milk, etc.

Taste: Taste a school hamburger, a pizza, buttermilk, bubble gum, ice cream, apple pie, spoonful of Milk of Magnesia or castor oil, taffy candy, chocolate cake, coke, lemon, sour milk, hot pea soup, iced tea. Show temperature, taste and consistency.

Exploring the Stage Space

Exercise: Space Walk
Form a large circle, then begin to walk around freely, moving into the open spaces. Move slowly and freely. You should feel a sense of stage space and relation to other people. Change speed: everyone with a touch of yellow clothing walk in slow motion, everyone with a touch of green clothing walk in double time, and everyone with a touch of red clothing stop. If someone is wearing more than one color, it can be "walker's choice."

Exercise: Moving to a Beat
Continue to move freely but add the beat of a drum or clapping of hands. The person in charge of the beat can change the beat every so often, and the people walking should react to the change in the beat. Then, play a record and move to the music. Change the speed of the record and move to the new rhythm.

Acting for Life

Remembering a Movement

Exercise: Repeating
Everyone closes his or her eyes except one performer and one observer. The first performer plans then pantomimes a simple action or movement, activity, how-to-do something or short story. Then, the observer does what s/he remembers, and a third person observes. When the second performer finishes what s/he remembers, the third person performs what s/he saw for the fourth person, and so on. (Somewhere between seven and ten performers should be the limit for this.) After the last person performs, the first person again performs the action to see how well it was followed. Discuss what was remembered and what was lost.

Exercise: Adding On
The first person does a simple movement. The second person takes the movement and adds on. Each performer continues to perform what was done before him/her and adds on his/her own movement. If possible, the movement should form some sort of story.

Exercise: Joining In
One performer picks a simple activity and begins doing it without telling what the activity is. As the other people observe what the activity is, they come up, one at a time, and join the first person and others in the activity. For example: painting a fence, washing a dog, baking a cake, performing an operation, etc.

Relating to Another Performer
Physically

Exercise: Simon Says
With one leader in front of group, play the game of "Simon Says." A leader gives instructions, and the group must respond only to the leader's directions when he begins with "Simon says." If a group member responds to a direction that is not begun with "Simon says," that group member is out and should sit down. The last group member standing wins. The Leader's right is your left, because, as you know, in a mirror, one person's right is the other person's left.

Exercise: Mirroring Partner

Pair off and sit opposite your partner. Performer A faces performer B. A initiates all movement, and B is the mirror. B reflects all of A's activities and facial expressions. While looking at B, the mirror, A takes a simple activity such as washing or brushing teeth. B follows the leader. Don't try to trick the other person. The object is to work together in harmony and have a sense of "being together." It is generally helpful to start by moving slower than normal speed in order to stay with each other. Then, after a short period, the teacher says "Switch," and you reverse the roles, with B initiating the movement and A playing the mirror.

Take your time. Don't rush. If you are the leader and the follower is out of sync, help your partner to become in rhythm with you again. Then, after a time, the players can instinctively change who is the initiator and who is the mirror and alternate rhythms.

Vocally

Exercise: Repeating A Line

Pair off. Person A says a line — any line — and the person B repeats the line exactly as s/he heard it in an effort to relate directly to the other person. The first line is repeated several times to establish a relationship. Then, a new line is said. Switch! B says a line and A repeats it, just exactly as heard. Don't interpret. The objective of this is to *listen and relate* to the other person, which is one of the most important lessons in drama.

Exercise: Instant Replay

Pair off. One person, A, initiates a story (*Cinderella, Goldilocks, Little Red Riding Hood*, the events of the day, a story from life or any how-to instruction can also be used). The other performer, B, follows verbally as closely as possible, picking up the inflections and rhythms of speech. Go slowly enough so that both of you can stay together. Then, when the teacher says, "Switch," change the initiator. For example: A starts, "Once upon a time there was a little girl. And she had a dream … " SWITCH. B continues, "She wanted to be a movie star." This is similar to "Relating to Another Performer — Physically." By using the words "fortunately" and "unfortunately," this can be used as an illustration of discoveries and reversals in storytelling.

19

Exercise: Mirror Exercise Combined with Instant Replay
(Physical combined with Verbal)

Tell a story of a daily activity, a children's story or fable or a how-to instruction. Go slowly to combine the auditory and the physical.

Emotionally

Exercise: Relating to Another Performer Emotionally

One person, A, says a line in a specific emotion. The second person, B, repeats the line as close to the same emotion as possible. Continue this for several times with new lines and emotions in order to establish a relationship. Then switch so B initiates the emotion-filled line, and A repeats it. It could involve some sentimental scene such as a wounded dog, an angry scene, a happy/joyful scene, etc. Continue this exercise until you are fully relating to each other. Since the performers are endeavoring to communicate, it is best to take time, stay focused and listen. This may also be done with gobbledygook, i.e. using nonsense words to express the emotions. (This will be explored further in Chapters 8 and 13.)

Chapter 3
The Stage and Acting Terms

The Proscenium Stage

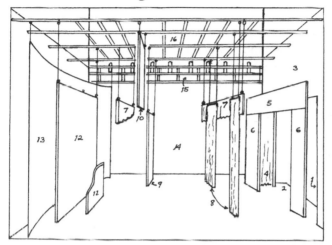

Cross-sectional perspective view from the right wing.

While there are different styles of stages that you may see in different theatres, the *proscenium stage* is a style that has been prevalent since the seventeenth century. Most school auditoriums and performing arts centers are built in this style. The audience faces the stage that has the proscenium arch. The proscenium arch is the arch that separates the house, where the audience sits, from the stage, where the actors perform the scene in the direction of the audience. There is usually a curtain to separate the stage or performing space from the audience area. There are many good possibilities for the use of scenery. (Other types and shapes of theatres are explored in Chapter 8 under "Projecting in Different Shapes of Theatres.")

Stage Terms
Terms in Diagram

House: (1) Where the audience sits.

Apron: (2) The section of the stage that extends in front of the proscenium arch.

21

Proscenium: (3) The arch that is between the audience and the stage where the scene is performed.

Act curtain: (4) The first curtain that opens and closes to designate the acts. Not all theatres have these.

Teaser: (5) The half curtain just inside the top of the proscenium. There is only one teaser, but it is the first of the borders. It is sometimes called the "first border." It regulates the height of the stage opening.

Tormentors: (6) The side curtains that are just upstage of the sides of the proscenium arch. They regulate the width of the stage opening. There are two.

Borders: (7) These are the short curtains that are hung along the top of the stage area to mask the overhead lights and pipes. These may also be painted sections hung along the top of the scene and used in conjunction with the wings and backdrop.

Legs: (8) These are the vertical curtains on each side of the stage that mask the off-stage areas or wings.

Wings: (14) The off-stage areas on either side of the stage that are not visible to the stage.

(9) A wing is also a leg painted like a scene and used with the painted drop or backdrop to form a painted scene. Used in musical comedies and opera.

Drop: (10) In a play with many scenes there may be many drops with different scenes on each.

Ground row: (11) A free-standing piece of scenery on the floor of the scene that masks the bottom of the cyclorama or row of cyclorama footlights.

Backdrop: (12) The last drop, which is a more fully painted scene at the back of the stage.

Cyclorama or Cyc: (13) (Pronounced: sigh'-klo-rah'-mah or sike.) The background curtain used to give a neutral background — often blue to resemble a sky effect. It could be across the back or around three sides of the stage. It could also be the back wall.

Pin rail: (15) The rail above the stage floor from which the curtains and drops are raised and lowered with the use of pulleys and a counterweight system.

Gridiron or Grid: (16) A series of heavy beams located above the stage at the top from which the lines pass to raise and lower the scenery.

Other Terms Not in Picture

Travelers: Stage curtains upstage of the act curtain that open left and right and are often used to set off areas of the stage for a play with many scenes.

Flies, fly loft or loft: The area above the stage and below the grid where the scenery, drops, wings and legs are stored out of the sightlines of the audience.

Batten: A long piece of wood or metal pipe that is hung above the stage and house areas from which the lights and scenery are suspended.

Flat: A wooden frame that is covered by unbleached muslin sheeting and painted to form the basic unit of scenery for most plays.

Jog: A narrow flat.

Backing: Flats or drops behind scenery openings to mask off-stage area and suggest other areas off-stage.

Hand props: These are personal items, carried on by actors, such as notebooks, letters, books, suitcases, a cane, etc.

Set props or set pieces: These are large built pieces of scene to represent rocks, trees and other special pieces. These are three dimensional as contrasted with ground rows and drops.

Wagons: These are platforms with wheels that are moved on-stage and off and stored in the wings.

Backstage: The part of the theatre that is not seen by the audience. It may include the green room, the dressing rooms, the shop, and costume and prop storage.

Green room: A waiting room for actors and actresses.

Strike: To take off a single item or whole set, usually after the play is over. To "strike the set" means put everything away.

Note: The flies, pin rail and grid are not always available in small theatres.

Acting and Directing Terms

The following list includes ways for a performer to gain emphasis on-stage visually. Most of the terms are more applicable to proscenium than other types of staging.

The Actor on Stage

Stage Right, R, and Stage Left, L: Refer to the actor's right and left when facing the audience. Some directors think stage right is stronger because audiences have a slight tendency to look to their left out of the habit of reading from the upper left corner. On the other hand, the front pages of many papers have the key story in the right hand column, so this may not prove to be the case. Test it.

Upstage, U or US, and Downstage, D or DS: These are terms that come from the days when audiences sat on a flat floor or stood on the ground (the Groundlings in Shakespeare's theatre), and the stage was raked, angled or ramped from lower in front (DS) to higher in back (US) so the audience could see all of the performers or the second row of a chorus. It also helped in creating depth perception when used in conjunction with a painted backdrop. It was not a steep rake, but it was not comfortable for performers to walk on an angled stage. Since the audience in the house area is now ramped, the stage is usually flat — except in some productions of classic plays from the seventeenth century. Modern movie theatres have gone from slightly ramped audience areas to stadium seating.

Above: Upstage of something or away from the audience.

Below: Downstage of something or toward the audience.

Upstage and Downstage Planes: Imaginary lines running parallel with the footlights (strips of lights located downstage near the front part of the apron and recessed in the stage floor, concealed from the audience).

Rake: The angle of the stage floor or house.

Symbols to write in the script:

C: Center
D or DS: Downstage, toward the audience
U or US: Upstage, away from the audience
L or R: Left and Right as performer faces the audience
X: Cross or move from one place to another
T: Table
Ch: Chair

Areas of the stage may arbitrarily be divided into six, nine, ten or fifteen areas. The diagram below shows fifteen areas.

UR	URC	UC	ULC	UL
R	RC	C	LC	L
DR	DRC	DC	DLC	DL

If this were a proscenium theater, the strongest area should be DRC (down right center) and the weakest UL (up left). Weak areas are thought to be off to the sides, because they are not in the center of the audience's vision.

If it were theatre-in-the-round (a stage configuration in which the audience sits on all sides of the acting area; the stage may be circular, square or rectangular), it would be possible to change the designations to reflect the face of a clock. For example, "Move to three o'clock" is left center or left and twelve o'clock is up center.

Body Positions in Relation to Audience in Proscenium Theatre (from strongest to weakest):

   a. Full front: that actor is facing the audience
   b. One-quarter front (frequent position when "playing to audience."): a position between full front and profile
   c. Profile: turned away from the audience, facing the wings
   d. Full back: turned upstage with back to the audience (Profile and Fully Back are about equal in emphasis, but have different values.)
   d. Three-quarters back: between profile and full back; thought to be one of the weakest body positions

Levels: Pertain to various heights above the stage floor. The attention should go to the person who is higher, for example, someone standing on a chair or platform.

Line of Direction: Pertains to the way an actor's body is lined-up or angled toward the person who is to get the attention.

Line of Vision: Pertains to an actor's looking toward the person who is to get the attention. Both line of direction and line of vision are often used in conjunction and are easily illustrated by the often-used situation of two actors forming one side of a triangle with "line of direction" and "line of vision" calling attention to a third actor at the apex.

Contrast: Refers to one person having a different body position (is on a different plane, in a different area or at a different height) than another person or group of people. Another aspect of this is the principle of isolation, which calls attention to a person who is not with a group.

Size or Mass: Usually the larger performer will gain more attention than the smaller performer. When there's a group, or mass and a single person who's different, there may be a balance in attention.

Color: The brighter colors (white, orange, red) will call attention quicker than other colors, particularly if they are contrasted with the background.

25

Ways to Gain Emphasis On-stage and Establish Relationships

Exercise:

Test the previous assumptions by actually standing on-stage and noting what members of the audience see. Compare the areas of the stage and body positions, relationship of the people, where attention is directed and why. The main object of doing this is to gain familiarity and comfort on stage. These guidelines are valuable to know when being directed or if you are blocking your own scene. They do not apply to someone who is moving or speaking. (See Chapter 11.)

Moving and Speaking: The two basic tools of an actor are the body and the voice. The body and voice project character traits, honesty of thoughts and emotions of the character while interacting with and showing relationships with the other characters.

Body Movement: Probably the most attention-getting physical principle is movement. It is for this reason that a performer should move when speaking and listen quietly and attentively when other actors give their lines.

The Voice and Speaking: Attention will go to the person speaking because audiences want to focus in on what is being said.

Directing Terms

Terms Involving Placement and Movement

Blocking: To "block the scene" is to establish home bases and territories to best show character relationships and tell the story of the play visually through the placement and movement of the actors on the stage. (See the Chapter 11 for more.) The dialog tells the story in words.

Places: This is the call for actors and crew to be in their positions at the opening of the act or scene.

Cross: This is to move from one place to another, and is indicated by the symbol "X" in the actor's script.

Cross down or Move down: Crossing downstage from where you are.

Cross up or Move up: Crossing upstage from where you are.

Counter cross: This means going in the opposite direction of an actor who has crossed. This is to balance the stage picture.

Open up or Turn out: To open up is to turn more toward the audience.

Cheat or Cheating: To angle your face or body slightly more toward the audience without appearing to do so.

Close in, Close up or Turn in: To turn away from audience and turn more toward other actors.

Dress the stage or Balance the stage: Both involve moving into open areas more equidistant from other actors.

Share the scene: Sharing the audience's attention with another actor(s) through body position (same plane, same level, etc.).

Give the scene: Calling attention to another actor to feature what s/he is saying or doing by moving into the weaker body position, looking or pointing, moving to a lower level, etc.

Stealing the scene: Taking the scene away from the person to whom it legitimately belongs. This might be moving upstage in order to force the other actor to turn three-quarters or full back to feature the upstage actor, or moving downstage closer to the audience and facing front to call attention to yourself.

Upstaging: Standing upstage of another performer so that the other performer is forced to turn 3/4 back and thus weaken their impact. (This is a form of stealing the scene)

Masking, Covering or Blocking (in a different sense): All mean hiding another performer by getting yourself between the other performer and the audience.

Gesture: This is the movement of any part of the body to help express an idea or clarify a thought.

Business or Stage business: Any action performed on-stage This usually shows a new insight to character and often involves a prop. "Bits of business" are small actions performed to show character. (See Chapter 4.)

Exit: Performers leave the stage.

Terms Involving Dialog

Cue: The action or dialog that immediately precedes another character's action or dialog.

Ad-lib: To make up a line of dialog that is appropriate to the scene when your own or someone else's line is forgotten, or someone has not entered on cue.

Improvisation: This means to spontaneously create a character and dialog that are based on a situation. (See Chapter 9.)

Hold it: Keep perfectly still.

Basic Guidelines for Traditional Stage Movement

Movement is a great attention-getter. Attention goes to sound and motion. Since dialog is important to advance character and plot, attention should generally go to the person speaking. Other people should not be moving during this time unless it is important for attention to go to the reaction of what is being said.

When *moving or walking* to the right or left, move on the upstage foot first in order to keep the body "open to the audience," instead of awkwardly crossing one leg in front of another and closing yourself.

In order to *balance the stage*, when someone crosses in front of you, you should go in the other direction to counter balance the stage. This is called *counter-cross*.

When *gesturing*, you should normally use the upstage hand or arm so that the gesture will not mask the body or face.

When talking to someone, *share the scene*. That is, stay on the same plane or same distance from the audience. If one person is upstage of the other and the person downstage has to turn away from the audience to talk, then attention will go to the upstage person because we see his/her face and body. S/He is open and the person downstage is "closed." When this is done, the person upstage is *upstaging* the other person or "stealing the scene." If someone does this to you when it should be your scene, simply turn and direct your lines to the audience.

When *talking on a telephone*, keep the telephone on the upstage side of the face in order not to mask the face. The mouthpiece should be held below the chin to avoid covering the mouth.

When *kneeling*, kneel on the downstage knee in order to keep the body more open to the audience. Put your weight on your upstage foot and then lower yourself onto your downstage knee.

Sitting and Rising. A conventional way to do this involves approaching a chair and getting close enough to feel it with the calf of one leg. Avoid looking behind you to see if the chair is still there before you sit. Then, by moving the leg back so that your weight is on the ball of your foot and your body is supported by your legs, you can stay fairly erect and lower yourself into the chair. Avoid sitting by backing into the chair with your rear end or rising by rolling forward. On rising, lean back and then shift forward to move your body's center of gravity over your feet. Then, you can stay fairly erect as you rise. Exceptions: if you are doing character roles that show eager youth, age, fatigue or a carefree attitude, then you have many possibilities.

Using Steps. When standing on or at the top of steps, don't let your toes dangle over the edge. Aside from looking unsteady, if there are lights from above, long shadows could be cast. When going up stairs, place your feet solidly on each step rather than just placing your toes on the edge and "rolling up," unless you are playing an eager, excited person who is anxious to reach the top.

Group Exercise

Everyone go on-stage to demonstrate and practice the techniques above. Then test and practice all the movements until they feel comfortable and natural.

Exercise: Using a Chair

Each member of the class can come on-stage and show one different way to use a chair in relation to character. This can be done by sitting on a chair or using it in different ways to show different types of characters and different attitudes in relation to the chair. Each person should show one way to use a chair and tell what type of character would do this.

Exercise in Basic Stage Movement

This is an exercise using the basic techniques that you have just studied. Plan the blocking and stage movement on the basis of the information given. Establish the basic location of Character A, the entrance point for Character B, the location of the chair and where the characters exit. Then, follow the script in planning the basic body movement.

You may play as yourself. Or, if you wish to base your performance on particular character traits, there are many possibilities to choose from in Chapter 13. Or, choose your own traits. For possible stage business see Chapter 4. You may also indicate familiarity with the area and weather and temperature both on-stage and in the off-stage area.

(Character A is discovered at C or LC doing some stage business in character. Character B enters from L or UL.)

B: Good morning!

A: (Startled) Oh! Where did you come from?

B: (Gesturing) From off-stage in the wings. I'm _____.

A: And, I'm _____. (Pause, as B looks at A) Where are you going?

B: I'm crossing you to play my big scene down right (or down right center.) (After B X's, B stops.) When I cross, you're supposed to counter-cross.

29

A: (Doing so) Oh, sorry.

B: No, no. Move your upstage foot first. (B begins to recite something, e.g.: "Oh, Captain, My Captain ... " or sing. A moves correctly, but keeps moving to chair at LC.) Don't move while I'm speaking. The attention should be on me and you're stealing the scene.

A: I just came over here to sit down and be out of the way.

B: Yes, but attention will go to the person who is moving. Besides, every movement should have a purpose. Stage business should reveal character.

A: Oh! You make me feel all sad and stupid ... like a loser.

B: Don't sit there and mope about it. (During the last two speeches, B X's to R of A)

A: You're right. I must regain control. (Rising) Attention will go to you if you're higher.

B: And to you if I'm turned in a three-quarters back position. I'll open up and regain the attention of the audience. (B turns front.)

A: That's not fair being farther downstage.

B: Not fair? You're the scene-stealer ... oozing all that self-pity. No one can feel sorry for someone who feels sorry for himself. (Moving away) I want nothing more to do with you.

A: (X-ing to B) No, I'm not a scene-stealer. Please don't say that.

B: Right now you're upstaging me ... again. (A X's DS.) That's better. I like people to share the scene with me. (B begins to recite, again, then stops) Why are you calling attention to me by staring?

A: I'm thinking about what you said, and reacting before I speak.

B: You should. I admire you for trying, but you're so needy that I want nothing more to do with you. I won't even speak to you. (Turns away and/or moves away)

A: Oh, please play the scene with me.

B: No, definitely no! You heard me the first time.

A: But, if you won't play the scene with me, who will?

B: I don't know and I don't care, and furthermore, I'm leaving. (B exits.)

A: Hey, wait for me! (A exits.)

This scene may be repeated many times in many different ways to practice different skills and techniques as you continue to learn about acting.

Chapter 4
The Body

" ... do not saw the air too much with your hand, thus;"
— *Hamlet,* by William Shakespeare

" ... suit the action to the word,"
— *Hamlet,* by William Shakespeare

Exploring Body Movement

Body Language

Body language is a form of non-verbal communication, and non-verbal communication is a major part of every aspect of your life. Understanding body language can be useful not only for a deaf person using sign language, but also for actors, teachers, businessmen, salesmen and animal trainers. As part of everyday communication we all, at times, use body language. We send out non-verbal messages all the time. Gestures, facial expressions and body movements frequently show what a person is thinking and feeling. Actions often speak louder than words. According to some people who have analyzed body language, it accounts for about 65 percent of the communication, while speech is 35 percent.

A person communicates all types of messages with different facial expressions, gestures, postures and body movements. The amount and type of gestures and meanings change with different cultures and different religions. Even the weather may also have something to do with gestures. For instance, the restraint often shown in Scandinavian cultures, where it is cold, is in sharp contrast to the flamboyance of the gestures often used in the warmer Italian culture.

Exercise: Exploring the Center of a Character's Movement
A body image is often registered by the way a person stands, walks or generally moves. This may be in such a way as to feature or center one part of the body over another. A small group goes on-stage and begins a slow "Space Walk." (See Chapter 2.) As you walk and change centers, *don't watch yourself.* Just relax and focus on the area to be centered.

1. Center your movement in your *head*, then, your *eyes*.
2. Center your head in your *nose*.
3. Then, find your center in your *shoulders*.
4. Then, shift to find your center in your *stomach*.
5. Then, center your movement in your *feet*.
6. Then, shift to feel your center in your *hips*.
7. Shift again to your *hands* and then your *arms*.
8. As you continue the slow walk, find *your own natural center*.

Discussion: Which center felt the most comfortable and most natural? What type of character might be shown by each of the different centers? Did you find a natural center for yourself?

Exploring the Use of the Hands, Face and Body

One of the questions often asked by student actors is, "What do I do with my hands?"

Exercise: Exploring the Hands

Point or gesture the following ways: index finger extended, two fingers, three fingers, four fingers, whole hand, thumb only, thumb on tips of fingers, palm up, palm down, fist, thumb and index finger together. Then, experiment: fingertips together, fingers interlocking and twiddling thumbs. Clench your fist, put fingers on forehead, on ear, on nose, on mouth, arms folded, hands on hips with clenched fists, then with open hands, etc.

Discussion: What kind of person, or what emotions were represented by each of the different ways of simply pointing and gesturing?

The hands and face and arms are the most used parts of the body. But to fully communicate, you need to use the whole body: arms, shoulders, body posture, movements, legs, standing and sitting, etc.

Exercise: Responding with Hands, Face and Body

Respond freely with gesture and facial expression to the following words as they are read: "NO!" "Stop!" "Absolutely not!" "You stop that!" "Who?" "Who me?" "Come on, follow me." "Why?" "I refuse to participate." "Now, now." "Shame on you!" "I beg of you." "Please!" "My prayers are with you." "I don't know." "Hi!" "Come here." "Get away." "Goodbye." "A-O.K." "We won!" "Quiet." "I don't want to hear this." "You did it!" "I can't tell you." "Don't tell." "Ha! You're crazy." "No comment." "Not me." "I approve." "Great. Perfect." "Never!" (For more on this subject see Chapter 6.)

Observing the Use of Hands, Face and Body

Find pictures in magazines and newspapers in which the people are using their hands or holding their bodies in interesting ways. Choose photographs in which the person is holding his or her head in a particular manner or has an interesting expression on his or her face. Note the pictures carefully. Imitate what you see and describe how it feels to pose in this way.

Observe how people around you use their hands, respond facially and move. Observe family, friends, others in school, in classes, halls, the cafeteria, at sporting events, etc., and how people express themselves through their bodies. This should expand your awareness and your observation skills to watch others. It will also expand the variety of possibilities for personal expression. (For further exploration of this activity, see Chapter 14.)

Exercise: Showing Emotions with Body, Hands and Face

Show or express the following traits or emotions in terms of the body, hands and face: puzzled, angry, suspicious, nervous, curious, shy, flirtatious, embarrassed, agreeable (nod), not agreeable (shake head), fearful, joyful, sad, angry, doubtful, worried, bored, proud, fatigued or world weary. Then, smile and again experience the emotions above while still smiling. (See exercise in Chapter 13.)

Discussion: How does each emotion feel? How does the meaning change for each of the above emotions when you smile? Is there any special meaning in any of these gestures? What kind of person gestures each way? Do you have the feeling that there is a mismatch of meaning and body posture, or that it changes the meaning?

You reacted to these emotions instinctively. This should help you in everyday life to become more aware of what you do with your body, what gestures or movements you use to communicate with others. Future chapters will deal with techniques for discovering or enhancing the use of the body through deeper emotions, thoughts, images, motivations and intentions.

Exercise

Describe the following without words: monster movie; cooking; stomachache, allergy or other illness; sporting event; different ages of people involved; an emotional reaction to something; etc.

Exercise

Do another space walk to show changing body movements. Move slowly into the open spaces. Then, everyone with blue or green move sadly, red and blue move cheerfully, others move sideways. After a few minutes of exploring space, do another space walk. Taking time for each, change your body movement as you walk like a: rag doll, tin man, dancer, one-year-old child, robot, eighty-year-old person, a person with a bad leg.

Gesture

A gesture is the movement of any part of the body to help express an idea or physically clarify a thought or line of dialog. Every gesture needs to have a definite purpose. If there is no purpose, there should be no gesture. There's nothing wrong with relaxing your hands at your sides or putting them together, in a pocket or holding a prop: glass, book, pencil or a piece of costume such as a hat, glove or cane. All of these can appear both natural and comfortable. (See section on Stage Business in this chapter.)

Pantomime
Defining Pantomime

Pantomime is the expression and communication of ideas, experiences, characters and small stories through the use of the whole body. This is an activity that is performed without words and without real objects. The performer *shows*, but does not *tell*. The physical movements are usually more stylized and more theatrical. Performers should create action that involves the whole body. The actions need to be detailed and clear in execution. Therefore, they may be slower and bigger or more exaggerated than normal in order to show the size, weight and shape of objects. The performer uses illusion to suggest and/or represent persons, spaces, environments (places) and objects (things).

While pantomimes may be based on real people, actors may also be mannequins, monsters, robots, extra-terrestrial creatures, clowns or animals such as cats, dogs, etc. Performers may also create movements that represent inanimate objects or machines, sound and movement, such as a gumball machine, pencil sharpener, typewriter, washing machine, car, etc.

Pantomimes may include sensory awareness: tasting (a lemon), touching (threading a needle), hearing (a voice inside a desk), seeing (a crawling bug), smelling (sour milk) and/or emotional attitudes such as fear, happiness, shyness, anger, loneliness, etc.

In preparing to perform the movements, the action may be practiced and rehearsed with real objects to experience how it feels to do that activity. Then, take away the objects and see if you have a sense memory of all the details. See in your imagination all the objects or "things" used in the pantomime. (For further exploration of images, see Chapter 14.)

Do your regular warm-up exercises, particularly those that involve stretching and movements that involve the whole body. Warm-up movements might involve lines and directions: up and down, back and forth, left and right, bending over, turning around, going in reverse. Or performers may have a change in tempo: slow motion (like TV replay) or normal or double time (like silent movies).

There may be vocal sounds, sounds from instruments or machine sounds, or music may be used as background or even "playing the room." (See Chapter 2.) In this respect, pantomime is akin to dance in the arts and figure skating and gymnastics in sports. While there is no dialog called for, music is often used as background for these sports and dance.

Introductory Group Activities

Exercise: Joining In

One person chooses a simple activity and begins doing it without telling what the activity is. As the other people observe what the activity is, they come up one at a time and join the first person and others in the activity. Examples might be painting a fence, washing a dog, baking a cake, performing an operation, cooking something specific, repairing something (engine, watch, etc.), sewing, carpentry, etc. Some people may work on their own while others may work together. Either way is fine.

Exercise: Naming the Activity

As an alternative approach, the leader or the person who began the first activity names someone. The person who was named then states an activity. For example, "You are cleaning your desk or room" or "trying on different clothes for an event." Then, everyone begins to pantomime cleaning a desk or room or trying on different clothes.

Exercise: Planning a Machine

Divide into groups of 4 to 8 people and plan a machine. All parts of the machine should be dependent on each other, that is, interdependent parts. Each piece of the machine runs because another part does something to another part or parts. Then, in addition, each part makes a sound. This should be planned quickly in about ten minutes.

Pantomime Exercises

Pantomimes may be done with one, two, three or more people in the group. Choose one activity from the list below, and, with or without a partner, pantomime the activity. In each of these pantomimes establish a beginning, middle and end to the story. Create a conflict by having something go wrong with the activity, such as a problem or obstacle to overcome. Take your time in practicing and performing so that all movements are clear. Remember, you need to "see" and "feel" the size, weight and shape of all the objects in order for the audience to see and feel them too. And you need to show — not tell. Your performance should be evaluated on the basis of character, story, ideas and whether "we see" the objects.

Performing alone should be about two or three minutes minimum, and duos or trios should be a minimum of about four to six minutes. Take your time to develop the story.

1. Fixing breakfast, burning something.
2. Changing a tire on car or bicycle.
3. Reluctantly cleaning your room or other parts of house.
4. Learning to drive, roller-skate, play tennis, golf, etc.
5. Watching an exciting movie while eating snacks.
6. Decorating a Christmas tree.
7. Playing a game: pool, ping-pong, solitaire, etc.
8. Doing homework and being interrupted by a bug.
9. Making a sandwich.
10. Wrapping a gift.
11. Doing laundry, ironing clothes and testing the iron.
12. Taking pictures of family.
13. Washing the dog.
14. Washing dishes and breaking one.
15. Building something with a hammer and saw.
16. Performing in a circus high wire act.
17. Discovering some money on the sidewalk.
18. Changing a baby's diaper.
19. Getting dressed to go on a date.
20. Moving as a robot.
21. Being allergic to something.
22. Talking on telephone while _____.
23. Flying a kite.
24. Swatting a fly or catching a butterfly.

25. Playing a sport.
26. Tending a baby: feeding, etc.
27. Starting a campfire.
28. Reacting to tear gas or bad smell.
29. Learning to ride a bike or skateboard.
30. Performing an operation.
31. Learning to drive a car.
32. Fixing or repairing something that is broken (car, watch, vase, etc.)
33. Finding something on the internet and registering the emotion it causes.
34. Create your own pantomime.

Note: This activity may be repeated frequently in order to practice pantomime, become aware of basic body movement and build up a backlog of ideas for stage business. Some activities or tasks labeled as pantomime might be used as stage business by adding the real objects needed and making the movements realistic. Likewise, some of the activities or tasks labeled as stage business may be used as pantomime by setting aside the real objects and taking a little more care: slower and larger, without losing the size, weight and shape of the objects.

Stage Business

Stage business is a physical activity, or what your character is doing during the scene while talking or listening. You can *do* something physical which is something you can control.

To "act" means "to do" or to perform an action. In these terms, acting is what happens in each moment of the scene. This also is what gives the scene a fresh, spontaneous feeling of "nowness" — an illusion of the first time. So, one aspect of acting on-stage is to have something to do — an action, physical activity or task to perform.

Stage business is usually an activity or task that involves use of real objects or props that are "realistic," and the action is often performed while one character is having dialog with another character. The action doesn't need to be referred to in the dialog. There are many possibilities for logical and motivated approaches to stage business.

Your stage business should define and enhance your character and be relevant and appropriate to your character, even though there may be no direct lines of dialog that refer to what you are doing. The stage business may parallel what is being talked about. (For example: trying on clothes while discussing how you might appear on a date or eating food while talking about losing weight.) However, stage business doesn't need to be related to the dialog. That is, you can be doing something different than the dialog. Whatever you do, it should be related to character, the plot or the theme.

In the comedies of high society characters of the 1930s and 1940s, characters were forever fixing drinks or lighting and smoking cigarettes. This stage business has become a cliché.

In some cases, what you are doing might be the exact opposite of what you are saying and show the inner truth that is not consistent with the dialog. Or, the business may reveal character, but not run parallel with the dialog. (For example, talking tough while biting fingernails nervously. Or a person pretends to be happy with his present state of life while rearranging furniture and dusting.) Or the activity may show some hidden agenda. (For example, a woman who is complaining about her husband while she is angrily chopping vegetables.)

Exercise: Stage Business with Dialog

Choose a brief scene, exercise or monolog and a specific physical activity, task or stage business that your character might be doing in the scene. This is something that should be consistent with your character and something that you personally might know about. This gives you a focus for concentration.

Environment, Location, Weather or Time of Day

In addition to showing an aspect of character you might also show background conditions such as weather or time of day. Show hot sticky weather by wiping away sweat or cold by bundling up with a blanket or scarf. Come from outside where it is raining, prepare for weather by putting on a coat, hat and scarf, or trying on different hats before leaving, or use an umbrella for your exit or for your entrance.

You may need to show the basis of business you may have in a place such as a restaurant or store that sells items to handle and test. Or, show what the environment is like. You may be swatting flies or bugs or indicating the time of day.

Exercise: Character Traits that Show Personality
Show activity that is the result of an emotional reaction to fear, anger, love, etc. Show a relationship or business with a friend, love interest, servant or master.

Hold or play with dolls, fuzzy animals, etc.

Clean and put on glasses or sunglasses.

Sew, knit, etc.

Write letters, type, sharpen pencils, etc.

Work crossword puzzles, a jigsaw puzzle, etc.

Watch TV then look out of window and see something, etc.

Type, file, operate a computer, etc.

Related to What is Happening in Scene

Fixing food and/or drink, making a sandwich.

Eating: candy, chips, nuts, sandwich, banana, etc.

Drinking juice, soft drink, beer, tea, coffee, etc.

Cleaning or straightening the room, vacuuming, dusting, scrubbing floor, ironing, removing crumbs, etc.

Packing: suitcase, backpack, picnic lunch, etc.

Looking at cans in cupboard or cooking something.

Sorting the laundry or putting the groceries away.

Waiting for bus, a friend or someone special.

Arranging for dinner guests, etc.

Comb hair, pick teeth, brush teeth, blow nose, put in eye drops or brush lint off of clothes. Fuss with clothes, adjust tie or bite nails. Put on fingernail polish, file nails, etc. Tie or adjust a tie or try on a piece of clothing.

Physical Conditions and Personal Activities

Show fatigue or headache by rubbing eyes, temples, aching muscles, stretching. Massage your head, neck, shoulders or those of another person.

Show nervousness by pacing, fidgeting or scratching. Show an emotion such as pride, envy, fear, anger, joy, etc.

Exercise: Occupation as Basis for Activity or Task
The stage business may be connected with a character's occupation or career and involve studying or working on project. What business would be appropriate for the following: doctor, lawyer, architect, athlete (choose specific sport), student, custodian, secretary, writer, teacher, etc.?

Exercise: Hobby, Sport or Activity

Read, paint or draw. Strum guitar, dance, run in place, relax, exercise, etc.

Do some exercises or physical workout (with or without a machine).

Practice a sport, swing a golf club, tennis racket, etc.

Perform some craft: whittle, paint, etc.

Play games: board, computer, ball, solitaire, chess, checkers, etc.

Tend to houseplants: water or trim, etc.

Fix or repair something: toy, car, wiring, etc.

Exercise: Observing Actions

Observe a character on TV. Turn on a sitcom or drama, and then turn off the sound. Watch the scene. See if you can tell from body movement, facial expression and gestures what is happening in the scene. Then, show the class and see if they can tell.

Exercise: Observing Actions and Dialog

Observe character in a movie or on TV. Observe and note what a character is doing (stage business) and saying (dialog), then demonstrate this to the group and explain the circumstances. (For further exploration of observing people on-stage, in film and in life, see Chapter 14.)

Exercise: Using a Chair

Use a chair in as many different ways as possible to show different types of characters and different attitudes. Each member of the class can have a chance to show a different way to sit or use a chair. Don't repeat anything that anyone else has done. As each person comes forward to suggest one way, eliminate that way so the next person needs to find another way. What does each new way suggest in terms of the type of person who uses the chair that way? What attitude or character trait is suggested? Remember these possibilities when you are performing scenes and incorporate the use of the chair with your character.

Charades

Charades is a form of pantomime, a game to communicate ideas. It is an excellent form of communication by body gestures. There is a lot of creative thinking and associated thinking in communicating ideas, both by the person doing the charade and by the team guessing. The value of charades is not only in more effective communication with the body, but also some new awareness of subjects in education and popular culture. It can be an excellent education tool. This can be a very educational activity and an ongoing process that can be used on a Friday afternoon or even at lunchtime.

One player performs a subject or topic in pantomime in an effort for his/her team to guess what the topic is. The team with the shortest total time wins. Charades develops skills in communication and in listening, focusing, concentrating and thinking in associations. Since so many people play charades you may have your own rules or guidelines. However, before you begin you should establish agreed upon basics or guidelines for the way you play. Here are some things to consider.

Choosing the Charades

The charades are best if they can reflect something of the background of the participants. Since there are no words allowed by the person giving the signals, a system of pantomimed symbols needs to be established for communication of the category or subject. Discuss and agree on some of these frequently used categories. Write down both the title and the category.

These are listed on 3 X 5 index cards or slips of paper for the other team members to act out. The participants should generally be aware of the topics. They should be "tough, but fair." It might be prudent for the director to monitor some of the choices to determine that they are appropriate for the participants.

Communicating Information

Establishing Categories

A wide range of subjects or topics for charades is possible. Some frequently used categories are listed below. As a group, practice these signals:

A Play: Signal a curtain going down as one hand lowers vertically onto the other hand placed horizontally like a stage floor. Or, draw a proscenium with fingers in a motion that is sort of like a swag curtain.

Book or Novel: Two hands placed together and then opened like a book.

Song: Arms out, hands open, head back, mouth open.

A Quote, TV Ad or Slogan: First two fingers of each hand make a quote sign in the air.

A Movie: A motion like an "old style" movie camera where you wind it from the side.

Old: Stroke imaginary beard.

Shakespeare: Shake hand as if you have dice, then throw a spear.

Lines from a Song, Poem, Story or Play: Fingers move like lines through space.

TV Show: Outline screen, turn knobs and stare at imaginary screen.

Animal: Dog (scratch head), cat (hold in arms and pet with long strokes. No sound effects), zoo (pantomime movements of animal, e.g. elephant with trunk and lumbering, loping walk).

Sports: Baseball (pitcher and batter), football (quarterback throwing football), basketball (dribbling).

City: Move as if to sit down and then "stretch it" (see below).

Symbols.

Practice special symbols. As your team begins to guess, you will need some special symbols. As the symbol is read, show physically how this is done.

Show total number of words: Hold up number of fingers. (Establish limit with a suggested total maximum around 10.)

Indicate which word: Hold up number of fingers, one for the first word, two for the second, etc. Choose key words instead of articles and prepositions such as "a" "and" and "the" and "by," "for" and "on."

Show how many syllables: Place number of fingers in crook of arm or elbow or on forearm.

Indicate which syllable is first: Place number of fingers in crook of arm or on forearm.

The whole thing or concept: A sweeping circular motion to show all encompassing concept.

Little word or words (articles and prepositions): Place thumb and index finger about one inch apart.

Idea of: Put finger on temple.

Sounds like: Pull earlobe and then act out. For example: "sounds like," then, hop, and they say, "Hop?" and you nod or point and they guess, "Cop ... ?" "Top ... ?" "Mop ... ?"

Past tense: A sideways motion with open hand that indicates "go back."

Opposite, reverse or flip it: Turn hand over and back to indicate "flip side." For example, "girl" is "boy" or "Istanbul" is "Constantinople."

You're close: Coax the guessing group to continue by indicating "come on now," "that's it" or even "that's the idea."

Sort of: Flip hand back and forth and possibly shrug shoulders.

On the nose: Index finger to nose and point to the person in guessing group who made the right guess.

Stretch: Put fingertips together and then pull apart like pulling taffy to get group to make singular a plural or add a "y" ending. For example: "sit" becomes "city."

Shorten: Make a short chopping motion. For example: chop "er" off of "mother" to get "moth."

Forget the approach I was using: Make stop sign or move hands from close together to away from each other with palms down in a sweeping, rejecting motion.

The guessing group should not be allowed to go through the alphabet, because this violates the spirit of the game.

Choosing Teams

Team size is best between four to nine (five to seven is optimal). With a large class there may need to be four teams. In this case two teams would have a contest, then the other two. Choose the teams arbitrarily by numbering off or drawing numbers. Mix the gender on each of the teams (don't pit the boys against the girls). While some team members might be good at acting, others may be better at guessing, and others might be good at creating ideas for a list of charades.

Then, the general procedure that follows is for a member of one team to pick a charade from the group of charades created by the other team and act it out for his/her team in the quickest way possible. The teams should alternate taking turns until everyone has acted.

Time Management

As soon as one team finishes, a member of the other team should draw a topic to move the game forward rapidly. Give the new person 2 minutes to figure out how to act out the charade. Meantime, you can wind up the previous performance with comments and discussions. Allow 3-4 minutes for the person to act out the charade.

Record the time it took each team to guess the charade as the score.

TEAM	CHARADE	TIME IN SECONDS
Person	Name of Charade	Score

After everyone has performed, the team with the shortest total time wins.

Other Guidelines

By the definition of pantomime, no props are to be used, even those found on people or in the room. No spelling out of words ("does it start with "a," "b" or "c"?). No going through the alphabet when you have a "sounds-like" (a no-no practice that usually begins with guessers who are frustrated by not getting anything, and the actor is just standing). No direct questions: "Is it Chaucer?" "Tennessee Williams ... ?" The questions can only pertain to clarification in the game: "Do we have the third word?"

Charades may be played at any time. With ten minutes at the end of a period, it could be performed informally with one actor drawing a charade from an ever-present bucket, and acting it out for the entire class to guess. Or, teams can be organized and have a competition on a Friday afternoon or at lunchtime.

Discussion: What are the similarities and differences between the following: pantomime, stage business, charades and body language? Discuss in terms of dialog, and body movement and rehearsed and spontaneous movement and performance.

Chapter 5
The Voice

The Vocal Instrument

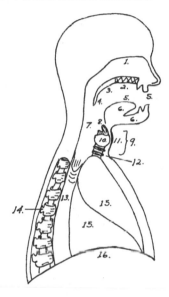

1. Nasal cavities
2. Hard palate
3. Soft palate
4. Uvula
5. Lips and Mouth
6. Tongue–Jaw
7. Pharynx
8. Epiglottis
9. Larynx
10. Thyroid gland
11. Adam's apple
12. Trachea (windpipe)
13. Esophagus
14. Spinal column
15. Lungs
16. Diaphragm

Voice Terms

Diaphragm: The body partition of muscle and connective tissue located in the lower part of the *thorax*, or chest cavity, that is the center of breathing control or power supply. The diaphragm works very much like a bellows system.

Lungs: The two spongy air sacs, which in themselves have no power to expand or contract, to take in or expel air.

Trachea: The *windpipe*, by which the air travels to and from the lungs.

Esophagus: The muscular tube that leads from the pharynx into the stomach.

Larynx: The *voice box* is a cartilage formation (soft bone and muscle) in front of the neck. Inside the larynx are the vocal cords or folds or bands. These are muscle fibers that vibrate, sending out sound waves.

Thyroid: The largest cartilage of the larynx. The thyroid covers the larynx.

45

Adam's apple: The projection of the thyroid cartilage in front of the larynx and neck.

Glottis: The elongated space between the vocal cords in the upper part of the larynx.

Epiglottis: The thin, elastic cartilage behind the tongue and in front of the glottis. It covers the glottis during swallowing food so that food does not cause choking when caught in the windpipe.

Pharynx: The part of the throat between the mouth and the esophagus.

Uvula: The soft, loose end of the soft palate.

Resonating chambers: The three resonating chambers are the *pharynx* (located just above and behind the larynx), the *mouth* (the hard palate at the top acts as a sounding board) and the *nasal cavities*, which include the sinus cavities.

Articulators: The four articulators, the tongue, lower jaw, lips and soft palate are used to form vowel and consonant sounds.

Eating, Speaking and Breathing

To a large extent, speech is an overlaid function. That is, most of the vocal instrument or speech mechanism is primarily used for some other function such as eating and breathing.

Eating

Eating food involves putting food in the mouth, chewing with the teeth and tongue and then swallowing. The food passes back into the *pharynx* area, down into the *esophagus* and then into the stomach. The *uvula*, in conjunction with the *epiglottis*, helps you swallow.

Speaking

Breathing and speaking involve initiating a breath from the *diaphragm*, which is the center of breathing control. As you inhale, the diaphragm expands (pulling the air into the lungs), and as you exhale, the diaphragm contracts (pushing air out of the lungs). The forced stream of air goes through the bronchial tubes and up the *trachea* or *windpipe* through the *larynx* or *voice box*. Inside the *larynx* are the *vocal cords*, which are muscle fibers that vibrate, sending out sound waves that are reinforced by the *resonating chambers*.

The *resonating chambers* are the *pharynx, mouth* and *nasal cavities* and serve the same function as a megaphone. The size and shape of the resonating chambers determines the quality of the voice. The so-called "head" and "chest" resonance is probably *sympathetic vibration*. That is, vibration is set up in these areas because of resonance in primary resonators. This sound then is "articulated," or changed into vowel and consonant sounds by the *articulators*, which are movable parts of the speech mechanism.

The four *articulators* are the *tongue, lower jaw, lips* and *soft palate*. (The teeth are *not* articulators because they are not in themselves movable parts, but are used in conjunction with the tongue, lower jaw and lips.)

Articulation pertains to diction, or how distinct the sounds are formed. Slurred or garbled speech is connected with this. This is sometimes referred to as having a "lazy jaw" or "lazy tongue." *Pronunciation* pertains to the accepted dictionary usage of vowel and consonant sounds and the emphasis on the proper syllable. Pronunciation is often determined by region, and national dialects are connected with this. (See "Pronunciation and Diction" in this chapter.)

Breathing

There is a difference between normal breathing and breathing for speech, or breathing as an actor. Normal breathing involves a regular pattern of equal length in inhaling and exhaling. However, normal speech is only produced when air is exhaled. So, for an actor or person speaking, air is inhaled quickly and fully and exhaled slowly. In breathing for speech, inhale through the mouth so the air can enter the lungs more quickly.

Breathing with only the neck and collarbone muscles produces shallow breathing. Shallow breathing is usually indicated if your breath is in the upper part of your chest cavity. If you do this, you will notice that your shoulders rise on inhaling and lower on exhaling.

Breathing by only rib cage expansion and contraction is slightly better. Your rib cage expands on inhaling and contracts on exhaling. Slightly deeper breathing occurs by breathing with your chest cavity.

But for drama and personal health in life, the deeper, more controlled diaphragmatic breathing is the best approach in order to experience the fullest amount of air in the lungs and more oxygen in the body.

Discovering Diaphragmatic Breathing
For diaphragmatic breathing, lie on your back, or if this is not

feasible, stand against a wall. Relax. Place your hand, palm or fist in your stomach area, just under your sternum or breastbone. This is the area of your diaphragm. Press inward firmly and exhale as much air as possible. Then, quickly take in a deep, full breath, and at the same time expand this area. Again, pressing gently on the area, slowly exhale. As you do this, slowly count to see how long you can sustain the exhalation.

With increased control you should be able to add to the number you count each time. Continue this until you feel that you are consistently using diaphragmatic breathing. Note: It is possible that you may become slightly dizzy for the moment, because you will be getting more oxygen into your system. Just relax and breathe normally until it passes. The best way to adjust your body to the benefits of diaphragmatic breathing is to begin the pattern just before you go to sleep at night. It should continue through the night. In a short amount of time, you should be able to breathe properly without having to concentrate on it.

Four Ways to Change Sound and Tone

The four ways to change sound and tone are: *quality, pitch, volume* and *pace. Quality* is the sound or tone of the individual voice. *Pitch* is the relative highness or lowness of the sound. *Volume* is the relative strength, force or intensity of the sound. The *rate, pace, time* or *tempo* is the basic speed, or *rhythm*, in which you speak.

Placement for Different Vocal Qualities

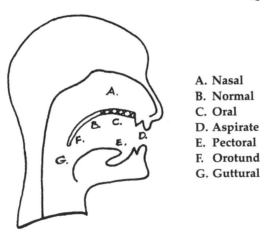

A. Nasal
B. Normal
C. Oral
D. Aspirate
E. Pectoral
F. Orotund
G. Guttural

Quality

Quality is the sound of the individual voice, which is determined by the size and shape of the resonating chambers. This also, to some degree, determines the placement of the air stream. There are seven basic qualities:

1. *Normal:* Used in everyday conversation. Your voice should have proper diaphragmatic breathing in order to cause the proper placement of an air stream to gain maximum resonance and flexibility. (Most sounds that are not normal are voice abuse. That is, they are not placed to give maximum resonance and flexibility.)

2. *Orotund:* Full, rich, deep, resonant and musical. It may show deeper emotions such as courage, patriotism and devotion or a huffy-puffy, flamboyant quality. Often used by old style, pre-TV politicians or ministers or by the wizard in *The Wizard of Oz*. The breath stream is in the back part of the mouth. You can find the area by making a gargling sound. Say, "Around the gurgle," and notice where the sound is formed.

3. *Oral:* Thinner and more delicate. It may show love, serenity, gentleness or understanding quality. Appropriate in depicting children and dainty, feeble, fatigued or delicate persons such as little old ladies. The breath stream is in the front part of the mouth and the lips. There isn't much resonance. Say "pretty petty pupils," and note where the breath stream is placed.

4. *Nasal:* This is a harsh, unpleasant quality. These are sounds that go through the nose that do not normally go through the nose. (Normally only M, N, and NG go through.) Used to depict gossips, vulgar or tough types or for whiny and talkative people. Say the word "morning" several times, or "going" or "wattuh" for water.

5. *Guttural:* This is a throaty, quality almost a growl. Used for old men and women, the villain and menacing roles that suggest evil. The breath stream is in the throat or pharynx. It is deeper than the orotund sound. Growl like a suspicious dog to find the area in your mouth.

6. *Pectoral:* This is a hollow tone to suggest horror or an unworldly effect, used for ghosts and witches. The placement is similar to oral quality but the pitch is higher, and vowel sounds are elongated much more. Try the words "Wooooe is meeeee and meeeee is woooooe."

7. *Aspirate:* This is a breathy sound, similar to a whisper used in moments of high tension. Placement of the breath stream may be normal like any of the others, but sounds are not resonated or vocalized as much.

In order to achieve the voice qualities described above, the breath stream is placed in the general areas of the resonators mentioned by changing the shape of the articulators.

Changing Vocal Qualities

Rehearse and perform a scene such as "Basic Stage Movement," (Chapter 2) with vocal quality that is different than your normal quality.

Pitch

Pitch is the relative highness or lowness of the sound. There are two ways to change pitch:

A. *Step method:* Going from one pitch level to another without intermediate pitch levels.

B. *Inflection or Slide method:* Changing pitch levels by going higher or lower in the midst of a word. You can only change pitch levels on a vowel sound (a, e, i, o, u and y), not a consonant sound. There are three types of inflection:

1. *Rising:* This can be used to show a timid person. Shows doubt, uncertainty of thought, or a question. Often used in comic delivery. Rising inflection on the ends of sentences is also noticed as a cultural type of delivery by a segment of the population known as "Valley Girls," theoretically originating from San Fernando Valley in California.

2. *Falling:* Used by a dominant person. A falling inflection on the ends of sentences shows completeness of thought and/or definiteness. Falling inflection is often used more in serious drama or sentiment.

3. *Circumflex:* This is a combination of rising and falling inflections. All on the same vowel sound, it goes higher and lower than established pitch level like a roller coaster. Used to convey inner subtle meanings and shades of meanings, and new awareness. "Oooohhh, now I see." Also, used for comic effect.

Monotony of pitch may be due to:

1. Inability to hear pitch changes.

2. Lack of flexibility in vocal mechanism. (Usually a combination of breathing, change in size and shape of resonators and placement of air stream.)

3. Cultural inheritance or preference.

Rate, Pace, Tempo or Rhythm: "Pick It Up!"

In acting, as in life, everyone — each person or character — has his or her own basic rhythm, tempo or pace of speech in terms of the way she or he moves and/or speaks. So, too, each character within the play might have a different tempo or rhythm. And, each play has its own internal basic rhythm. This tempo is not always the same, but it is a basic rhythm.

Different types of plays also have different tempos. Farces and most comedies move more rapidly, and the characters usually move and speak more rapidly. By the same token, note the pace of soap operas (sentimental dramas on TV) and the slow, controlled movement, the slow delivery of lines and long pauses between lines. Melodramas usually have a more intense, emotional and suspenseful driving tempo.

In any play, an increase in rate of speech can give a feeling of tension and inner excitement and build to a climax. (A more rapid tempo is often used with an increase in volume and the rising of pitch level to gain a climax.) Pauses are part of rate and, coupled with elongation of vowel sounds, interesting variety can be achieved.

Changing the Rate

Some directors, who become anxious over listening to actors play at the naturally slower pace of a drama or sentimental play and are eager to keep an audience interested, have endeavored to make scenes more exciting by snapping their fingers at actors and saying, "Pick it up!" They usually mean tempo, pace or speed, because they perceive that the actors are going too slowly, and the audience will be bored.

But if an actor then speaks more rapidly, the pitch often goes up and the volume also increases. This appears to give more energy and life to the scene, at least for a short period of time. However, playing a sentimental drama built around character, faster may not be playing the characters and scene honestly, and can distort the basic rhythm. The actors may also slur the words at the increased speed.

Since this is not a desirable result, if you are called upon to "pick it up," begin by increasing your energy and emotional intensity before you increase your speed of delivery. This should help toward solving the problem.

Volume

Volume is the relative strength, force or intensity of the sound. Volume depends on the violence with which the air from the lungs strikes the vocal bands or folds. This force is of two types:

1. *Explosive:* A sudden sharp pressure is emitted. Used in shouts, commands, loud laughter and screams.

2. *Expulsive:* The breath is released gradually and steadily in order to prolong a sound or sentence or groups of sentences almost indefinitely. Singers learn to sustain notes for long periods of time.

Voice Projection or "Louder!"

One of the major problems that students have is projecting their voices to all areas of the audience. When they can't be heard, the director sometimes says, "Louder!" Often the volume goes up for one word or line and then is lost again.

Good voice production through improved diaphragmatic breathing and good projection is a long-range process with many aspects. If one actor is actually talking to another one on-stage, the understanding may be that s/he has only to be heard by the other actor. Since the voice is directed at the other actor five feet away, the sound waves travels only five feet and in the wrong direction (toward the other actor, not the audience). If the director says, "Louder!" the actor may feel that s/he is already loud enough. In reality, the sound must travel at least fifty feet toward the back row of the audience while appearing to be in a casual conversation with a person who is close by. Another approach might be to think of "louder!" or projection — not as a voice problem — but as a communication problem.

If so, there are methods or techniques that can help almost all students in a very short time that are also valuable over a long period of time. They are:

1. *Directing, projecting or throwing the voice in the right direction:* This is to include people in all parts of the auditorium or room.

2. *Psychologically including all members of the audience:* It is one thing to project the voice. It is something more to relate to the audience emotionally and project the emotional and intellectual honesty of the character. (For more on this aspect of communication see Chapter 8.)

Directing, Projecting or "Throwing the Voice"

Exercise: Projecting Your Voice to a Partner

Form two lines on the opposite sides of the stage. Focus on the person directly across from you to be your partner. While you are facing your partner, exchange a word or one line of dialog. Aim the word or line at some particular part of the face, head or shoulders, and see if the line reached him/her. Did it hit where it was being aimed? In order to better understand directing or projecting the voice, don't tell where you are aiming, but let your partner tell you where it hit. Note that if a voice is thrown or directed "straight outward," the sound wave may do a nosedive into the stage floor.

Instead, since it is some distance to the other side of the stage or room, in order to reach there, the voice needs to be projected, or thrown, in a high arc, like a ball. Doing this, you may note that you begin to raise your chin and stretch your neck and speak more carefully to project your voice or words to your partner. Continue this process by taking turns projecting your voice directly to each other.

Then change partners and repeat the exercise several times, until you understand the skill in directing your voice.

Exercise: Projecting Your Voice to the Audience

A small group of performers should pair off in teams and find some area of the stage. Stand a few feet apart as if playing a scene.

1. Exchange several lines of dialog to each other while looking at each other.

2. After you have successfully communicated with each other several times, turn and face the director someplace in the back area of the auditorium and repeat this exercise by directing the same words or lines to the director.

3. Once again, face your partner on-stage. Only this time, while looking at your partner, actually deliver the line, or play it, to the director in the back of the auditorium. You will probably feel yourself "fudging" by turning both body and face "more open" or more toward the house area. The other performer will feel that the lines curve past his/her face into the auditorium or bounce off of the person or people in the audience back to him/her as it would in a game of handball.

This should offer a better understanding of the problem of projecting the voice and including the audience than trying to respond to the word, "Louder!" (For more information on including and relating to the audience emotionally, see Chapter 8, and repeat this exercise with new lines or script.)

Exercise: Gaining Vocal Variety
Vocal variety can be gained by changing pitch, volume, quality and rate, speed or tempo. Build up or down in pitch, volume, and time in each of the following groups of three sentences.

Where are you going with that suitcase?
Why are you going?
And what are you going to do?

There's something about you students that's familiar.
I believe I remember you from last time.
Didn't you witness that ugly, cruel murder?

I expected a short, cheerful, pleasant trip.
But it was a long, weary, tiresome journey.
And I'm exhausted to the point of insanity.

The *wh* is like hw or blowing out a candle. The *u* in students and suitcase is like the *u* in constitution. Make the word sound like the thing it represents with a change in pitch, volume, rate or even quality. Beware of saying were, wy, wat, sootcase, buhlieve, aboutchew, lastime, didunchew and stoodunts. For more words to note and practice see "Pronunciation and Diction" in this chapter.

Warm-Up Exercises
Using lips, tongue and teeth to help pronunciation and diction, say clearly, distinctly and rapidly several times the following:

Wee, woe, wah, woo, wee, woe, wah, woo, etc.
Rubber baby buggie bumper, etc.
Sue sells seashells by the seashore, etc.
Tall Tommy Teeny took tiny Tilly Tootie to tea, etc.
Shrew Simon Short sewed shoes — sixteen summers, spreading sunshine saw Simon's small shabby shop still staunch.
Pouting peevishly Pretty Polly Perkins persistently pursued Paul's ping-pong playing partner, Peter.

Make up your own sentences with sounds that are difficult.

Pronunciation and Diction

Discuss: Regional differences in pronunciation and diction. Read aloud and discuss the pronunciation of the following words. Remember, depending on your point of reference, that everyone has an accent, and there is no right or wrong. Do not make fun of someone who sounds different from the way you do. You don't need to feel defensive, either. Simply compare your pronunciation with others and the dictionary and discuss any differences. If there are more worthwhile ways to speak for life and drama, it may be worth the challenge to change. Meantime, just relax and celebrate diversity.

America	wash (no "r")	Washington
squash	water (did you	bottle
little	say "wodder"	often
just	"wat-tuh" or	grocery
it's cloudy	"wort-tuh"?)	athlete (did you say
been	any	"athalete"?)
many	get	ten
guess	where	what
when	why	white
wharf	similar	constitution
familiar	students	suitcase
Tuesday	pharynx	larynx (inks – not nix)
picture	pitcher	voice
oil	girl	curl
cow	now	ours
yours	believe	porridge
last time	first time	night's slow passing
right	bite	fight
social security	statistics	morning
this morning	them	going to
didn't you	couldn't you	wouldn't you
wolf	a	the
enough	escape	poor
roof	book	government
environment	route	data
harassed	exquisite	absurd
about you	interesting	accuracy
always	adult	aluminum
laboratory	library	February
warriors	telephone	amphitheater
sphere	diphthong	sophomore
diphtheria	probably	news
adult	ask	drowned
etcetera	height	length
jewelry	realty	nuclear

(Add your own.)

55

Accents

Depending on what is regarded as the norm, everybody, in a sense, has an accent. Different places, countries, regions, areas, have definite sounds that come from living in those places. People's accents are often determined by where they come from and/or how their families talked. Most playwrights write the way they talk. And actors, when speaking normally, usually have accents on the basis of their origins.

People from other countries who speak English all have many different variations of accent and pronunciations for different words. Other countries that speak English and have different identifiable accents are the Cockney in England, the West Indies, the Australian "strain" sound, the Irish accent or Canadian sounds. All have their origins in English.

Several different regions of this country with different accents are: general American speech from the Midwest, the Boston Irish sound, the East Coast or New York/New Jersey sound, the soft speech in the deep South and the west Texas twang sound. But, since we are a mobile society and hear TV speech, not all people from any one region have the same accent.

Actors who can "do accents" and impressions or imitations of people vocally can frequently do many. This may be something like singing on key. But there seems to be no relation between doing accents and singing on key. And people who can't naturally do accents seem to have a difficult time developing a feeling for doing them. This may be an area of acting in which, if you can do accents and different voices naturally, you can, and if you can't, you can't.

However, there are a number of books that help develop this skill. Sounding authentic has at least two aspects: forming the right sounds and establishing the rhythms of speech. Forming the right sounds depends on where the sounds are placed in the mouth and how they are pronounced and articulated.

Doing plays that were originally written in a foreign language present the problem of what to do with accents. For instance, there were many movies during World War II with Germans talking to Germans in English with German accents, which they would never do. Or, if you do a play by Chekhov (originally in Russian) or by Ibsen (originally in Norwegian) with a British accent for a British audience, you would of course, do it in English. But would you do it with a Russian or Norwegian accent? Why?

But then, if it's British English and there are servants, do the servants speak Cockney to indicate they are a lower economic class? Is it possible that this could not only be inaccurate, but also could be offensive to some group?

When a British comedy is performed by an amateur group in the United States "doing British accents" with each cast member having a different sound and being in and out of the accent, you can appreciate the problem. It is difficult for one cast to do the same accent, which is not their own, and do it honestly and accurately so that it doesn't call attention to itself.

But even with American plays played by Americans, how do you believably play New York or Boston characters in the south or vice versa? It's an almost unsolvable problem. Whatever you arrive at doing, all the people in the play or scene should sound as if they belong in the same play and not call attention to themselves by some strange sounding "tacked-on" phony accent. The ultimate answer might be "do whatever works for the production." Some actors have learned to speak with something called "stage diction." This is a somewhat cultured American speech sound with a touch of British diction. It is slightly mannered.

Ultimately, you should not listen to yourself, but instead think about what you are saying — not the way it sounds.

The I.P.A.

The I.P.A. is the International Phonetic Alphabet. There are characters representing sounds from all of the major languages in the world including diphthongs. (Diphthongs are two vowel sounds together in the same syllable, for example: about.) If you have a difficult time hearing and reproducing the correct or accepted pronunciation of words, then it is possible to use the I.P.A. as another approach to the problem.

> *"Speak the speech, I pray you, as I pronounced it to you,*
> *trippingly on the tongue: but if you mouth it, as many of your players do,*
> *I had as lief the town-crier spoke my lines."*
> — *Hamlet,* by William Shakespeare

Chapter 6
Hamlet's Advice to the Players

Below is Hamlet's advice to a band of strolling players from Act III, Scene 2 of *Hamlet*, by William Shakespeare.

Hamlet:

"Speak the speech, I pray you, as I pronounced it to you, trippingly on the tongue: but if you mouth it, as many of your players do, I had as lief the town-crier spoke my lines. Nor do not saw the air too much with your hand, thus; but use all gently: for in the very torrent, tempest, and, as I may say, whirlwind of your passion, you must acquire and beget a temperance that may give it smoothness. O, it offends me to the soul to hear a robustious periwig-pated fellow tear a passion to tatters, to very rags, to split the ears of the groundlings, who, for the most part, are capable of nothing but inexplicable dumb-shows and noise: I would have such a fellow whipped for o'erdoing Termagant; it out-herods Herod: pray you, avoid it.

"Be not to tame neither, but let your own discretion be your tutor: suit the action to the word, the word to the action: with this special observance, that you o'erstep not the modesty of nature: for anything so overdone is from the purpose of playing, whose end, both at the first and now, was and is, to hold, as 'twere, the mirror up to nature; to show virtue her own feature, scorn her own image, and the very age and body of the time his form and pressure. Now this overdone or come tardy off, though it make the unskillful laugh, cannot but make the judicious grieve; the censure of the which one must in your allowance o'erweigh a whole theatre and others. O, there be players that I have seen play, and heard others praise, and that highly, not to speak profanely, that neither having the accent of Christians not the gait of Christian, pagan, nor man, have so strutted and bellowed that I have thought some of nature's journeymen had made men, and not made them well, they imitated humanity so abominably.

"O, reform it altogether. And let those that play your clowns speak no more that is set down for them: for there be of them that will themselves laugh, to set on some quantity of barren spectators to laugh, too, though in the mean time some necessary question of the play be then to be considered: that's villainous, and shows a most pitiful ambition in the fool that uses it. Go, make you ready."

Analyzing Hamlet's Advice

Hamlet's advice to the players is really Shakespeare's advice to all performers. Although written in 1602, the advice on body, voice and emotions is still valid for actors today.

1. *"Speak the speech, I pray you, as I pronounced it to you, trippingly on the tongue: but if you mouth it, as many of your players do, I had as lief the town-crier spoke my lines."* This is advice not to mumble and "garble" your lines, but instead to use good diction and enunciation when playing a character so that the audience will understand every word that your character says. This was explored in Chapter 5.

2. *" ... in the very torrent, tempest, and ... whirlwind of passion, you must acquire and beget a temperance that may give it smoothness."* However emotional the character is, and however emotional you are playing the character, you still must be in control of your own emotions. For example, do not wave your arms wildly, flip your hands or toss your head without a purpose. Every movement should have a purpose. (See Exercise: Showing Emotional Moods in a Mini-Scene," in Chapter 13.)

3. *"Suit the action to the word."* This could mean any action or movement, but usually or at least, mostly, refers to gesture. The gesture, or movement, should match or reinforce the words in the dialog. When you "don't know what to do with your hands," you can suit the action of your hands, arms and body with what you are saying or with the words in the dialog. See exercise on "Suiting the Action to the Word" in this chapter. Some caution needs to be exercised when actually playing a character.

4. *"Suit the word to the action."* This means to make the words sound like the ideas or feelings they represent. (See exercise in "Suiting the Word to the Action" in this chapter. Also, see "Thoughts and Emotions," and the exercise "Showing Emotional Moods in a Mini-Scene" in Chapter 13.)

5. *"Hold the mirror up to nature ... "* This means, at least in part, that you need to portray people honestly and realistically in drama ... as they are in life. And in order to do this you need to observe other people, and yourself.

6. *"Speak no more that is set down for them: for there be of them that will themselves laugh, to set on some quantity of barren spectators to laugh, too ... "* This means that when playing a role, don't make up extra lines and stage business in order to get the audience to laugh. Don't break character just to be noticed. It will destroy the audience's concentration on the play, and it's very unfair to your other performers, and unprofessional.

Look, Think, Gesture or Move and Speak.

In acting, as in life, the thought and physical movement usually precedes speaking.

But, gesture and speech may move closely together. The gesture may precede the words slightly, or be at the same time. This sequence will probably come naturally.

But if it follows ("come tardy off"), it could bring laughs. For example, picture someone leaving. Then, notice the difference in the following: Gesture in direction, pause, and say, "He went that way." Then, gesture in direction and simultaneously say, "He went that way." Then, say, "He went that way," pause and gesture in that direction. How did each feel and look? Variations of the time spent on each can give a different feeling to the line. This may be seen in the presentation of nineteenth century melodramas that are satirized. Shakespeare also implies to keep the size of the action in keeping with the size of the role and distance from the audience. (For more on size and relation of dialog and gesture, see Chapter 7.)

Exercise

Observe and take notes on people. This may include family members, classmates at school, in class, hallways, the cafeteria and people in shopping centers. What do the people do with their body: their hands, their feet, their face and mouth and eyes? And what do the movements tell us about the person? Actually, you probably have already observed other people's physical movements, and your subconscious use of gestures and facial expressions that are similar to those of your friends and family.

Practice the movements of others and note how they feel. After the movements have been practiced or repeated for a while, they become yours and should feel perfectly natural if they are right for the character. This approach is particularly helpful in performing someone who is nothing like you are in age or type. Practice doing what you have been seeing, then show us the people you've been observing. Remember, it is demeaning to the performer to be cruel. (For more on this subject see Chapter 14.)

Exercise: "Suiting the Action to the Word"

Physical movement involves body, face, and gesture in such a way that the movement supports and reinforces the spoken word. Be as detailed and specific as possible. But, for exercise purposes, do not be afraid to exaggerate. Note that the memory of the line reinforces the memory of the movement and vice versa. Choose the proper gender.

The Performer:

Who am I, Ladies and Gentlemen? I am Queen Elizabeth/Emperor Napoleon, I am mother/father, teacher, student, doctor, lawyer, cowgirl/cowboy, custodian and minister. I am everyone and no one. I am the policeman who seizes the criminal. No, I am the beggar who is condemned by the judge. I command and I obey. I am a swaggering young woman/man about town, with hat cocked, plume flying and sword ready. Ladies and gentlemen, I am an actor.

The City

I am one of those employees who work way up in the sky on the twenty-fifth floor of the smooth-fronted office building. I'm the stressed-out, overworked employee who programs on my computer, answers the telephone and files letters. I take/give dictation, go on coffee breaks, file my nails/polish my shoes, comb my hair until the end of the day, when I check my watch and leave for home on the elevator. I buy my evening newspaper, see that it's raining, put up my umbrella, jump over puddles, get into a taxi and head home.

Outdoors

In a splashing, churning stream are slithery, snapping fish. Back from the bank is a tall, stately tree covered with fan-shaped, rainbow-colored leaves that shimmer when the high hot sun hits them. In the fall, when the air becomes crisp and cool, the leaves float slowly, slowly, slowly down to the moist ground. Underneath a nearby ugly rock is a little — very little — wiggly worm with two antennae that look from side to side, and then stare at you. I call my favorite dog, "Here, boy," and pet his heavy coat. Then, I brush off a tree stump and sit down with my fishing pole, throw in the line and after a few moments ... fall asleep.

My Uncle

Hi, there. Come on in. Sit down. No, no, not in that chair. Up, up, up! That's my uncle's "beautiful, personal" chair. My uncle is grouchy and mean. He hates everybody in the whole world. Except me, maybe. Sometimes he smiles at me — a stupid, idiotic smile — and says in a deep voice, "You're a good little kid — but I want you to get out of my chair!" I do. Quickly. My uncle's a miner. I don't mean like a little kid — I mean, like a grouchy old man who works way down in the ground in a mine. Yes sir, my uncle's quite a guy. Go on, sit in his chair. He won't be home till later.

Write your own brief story or exercise that uses words that are conducive to "Suiting the Action to the Word" and "Suiting the Word to the Action."

Exercise: "Suiting the Word to the Action"

This is an exercise in making the word sound like the idea it represents. Pick any 25 words or phrases from the list below and read them aloud. Take your time between each. Be specific rather than vague and general. It can give an added shading of meaning to picture someone who is like the quality described. Or, you may act out the words as a character with that quality. You may add a noun or verb if you feel it helps. Some are similar. For variation, do not put like words together.

ugly	beautiful	crazy
bubbly	gnarled and twisted	funny
dumb	hateful	winding
long, long, long	roar	whirring
martyr	stinky	cautious
riff-raff	watchful	brokenhearted
glob	roly-poly	rugged
dangerous	mean	vulgar
sullen	cold	vengeful
clod	dull	prying
suspicious	cuddly	sleepily (with yawn)
faster and faster and faster	did oo wannum din-din	sycophant silly and giggly
weak-willed	wishy-washy	evil
goody-goody	lusty	lout
lazy	loose	lumbering
frowning	smiling	grumbling
innocent	tough	uptight
apologetic	lonely	accuse
piggy	wiggly	heavy
slob	twinkle toes	home
kiss	soft	worrywart
oddball	nervous	boring
fearful	precise	floozy
scatterbrained	thundering	sweet
luscious	tsk, tsk, tsk	bumpy
messy	militant	ick! or icky!
wheezy	upset	doubtful
tired	worn out	prissy
cynical	conniving	humbling
cute	pest	fat
skinny	hesitant	tearful
angry	sad	thoughtful
healthy	sick	

Audition Exercise

Practice reading the form below with a variety of emotions for possible auditions. Directors are looking for certain types of people that register believability in terms of physical type, vocal type, character traits, emotions and acting ability. While this audition form is short, it offers enough information for the committee to make a valued judgment. Suit the action to the word and the word to the action in the following material. That is, make the character traits and emotions sound and look like the words and be believable. Take your time. If it is helpful, take a slight pause after each sentence.

Audition Form

Hi, My name is _____. I've had (choose one) a lot of/a variety of/almost no/ some experiences in acting.

I like playing proud, noble protagonists for a positive experience.

But, I can do happy, (chuckle) cheerful, comedy roles, too.

Or, I can play sad, (almost tearful) serious, soap opera type roles.

I also like very friendly, romantic, flirtatious types, too.

And, I can also act suspicious, melodramatic, villainous characters. As well as lazy (yawn) tired, boring parts.

Or, I can play shy, meek, hesitant characters.

Or, sometimes even perform mean, angry, vicious types.

And, I can also play dumb, stupid type character parts.

But most of all I like to play _____ type characters, in an age range of _____ to _____.

Thank you.

(This exercise may be repeated when studying Chapter 13.)

Chapter 7
Practical Skills and Considerations

"Acting is fine, if you don't get caught at it."
— Spencer Tracy

Body and Voice

Size of Performance

Size of performance refers to how big, exaggerated or theatrical your gestures, movement, voice and emotions need to be for your performance. This is determined by several factors.

Size of Theatre or Distance from Audience

A performance needs to be bigger in a large theatre. Acting in a large theatre where you are some distance to the audience calls for larger body movements, more voice projection, more clarity of pronunciation, and more intense emotions. However, you need to beware of playing over the heads of the audience instead of directly to them and not being truthful as you increase the size of the emotions. A smaller performance is usually called for in smaller theatres (99 seats or less), and smaller emotions are needed. But you still need to be honest and project your voice and emotions.

Style or Type of Play

Classic plays such as Greek, Roman or other period plays of Shakespeare, Moliere or the seventeenth and eighteenth centuries are usually larger, more stylized or more theatrical than modern realistic plays. (See Chapter 12 for more on naturalism and theatricality.)

Type of Character

Some character traits call for more theatricality: a braggart warrior, country bumpkin or salesman needs to be bigger than a shy introvert.

Number of People on Stage

When there are crowds or large musical numbers, you may need to be bigger, or more theatrical, vocally and physically in order to be seen and heard when delivering lines.

Acting for Film

In performing for TV, commercials or motion pictures, the size may be smaller since the projection is only to the camera. But the performance needs to be even more honest because the camera registers your inner thoughts. (See Chapter 20.)

Emphasizing an Idea

You may emphasize words or an idea by changing what you are doing physically, vocally or emotionally. The change calls attention to what you are doing. The choice of what you do depends on what you want to emphasize, or point out, or what your intention, or objective or subtext is. (See Chapter 15.)

Physically

Any change in physical movement should call attention to what is happening, being said or to the idea you want emphasized. For physical movement you may stop moving, start moving, or change the size of the movement: smaller to bigger, bigger to smaller, slow to fast or fast to slow, etc.

For example, if you are sitting thinking what you are going to do next about some problem, then, suddenly make a decision, you could give a definitive slap of your thigh and rise. Or, you might be walking nervously, then stop, because you've "thought it through," and now have an answer. Or you might be trying to decide which way to turn or which direction to go in an issue or with a person.

Vocally

You may emphasize an idea, or *point a line*, by a change in your vocal delivery. You may go slower to faster, faster to slower, use pauses or broken sentences in different ways or elongate vowel sounds. These are all ways to change time, rate or pace. If you are talking softly, you may hit or punch a word or line. Or, you may go from loud to soft, slow to fast or fast to slow, etc. Also, changes in pitch, volume or even quality of voice may also be used to call attention to an idea.

Exercise: Emphasizing an Idea #1

Read the following: "I'm not sure who committed the crime. I still suspect several people. It could be the crazy uncle ... or the jolly aunt ... or the suspicious-looking butler ... or perhaps even the detective. In putting together the various pieces of information ...

like who poisoned the wine, or who got the millionaire to rewrite his will, or who wanted revenge, I would say ... if I had to decide on one right now, it would be _____."

Discussion: From the way the above was read, who do you think committed the crime and why?

Exercise: Emphasizing an Idea # 2

Choose a short paragraph from an exercise or scene of your choice and illustrate how a word, a line or an idea can be emphasized by a physical or vocal change.

Special Voice Skills

In acting, as in life, people stumble on lines and backtrack and grope and fumble for the right words. If this happens to you in a play, treat it as natural. And to a limited extent, if any hesitation is motivated by the character, it is possible to plan this as an effect to show character or call attention to an idea. Here are some possibilities for variety and emphasizing ideas.

"Putt-Putting"

This would mean that you purposely add hesitancy to your lines through backtracking and groping. Take a simple line like, "I should do something. But, I don't know what to do in this situation." It might sound like this, "Well, I, uh ... uh, should uh ... ummm, do something. But, but, but, I, uh ... don't ... I just don't ... know what to, uh ... do ... in this, uh ... " Well, uh ... *whatever you do, don't overdo!*

Phrasing Speeches

Audiences like to be surprised. It's possible to breathe at a time that the audience least expects it: at the obvious places. Or you may break up the speeches at ... unconventional places.

Exercise: Using a Change in Phrasing Sentences for a Dramatic Effect

First read this without the ... (slight pause). Then, read it with the pauses. "When I returned home I found ... the front door slightly open. And stepping inside ... I noticed ... the only light on ... in the entire house ... was in the family room. The TV was still on to the test pattern ... Then ... I saw ... someone ... slumped over in the big armchair, with arm falling to the side. As soon as I reached the person, I realized ... it was my _____ ... who was ... sound asleep."

Rhythm

Let your thoughts and your actions precede your speech. Don't rush or hurry your performance. Don't stumble over your lines. Keep the lines "out in front of you, so that you are underneath and behind the performance." Some actors focus on being clear and understood by speaking slowly, clearly and distinctly.

Pauses

When pauses are indicated in the script, pause. The playwright wrote those pauses because she or he heard them as part of the rhythm of the character and the scene. They are important to establish the overall rhythm of the play. The time can be filled with thoughts, looks and movement that further expand interest in your character. Use pauses positively to enhance your character and the play.

Secrets

Withholding something or having a secret can give your character and a scene a special quality. This can apply to ambiguity or showing several sides to a character.

Picking Up Cues

Your "cue" is the other actor's line that precedes yours. Most of the time you will need to follow by delivering your line quite closely to establish an interesting rhythm. This is particularly true of a farce-comedy. In order to do this, you need to take a breath while the other actor is speaking so that you will be ready to deliver your line. This is also a good time to convey thoughts and physical reactions to the other actors' dialog.

Caution: While anything is possible, not everything is necessary. While these techniques can be effective, offer surprises and make dialog sound more interesting and more dramatic, a simple, straightforward delivery of your lines, in most situations, may be the best. But, you still need to use your good judgment and stay honest and truthful to your character. Don't let your technique show. It is only important to know more skills, if needed. But, it's equally important not to overdo these techniques!

Entrances and Exits

Your character has a life outside of the space on-stage where the lines are delivered. Show some aspect of that life by making your entrances and exits purposeful.

Entrances

In acting, as in life, you only make a first impression once. So, plan to establish your character with your first entrance to show who you are, where you are coming from, why you are entering the scene at this time and something about the off-stage environment.

You can show the weather, time of day or current concern. You might show the weather by sweating from the heat, shivering from the cold, brushing off rain, straightening your hair from the wind, etc. Or, you can give some indication of an occupation, hobby or concern over personal appearance. Or, you can be in the midst of an activity such as eating, reading or just looking for something. You might also show some character trait or an emotional state. Whatever you do, it should be plausible for your character in that situation.

In acting, as in life, when you first enter a room, you probably look for people you know or people like yourself for both comfort and safety. Do you notice gender, age, race, ethnicity, etc.? It is natural to want to be near or next to a friend or group of friends that share your common outlook on life in order to have a feeling of both safety and comfort? What would your character notice? Would it be the room, the change in the environment or a person that is already there? Is the person you see familiar, an old friend, a lover, a stranger, a parent, an enemy, or what? The way you react to this person will establish your relationship, and the audience will note this.

However, when you show the audience who you are, you don't need to show everything at that time. Show just enough to be believable and create an interest in your character. Frequently, the playwright will give you a line to show your basic objective. For example, your character might have a line such as, "Ah, there you are. I've been thinking over what you said, and my major concern on this subject is ... (the money, my family, my job)."

Exits

When you exit, know why you're leaving, where you are going and why, and what are you going to do and why. The way you exit, quickly, slowly, hesitantly, etc., can show both the whys and wherefore. And finish the scene before you leave.

In Different Locations or Environments

Closely associated with entrances and establishing your character is establishing your familiarity with the location or environment, both the space itself and the people whom you see there. For instance, if a scene is set in "your house," a house belonging to your character, then you can show that you are familiar with the surroundings by the way you move around and relate to everything. If this is your house or your room, you would probably not look for the light switch and bump into the furniture. In fact, you might even reach for things without looking. This takes some practice.

By the same token, if you are entering someplace for the first time, and your character is unfamiliar with the environment, you might look around to explore the space and make thoughtful evaluations, even though you, as an actor, would be familiar or know where things are. Or, you might look around for something before you found "what you were looking for." Or, you might purposely do the "wrong thing" several times before "discovering" the correct thing.

Reading and Writing

Reading or writing something in life usually takes longer than is allowed for on-stage. And for most people to watch someone read or write something is like watching the grass grow. The dilemma is this: if you do it realistically, it can be dramatically boring. If you do it too quickly, it's not believable. You need to find a balance.

However, it is still best if you can actually read, or at least speed read, rather than just glance at the paper or book. And, it is better to actually write words on the paper more quickly than normal, rather than scribble something. This is particularly true for performing in theatre-in-the-round where the audience is so close they can see what you are reading and writing.

To realistically lengthen the time, one answer can be to compromise the length. Or, you can fill the time by reacting emotionally to what you are reading or writing. You can show this with body movement and gestures or use of book or paper or pen and/or facial expression to indicate thoughts about what you are reading or writing. Don't "mug." Just think. It might even be possible to add an "ummm," or "huh" or two as you react. (For more on emotions and images see Chapters 13 and 14.)

69

Eating and Drinking

Eating on-stage can be a problem for actors, director and prop crew. For actors to be seen while passing food at a crowded table and to be clearly understood while actually eating food and delivering lines is an acting problem in many plays. You need to space the timing of eating so that you don't put food in your mouth just before you have to deliver a long speech. You can spend much time in cutting and organizing food on your plate and very little in actually eating. You can also bring a fork toward your mouth, stop, lower the fork, deliver the line, start again, stop, etc. Then, ultimately, take a small bite. So, if you need to eat and talk, take very small portions of food and chew as vigorously as your character might chew.

As a suggestion in rehearsal, only pantomime eating. Remember, food is also a problem for the prop crew. They either need to buy it or prepare something. It can be very distressing if you gobble down a bag of potato chips during rehearsal. It does nothing to enhance you as an actor, and does even less to endear you to the prop crew if the prop crew has to go to the grocery store and purchase another bag of potato chips. Also, don't eat any food while it's on the prop table. You'll be doing yourself a favor since some of the food may be "faked" in some way.

In terms of drinking, small portions are also best. Colored water, tea, cold powdered coffee and powdered milk often serve for a variety drinks. You don't need to gulp.

Playing drunk

When people are drunk in real life they are slightly out of control. In life, people do not want to appear drunk. So, if you need to appear "drunk," don't overdo it. Just totally relax your whole body, then, try to control your movement and speech and not appear drunk. Less is more.

Laughing

Laughing is generally a positive emotion. To accomplish this you need to, first of all, relax and inhale. Then, you need to exhale by tightening or contracting your abdominal muscles in short bursts of air so that the laughter comes out on vowel sounds. There are all types and variations of laughs or ways to express delight. While smiles may come rather spontaneously, laughter is a little harder to make believable. However you choose to laugh, the laugh should be honest and believable in terms of the character and the situation.

Group Exercise 1

As each of these types of laughs is read, perform them. Start with a smile, now chuckle, giggle, give a stifled laugh, a snicker, a "wheezy" laugh, an evil, sinister snarl, a guffaw and a "belly" laugh.

Group Exercise 2

Remembering the exercises from Chapter 5, change pitch, volume, pace, and finally quality as you go through a group of vowel sounds such as "Ha, ha, ha, hee, hee, hee, heh, heh, heh, ho ho, ho, haw, haw, haw," etc. In pitch you can go from high to low and low the high and then circumflex. Then, change volume and speed. All this may be done as a group activity.

Individual Exercise

Laugh while saying a simple line such as: "This is a really strange day, and a lot of weird things are happening."

Crying

The basic breathing technique of crying is similar to laughing, but the inhaling is more like gasping for breath. The basic physical feeling of either laughing or crying begins in the diaphragm area with the expulsion of air.

Some techniques may include: the muscles may grow tense, the hands may clench, the face may "cloud up," be contorted and register real pain and distress, the lip may quiver and you may even bite a lip or finger in anguish. Because you are gasping there may be a "catch in the throat." It might be helpful in stage crying to bite your lip, pinch yourself or dig a fingernail into another finger to create a small pain.

As with laughing, the crying should be believable for that character and within the context of that scene. These are reactions that should not be tacked onto a character artificially. By the same token, you are an actor who should be in control, and not someone who loses control with a tear-drenched performance. In order to make it honest, begin with the character in the scene and the thoughts and feelings of sadness, loneliness, loss or whatever happened that made your character need to cry.

Crying may be difficult for many, since our culture tends to view people who cry as either weak or having lost control of their emotions. (This possibly began when an angry parent or sibling said to a small child, "Quit crying," or "Get a hold of yourself!") Most people don't want to cry in front of others. Just as drunks try not to appear drunk, most people try not to cry. Crying, like being drunk, is a state in which someone has lost control.

When trying to cry as an actor, you are often trying to control the emotion and "make it happen." Some people can do this. But trying not to cry is more life-like. In terms of crying, you can say to yourself, "I'm not going to cry. I'm not going to cry!" The attempted restraint is more life-like, and even if it doesn't bring tears, it should appear more honestly real and create the feeling you are about to cry. As with laughing, there are many types and variations of crying. Both laughing and crying need to be practiced and the feelings and experiences remembered and internalized to produce believable laughing and crying. (See Chapter 13.)

Group Exercise
Do each of the following: whimper, sob, give a stifled gasp, wail, weep out of control.

Exercise in Laughing and Crying
Choose a short scene. This might be "Suiting the Action to the Word," "Emotional Moods" or any group of ten to fifteen lines. Then, laugh or cry as you deliver the lines. Still another method, based on emotional memory exercises from the techniques of "The Method," is to remember a situation in the past that caused you to cry or laugh. With some practice you should be able to improve these skills. (See Chapter 13.)

Switching Electrical Appliances Off and On

Many plays call for characters to turn on or off lights, appliances, TV sets, tape recorders, etc. If it is "practical," it means the performer actually controls the power. If, however, the power originates in the control booth, then the switching on and off needs to be coordinated with lights and sound (for records and radio). Since the light and sound control people are watching you, you may need to help by holding your hand on a switch until the lights or appliance go on or off rather than quickly flipping the switch.

Using a Telephone
On Answering the Phone

The ringing of the phone needs to be coordinated with sound control. It needs to come on or before the end of the dialog that is the cue. And it needs to stop when or before the phone is answered. If the ring comes slightly early, there is no problem since most calls are not answered on the first ring, anyway. So, if you have more dialog, a second or even a third ring is believable. However, if for any reason sound control might be late in ringing, it can be helpful to decide in advance what you will do to fill the time by improvising dialog or stage business until it rings. And, if you know that the news on the phone will be negative, for example, the news about some accident or disaster, then it can be dramatically interesting to approach the phone in a cheerful mood. When the discovery of the negative news comes, it can create a dramatic reversal. This would be in reverse to the good news. Since most people don't answer the telephone on the first ring, if you're actually calling someone, allow time to let it ring several times before someone would answer, and you begin talking.

Talking on the Phone

It's best to hold the phone on the upstage side of the face or low enough on the face so the audience can see your mouth. If the audience can see your mouth move, they can actually "hear better," because it adds the visual to the auditory. (See Chapter 8 for ways to create someone being on the other end of the phone to make the conversations believable.)

Takes and Double-takes

These are comic reactions to a situation. Essentially, "a take" is a surprised, often delayed, comic physical reaction, mostly facial, to something unexpected that someone says or does or a reaction to something unexpected that happens. The head turns with a look of, "What?! I don't believe this!" For instance, if someone volunteers you to do something you don't want to do, or that person brags about you and says something that is exaggerated or outrageously untrue. For instance, someone says,. "S/He just loves to go camping and hiking and all those things in nature." If you don't like camping or hiking and think of "nature" as something with a lot of bugs, it could produce a large take. A double take involves two looks, one of slight disbelief followed by a bigger facial response of surprise. For example: a friend or parent volunteers you to play tennis in a tennis tournament and says, "Oh, yes, s/he just loves tennis. S/He was a champion in high school," when in fact you never played tennis, didn't enjoy it, and you certainly weren't a champion. Your first surprised response would be the registered thought, "Love tennis?!" and an even bigger response to being "a champion in high school!?"

Stage Fighting

When called upon, a stage fight needs to be carefully choreographed in slow motion in order to produce maximum effect and safety. A director can help work this out.

Fist Fighting

Decide who hit who when, how, where, and why. The planned hit, which is a near miss, needs to result in a sound which can be produced by the recipient slapping hands (unseen) or clicking the tongue as "the blow" jars the jaw or body. The recipient reacts in response by falling away from the hit. Then, keeping the same patterns of movement, tighten the fists, firm the muscles and increase the speed to normal and practice until it appears realistic.

Slapping

This is similar in technique to a fist fight, except it is possible to cup the hand, relax the wrist and avoid hurting the recipient. Make contact to the jaw of the person who is retreating. This can create a sound and look real. Avoid hitting in the area of the ear. This also needs careful practice for safety reasons.

Stabbing

The knife in a stabbing should be a rubber knife or child's toy with a retreating blade. One area to "stab" can be in the underarm area, between the arm and the chest. On the stage, at a distance, this can give the appearance of "going into the body." The recipient of the stab needs to pull away from the stabbing just as the stab blow is delivered. If the knife goes in the stomach area, the recipient can double over and grab that part of the body and pull in or away from the stabbing for added effect. This is often hidden in some way by committing the act in a corner of the set away from the audience or behind furniture and/or by the actors themselves. Protection or padding can also be helpful.

Falling

In falling, you need to stay relaxed and crumple in short movements. By dropping your head as you hunch forward, bending at the waist and dropping and pulling your arms inward and downward to break your fall as you bend your knees, you can fall slowly but believably without hurting yourself.

If possible, as part of the pattern, use furniture to brace yourself and break your fall. Fall with your body parallel or head downstage to the audience, rather than feet aimed at them. For safety, use gym mats or some type of pillows when practicing this technique.

Dying

After being shot or stabbed and grasping toward the wounded area, the death that follows needs to show weakness and pain. This should be played slowly with agonized movement and a shortness of breath with a slow, choppy, hesitant and gasping delivery of lines.

Playing Love Scenes

These scenes are often difficult for actors because they are showing affection publicly for something that is usually private. And the private activity is usually between two people who know each other very well and who have gained a trust over time. But this is not about you. It is your character that is in love, and you are the actor showing this affection. As an actor, you need to show these people are really in love.

These scenes need to be planned about halfway through the rehearsal schedule in order to be comfortable. Starting too late can leave actors flustered, resulting in lines being dropped. And, starting while actors are still walking around with scripts in their hands, before they really know each other, is usually too early. It's usually easiest to begin to work privately and separately with the director to choreograph the scenes. You can begin by standing close in a dance position with both people looking in each other's eyes. The kiss can follow from here, or the female can turn slightly upstage to mask the kiss, which may or may not happen.

Treating Mistakes as Normal

In acting, as in life, people make mistakes. Items can be lost or misplaced. People drop things, break things, lose things, bump into furniture, forget what they were saying, etc. Things go wrong, people don't arrive when expected, things aren't where you thought they were, drawers and doors stick, clothes get torn, you trip on rugs, etc. This is normal in life, and it happens on the stage. So, if mistakes happen to you on-stage, treat them as normal.

If something falls on the floor, pick it up and keep playing the scene. If lines are dropped or momentarily forgotten, stay calm, and do whatever is necessary to continue the scene whether it's your fault or someone else's fault. The audience doesn't know the lines or the action, and if you treat the situation as normal, they will probably assume it is normal. If you are rehearsing and get totally lost in what you are doing or saying, the director will often stop the rehearsal and backtrack to "fix the problem."

However, sometimes the action will not be stopped, so it's best to keep going, stay in character and fix the scene without breaking the continuity. You may need to improvise dialog or action in order to maintain character and a flow of the scene's rhythm until you get back on track. If you learn to work through a problem, it can prepare you more quickly for performance. Be prepared for whatever happens, but honor the moment.

Mistakes can actually be planned in order to make things that go wrong look even more like normal behavior. *Plan what you are going to do, then do something else — at least initially.*

Breaking Character

This means you stop your concentration on acting your character and do something else that is not part of the scene. You become yourself, or you may do something that is distracting, like stopping, becoming yourself, complaining about something or laughing. You may use the excuse that you don't know your lines, or the blocking isn't right, or you want to discuss your character's motivations. Whatever you do, it will probably not help the scene. Try to avoid breaking character. If you just stay with the scene and in character, you will help the other actors and yourself to create a better scene.

Whatever You Do, Do Definitely

For example, if it's being uncertain and insecure, then be definitely uncertain and insecure in order to project the quality. It's better to have a good actor playing a shy person rather than a person who is usually shy. It's better to have a good actor play a clumsy person rather than a clumsy person trying to play a clumsy person. (For more on character traits and emotions, see Chapter 13.)

Exhibitionism

"Showing off" is a need or want to be noticed to attract and focus attention on yourself rather than the character. It is often doing the wrong thing at the wrong time for the wrong reason —

possibly because of personal needs and insecurities — and it has nothing to do with the play. It has no place in performing. Honor your character and the play.

Being Self-Conscious

Being "self-conscious" means being "conscious of yourself." You may feel the audience is looking at you and wanting to judge you negatively. If so, this general insecurity can make you feel uncomfortable or embarrassed, which can make you feel fearful of failing. This is a natural reaction.

It's been reported by some pollsters on surveys that many people are more fearful of getting up in front of a group or an audience than they are of death. So, if you feel slightly insecure about playing a character on a stage for an audience, you are probably in the majority. The reality is that most audiences want you to succeed.

In order to *not* be self-conscious, it is best to focus outwardly on other performers in the scene and listen, really listen, to what they are saying and respond truthfully. You can also focus on your stage business and the action of the play. And, if you focus on the audience in terms of giving them your very best performance, that should also take away your feeling of being self-conscious because you won't be focusing on or thinking about yourself. Instead you will be giving something of yourself. It is better to give than to receive.

Skilled performers in other areas (athletes, musicians, etc.), who have trained and internalized their skills are not only not self-conscious, but they enjoy performing.

If the scene is about the other performer's character and you mainly need to show your reaction, then give the scene to the other actor. If you are sharing the scene, then share the scene fairly with the other actor. If it is your scene, then take the scene and give it your best.

If you are prepared, you should not feel self-conscious, because being prepared can help you relax and give you confidence. And confidence can improve your performance. So, if you are prepared and generous in sharing your performance with other actors and the audience, you will receive your rewards and there will be no need to be self-conscious.

Chapter 8
Listening, Relating and Projecting

"In every theatre audience there are three people sitting way in the back. One is blind, one is deaf, and one doesn't care. It's up to you to reach all of them."
— Anon.

"Make another member of the cast look good, and you will not only receive back the gift, but you, too, will look better."
— Anon.

"People listen, but don't always hear what's being said ... even people who say ... 'I hear you.'"
— Anon.

Listening and Relating

When developing a character you may start by analyzing, researching and developing a specific character as your approach to a whole script. But, you will need to use the basic skills of listening, relating and projecting to rehearse with the cast and perform for an audience. (See Chapters 13–16 in Part C for techniques in character development.)

While it is important to develop your personal characterization, it is also equally important to listen to other characters, relate and react to them honestly and project your performance to them and to the audience.

In acting, as in life, it is difficult to learn anything about other people if you're talking all the time. Talking is focusing on yourself when giving information. Listening is how you learn about other people and the world around you, both on-stage and in life. Listening can be a wonderful character trait for every day life.

Listening establishes an emotional relationship that helps everyone. Listening carefully to other actors on-stage can help you better understand how to play your character and deliver your lines. It's not only the words you hear, but also the emotions, feelings and thoughts behind those words.

Acting should be a two-way exchange, or sharing of ideas and information with another person, that involves body, voice, character traits and emotions and images. By honestly listening and responding to what other actors are doing and saying and how they are saying and doing it, you create a relationship or emotional bond with other actors and their characters. Giving emotional support to other actors should help you receive more emotional support and further define your character. This, in turn, helps both of you in playing scenes together and makes you both look better.

Listening establishes a rhythm and helps you relax. Listening honestly and carefully and focusing your attention outwardly on another actor rather than inwardly on yourself should help you be less self-conscious. Therefore, it should help you relax, because you are not watching or listening to yourself. This relationship not only establishes an internal rhythm but also helps the scene to be more realistic.

Repeat Exercises

Look again at Chapter 2 and the sections that involve "Relating To Another Performer — Physically," "Relating to another Performer — Vocally" and "Relating to Another Performer — Emotionally." Perform these exercises again with a new focus on listening and relating.

Exercise: Listening and Relating to Another Performer

Pair off. One person tells something about him or herself, and the other person listens and rephrases the line to say the same thing. Don't interpret. Just repeat with the same feeling in which it was stated. Don't change emotional intensity. The purpose is to listen and relate so that there's an emotional relationship and relaxed communication.

Example:

A: I got up this morning.
B: You got up this morning.
A: Around seven.
B: Around seven.
A: I had a good night's sleep.
B: You had a good night's sleep.
A: Then, I had breakfast.
B: Then, you had breakfast. (Continue this.)

Other subjects might include:
"Going to Classes"
"Getting Ready for a Social Outing"
"Cooking Something"
"Describing a Work Day" or "Describing a Hobby"

"Family Trip" or "Summer Camp Experience"

"How to play": sport, art, drama, painting, or music.

Switch the person who initiates the subject. This exercise may be repeated many, many times with different people. You may find that you relate to some people better than others.

Exercise: Listening and Relating in a Scene

This may also be used as a rehearsal technique when working on a real scene.

A: Say the line.

B: First repeat, and then deliver the new line.

For example:

A: "Oh, where did you come from?"

B: "Where did I come from? Off-stage in the wings."

A: "Off-stage in the wings? Where are you going?"

B: "Where am I going? I'm crossing you ... " (Continue this.)

Duo Exercise: Listening And Relating

Two people should choose one scene such as "Suiting the Action to the Word," (Chapter 6) or "Introduction to Emotions in the Mini-Scene" (Chapter 13). One person does only the physical movement and one does only the vocal part of the exercise. Since you need to form a bond, you need to listen and relate so you are together. After you have successfully performed with one combination, switch roles vocally and physically and perform with the new combination.

Thinking and Reacting
Listening and Thinking Are Also Acting

What are you thinking while acting? If you are thinking, "What's my next line?" you are not acting because you are not listening. If you don't have anything to do — no lines, no business — then it's okay to do nothing physically. But doing "nothing" does not mean that you are just waiting for your turn to speak. Because if you are part of the scene on-stage, listening and watching what others are saying and doing, then you will be reacting to this, even if it is simply by thinking. Thinking shows in your eyes and face, (Remember: The eyes are the mirror of the soul — or show what the mind is thinking) and this is doing something. But, don't mug! That is, don't make faces and react in an artificial way, as if you are listening. If you have few or no lines in a scene, think what you would say if you could speak. This may register even more strongly than if you have lines to say.

In drama ... as in life, the person talking can usually tell if you're truly listening or just pretending you're listening and faking a reaction that you don't really feel. Relax and stay focused on what is happening.

So, how does an actor learn to listen? First of all, your lines and characterization need to be so internalized that you are confident and relaxed in your performance. Then, by truly listening you can relate emotionally to the other actors and give a natural response, which creates a natural rhythm in the scene. Finally, you can simulate a life experience by paraphrasing in thought what the other actors are saying and doing and respond spontaneously, honestly and emotionally.

Exercise: Listening and Responding Only with Thoughts

The listener just thinks the response rather than speak the lines of dialog. For example: A is the speaker and B is the listener. Just think, don't mug.

A: I'm going to get married.

B: (With surprise and emotion, thinks, "Get married!? Who is it?")

A: Yes. To a wonderful person.

B: (Thinking, "Who is it?")

A: (For Female) Well, he's tall and strong and handsome and kind and friendly and nice.

(For Male) Well, she's very attractive and she's sweet and smart and friendly, and she likes me and I like her.

B: (Pictures images and thinking, "Wow! — Who could this be?")

A: Do you know_____(make up name)?

B: (Picturing this person and thinking, "Wow, I can't believe it!")

(Continue this.)

Exercise: Paraphrasing Thoughts to Respond

When you listen honestly your thoughts are often paraphrased. That is, you think a shortened phrase of what is said. You can often use key words or a shortened phrase.

Example #1

A: I've got something important to talk over with you.

(B thinks, "Oh? Important?")

A: Actually, it's, uh ... somewhat of a secret.

(B thinks, "Secret?")

A: It just sort of happened last Saturday.

(B thinks, "Happened ... Saturday?")

A: I'm ... well ... (Pause)

(B thinks, "What is s/he trying to tell me?")

A: I'm getting married.

(B thinks, "Married ... ?" Wow!)

A: And I'm quitting my job, and we're leaving and moving to Hawaii.

(B thinks, "Quitting ... Leaving ... Moving ... Hawaii!")

A: Are you surprised?

(B thinks, [come up with your own reaction])

If this does not come instinctively with practice, then it would be helpful to write the thoughts and memorize them along with the spoken lines. Or, prepare the scene with the lines memorized and say them. Then, rerun the scene with only the thoughts. In addition to adding honesty, this helps the rhythm of the scene, and the thoughts will show what the mind is thinking because the "eyes are the mirror of the soul."

Example #2: Using Short Phrases or Key Words

A: I have news about your friend (depending on the context of the scene and character).

(B could think, "News?" "Which friend?")

A: You remember Catherine.

(B thinks, "Oh, Catherine. What news?" and the thought registers with the emotion felt toward Catherine.)

A: Well, she went to a wild party.

(B thinks, "Wild party? Catherine?")

A: Yes, and on her way home she had an accident.

(B thinks, "Oh, no. Not an accident!")

A: And she was badly hurt.

(B thinks, "Oh, no. Hurt. Pain.")

A: But that was last week and she's much better now.

(B thinks, "Oh, good.")

A: And she wants to see you.

(B thinks, "Oh, good, I'd like to see Catherine.")

B: Where is she now?

Listening and Relating on the Telephone

In life, unlike acting, when talking on a telephone, there is someone on the other end who is actually listening and speaking. You know and are able to picture the person with whom you are speaking. A phone conversation is essentially a dialog.

However, on-stage, no one else is really there. The playwright has given the actor only half of the conversation with enough of the heard dialog to make sense of what is being said on the other end of the line. But the audience must believe there is someone on the other end of the telephone who is actually listening and talking.

Too often, because the actor speaking doesn't "hear" what the person on the other end of the line is saying or have an image of anyone, phone conversations are not believable. Because of that, the performer on the telephone often leaves too little or too much time, with little sense of rhythm in the conversation to give a sense that there is someone actually there.

In order to make the phone conversation realistic and believable and establish a proper rhythm to the scene, the speaker needs to have an image of the unseen character, know what that other person is saying and allow time for that person to say it.

The listener needs to focus on what is being said and respond honestly to the thoughts, emotions and images that are projected by the speaker. So, *in acting, as in life,* you need to have an image of the person and respond to what the other person would be saying. This is similar to the dialog problem. In this case, you need to picture the person you are talking to on the telephone and think the line that the person would be saying.

Exercise: Telephone Conversation

This is a solo monolog. This combines several skills that are used in changing emotions and images and the use of a telephone. Pantomime the telephone.

Person on Phone

(Phone rings.) Hello? (Beat. Puzzled.) Who is this? (Beat. Chuckle.) Oh, Pat. You don't sound like yourself. (Beat. Sympathetic.) Do you have a cold … or something? (Beat.) What? I can't hear you. Did you say danger? (Beat. Stage whisper.) Why are we whispering? (Beat.) Watch out for what? (Beat. Suspicious.) What are you trying to tell me? Is there someone there with you? (Beat. Annoyed.) Well, who is it? (Beat. Surprised.) Hello? Hello! (Angry) S/HE HUNG UP ON ME! (Hangs up slowly. Beat. Thinking what to do next. Suddenly there's a loud sound off-stage.

83

(Startled.) Who's there? (Beat. Fearful.) Who are you? What do you want? (Beat. No answer. Then, angry fearful.) Come on out where I can see you! (Beat, then relief.) Oh! — It's you! (Then, angry.) DON'T EVER DO THAT AGAIN. HEAR ME? DON'T!

In order to create this illusion most effectively, write out the lines that are being said by the unseen character, then memorize them and think those thoughts when the unseen character would be speaking. Thinking the thoughts being said creates the thought process of listening. This should establish a natural rhythm of the dialog, and prepares you, as the speaker to deliver the next line with the right emotional and intellectual tone.

In Summary: Write the dialog for the other unseen person, then memorize these lines and think the unseen person's lines before you speak your lines. At the same time, have an image of the other person as you "listen to," or think the other person's lines.

Including and Relating to Others: "Vibes"

Vibes is a word that is short or slang for vibrations, or the feeling of an emotional connection or relation with another person or actor. There are good vibes and bad vibes, positive and negative feelings in relation to others. When people say they are getting "negative" or "positive" vibes, it is this experience they are talking about. This is akin to the technique of "Projecting the Voice" in Chapter 5. This includes not only a vocal projection, but also a psychological or emotional inclusion and projection to another person, actor or audience.

For instance, have you ever gone into a store and not wanted to be waited on by a clerk? If so, you find yourself forming a psychological barrier between the clerk and yourself. It's like the feeling of being inside a bubble. Or, just the opposite, you want a clerk to wait on you, so you set off "relationship vibrations" in order for the clerk to notice you. These may not be anything physical or verbal, a psychological projection or opening out in the direction of the clerk.

In acting, as in life, people like to be included. One of the objectives in both should be to develop healthy relationships. In life, when you are among friends talking to each other, you know when you are "included" in the conversation whether they look at you or not. You can usually feel the thoughts and emotions directed toward you (or not). Just as you want to be included, so do other performers on-stage, and members of the audience.

Likewise, teachers often have ways of psychologically or emotionally focusing attention on single students or groups in a class. For example, there can be strong vibes or feelings of communication between a teacher and bright, cooperative students who are eager to learn, and special attention may often be focused on these students. At the same time, others who have unsatisfactory behavior may also attract attention unless or until there seems to be no hope for their positive involvement. Then, they can get "cut off" from the communication. This also applies to auditions when you need to project to the director conducting the auditions.

For instance, if you are telling a story to another person — or another character in a play — and a third person comes up to hear the story (the audience) and you want them included, then you also need to include them and project your character's emotions in their direction. Since acting is communicating, what is established in the communication between two actors is also communicated to an audience. Communication with the audience is more indirect than direct.

So, when communicating with other people, friends, performers and the audience, you need to relate to and include them emotionally and think positive thoughts about them. If doing this is not instinctive, it is an important skill that needs to be learned for anyone talking to or appearing in front of groups, whether they are performers, teachers or sales leaders.

Reacting and Responding

In life, you relate, react and respond to other people on the basis of *what* they say and the *way* they say it. But, life is unpredictable. In life you don't know what's coming next in conversation. In life you have no emotional preparation for response. Therefore, you act and react truthfully to what other people do and say.

But a script is predictable. In a play, the playwright has given actors the dialog, or *what* to say. But the actor, as an interpreter, determines *how* it is said. You, as an actor, know what's coming next. But your character doesn't. And if your character doesn't know in advance what other characters are going to say and do, how other actors are going to say it or what they are going to do physically and emotionally, then how can you honestly "prepare" for something that should be a surprise? Theoretically, you can't.

Rather than prepare an emotional reaction, you need to stay

open and receptive to what is happening on-stage at the moment. You need to listen and relate to other actors' emotional interpretations of their characters in order to react and respond realistically and truthfully with your character.

Listening, relating, reacting and responding to another actor should be more that just physical, emotional, sensory or intellectual. It is all of these in different proportions at different times.

Even with successive rehearsals your emotional relations with other actors may change, which in turn would alter your performance. Trust your instincts and stay in the moment as you listen, relate, react and respond spontaneously. This should give the illusion that the scene is happening for the first time.

Relating and Projecting to an Audience

While listening and relating in relationships between characters are important, less attention has been paid to developing skills that include relating to the audience, and to the camera in film acting. Ultimately, you will want and need to communicate your character and the play to the live audience and involve them in the production. It can be difficult to practice this skill because they are not there during rehearsals. If the director is listening, you can relate to him/her, but that is only one person. So, you have very little to relate to, or rehearse for, until you open the show when the audience comes to see the play. You owe it to the audience to involve them by projecting your most realistically honest and theatrically truthful performance to the people who came to see you and hope to see a good performance. You can say to yourself, "These nice people have come to see me. So, I want to give them the best performance I can give." This should also help you be less self-conscious and more relaxed and confident as you focus on giving your best performance.

If your performance or character is not reaching other performers or the audience, either vocally or emotionally, then this is a skill that needs to be practiced. Including the audience is a valuable skill, and with a little practice you should be able to accomplish the technique more quickly than you might have imagined.

Playing to a Specific Person

When you perform for an audience, playing to a specific person can enhance your performance. You may know that they are in the audience, or you might imagine that they are there. Either way it should help to keep your performance fresh because you want to play your performance to that person who will be seeing you in that role for the first time.

Projecting to an Audience

You also need to establish an emotional connection or relationship with the audience in order to project your character and story. Since acting is communicating, then what is established in the emotional communication between two actors also needs to be communicated to an audience — more indirectly than directly.

On several occasions, I have seen performers audition for roles. In an effort to impress the director who is casting the play and be chosen for the cast they have projected their character directly to the director in the middle or back of the house who is listening to the audition. In observing this, while sitting near the director, I was moved emotionally by the performers who were auditioning because they were projecting or playing their performances "out front" to me. This was not only vocal, but also emotional and psychological.

Then, they were cast. They learned their lines and rehearsed. Sets were built, costumes were constructed, lights were added and they performed for an audience. However, in the performance, they played *only* to the other performers on-stage, and their characterizations were never projected beyond the curtain line into any area of the audience. I heard their voices, but their emotional performances did not project to me or reach me.

In viewing these two situations I was struck by the disparity between the actors' projection in relating to the audience in the audition and how little reached or moved me when they were fully rehearsed for their full stage production.

On the other side of the spectrum, at the intermission of a Shakespearean performance by a famous Shakespearean actor, people from all parts of the theatre were heard saying, "He was playing all those scenes directly to me." This is an important basic skill that needs to be practiced.

While developing your character and the relationships between characters is important, less attention has been paid to developing skills that include relating to the audience, or the camera in behaving for film. This also needs to be practiced.

*Exercise: Projecting to the Audience Vocally,
Emotionally and Psychologically*

Begin by repeating the exercise in Chapter 5 that involves projecting the voice. Remember, it is like throwing a ball.

1. Say your line directly to the teacher or director in the audience area.

2. Then, look at the other performer on the stage, but still direct the line to someone in the audience.

3. Then, deliver the line as if it is going out to the audience and bouncing off of them back to the person on the stage. This way you include the audience by delivering your lines to the other person(s) on-stage at the same time you would be including the audience.

4. As the next step, have several people move to different areas of the house or auditorium. Then, as a performer, look at them and focus on them until you have an emotional connection to them. (This has some of the relationship qualities that you first experienced in the "Mirror Game" in Chapter 2.) Then, remembering the image of them and the emotional connection to them, again play the lines or scene to all areas of the room or auditorium. Watch what happens.

Discussion: Did the actor reach you vocally, emotionally or psychologically? Were you surprised at how quickly the actor was able to project his/her voice and include the audience more effectively than by just getting the direction, "Louder"?

Since communicating with other performers and audience is an important aspect of acting and life and takes time to learn, this can be repeated with every new scene. Combine this information with "Basic Acting and Directing Terms," "Ways to Gain Emphasis" and "Basic Stage Movement" (Chapter 3).

Listening to the Audience While Performing

In line with projecting your performance to the audience, it is also important to listen to the audience while you are performing. Since you are playing or projecting to them, they are also part of your scene. As you project to them, their energies and attentions are in turn focused back toward you and the person(s) with whom you are sharing the scene on-stage. The audience should be involved and attentive as a participant in the scene. If the scene is working, this experience of relating and sharing emotions can be very exciting.

If the audience is not attentive (coughing, shuffling, talking, getting up and leaving the theatre, etc.), it probably means you are somehow not projecting or communicating your performance, your character or the story, to reach them. You may be projecting your performance "over their heads," or not in their direction at all. Or, you may not be "including them psychologically."

In these cases, without breaking character, you may need to change some things. If it's a vocal problem, you may need to speak slower or faster (less likely), sharpen your diction and be more deliberate in speech. Or, you may need to relax, concentrate more, perhaps re-focus your projection, be more honest in thought and be more or less intense in emotion.

In Summary: A good actor is consistently aware of what is happening all around and relates to other people and the environment. Being aware of what other performers are doing, thinking and feeling is important so that you can respond spontaneously and honestly. Responding honestly in terms of that awareness is what enhances your acting performance.

Relating To Another Performer and the Audience

This is a three-way or triangular communication. You project the performance to the audience, and it bounces off them to the other performers, who in turn respond to you through projection to the audience. This is a very exciting experience when it happens and everyone is communicating.

In that sense, acting is more like racquetball, with the wall being the live audience. Two players hit a ball (or deliver a line) off a wall, and it bounces back to the other player. In film, the wall is the camera.

The Fourth Wall

The fourth wall is the imaginary side of a fourth wall of a room, which has been removed so that an audience may look into the lives of the characters in the play. When actors are facing the fourth wall, they are facing the audience.

Since it's a play in the theatre and you are performing for an audience who is in the direction of the fourth wall, it's appropriate to do what is theatrical and natural by facing front, as long as you don't overdo it. There is no "fourth wall" in shapes of theatres other than proscenium, such as theatre in the round or central staging.

Actors' Relation to Each Other and the Audience

Actor 1   Actor 2

Audience

Fully Developed Character: Good use of *body, voice, character traits, emotions* and *images.* (It's all interior, and this performer is not listening and relating to other performers or the audience.)

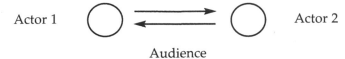

Actor 1   Actor 2

Audience

Two Fully Developed Characters in a Two-way Communication of Listening and Relating to Each Other. (These characters are not projecting to or including the audience.)

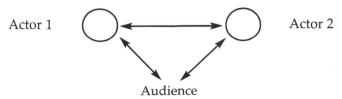

Actor 1   Actor 2

Audience

Two Fully Developed Characters, Communicating with Each Other and Projecting to the Audience in a Three-way Communication.

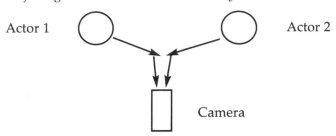

Actor 1   Actor 2

Camera

Two Fully Developed Characters Playing a Scene Close and Intimate to Each Other and Including the Small Focal Point of the Camera. Note that on the stage, the actors project to the audience in a wide area. But for film it is to one small point of the camera lens. For further exploration of playing for the camera see Chapter 20.

Projecting on Different Shapes of Stages

There is an optimum way to present every play, and no one style of theatre is best for all styles of plays. As you develop skill in the use of the body, voice and emotions, you may need to adapt to differences in the distance and direction that performances will need to be projected.

Proscenium Stage: Proscenium means in front of the scene, and a proscenium arch with a curtain divides the house area where the audience sits from the stage area where the scenes are performed. This type is most prevalent and best known. It is the style that you see in most elementary schools and junior

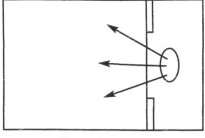

Proscenium Stage

highs. It is often part of the "cafetorium." It is the style on which we have based most of the work in this textbook.

End Stage: This is again a style where the audience focuses on the stage from one side only, but there is no proscenium arch and no wing space. Without the divider of the arch and the curtain, there is more intimacy with the scene. These are quite prevalent in small towns in England.

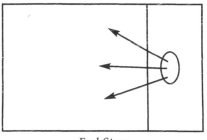

End Stage

Center Stage: Two-sided: This is a two-sided arrangement. The audience faces the center performance area from two sides. They see the performers' back, front or profile. What is a back to one side is a front to the other. There is little use of scenery as background, because the main background is the audience on the other side.

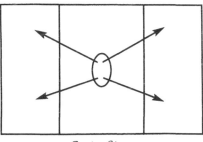

Center Stage

91

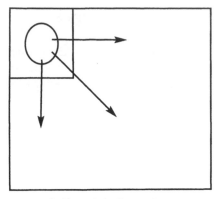

L-Shaped Audience Area

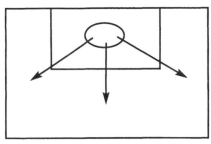

Thrust Stage

L-Shaped Audience Area: This is the type where the audience sits in an L-shaped configuration. This is frequently used in a small to medium-sized space. The actor projects in two or three directions: the two sides and possibly the corner where the two sides join. This allows for some scenery considerations, but actors have a tendency to play to one area or another.

Thrust, Open Stage or Horseshoe: This is basically a shape in which the audience is around three sides of the performance space. This is the style of the classic Greek and Shakespearean theatres. The same amount of people can be closer because they are in a wide arc. But to reach the whole audience the actor has to project a wider performance. What the audience sees from the far left is different than what the audience sees from the far right. The sound may be better, and the audience may feel more involved emotionally because they are all closer to the action. It is more "theatrical" and works well for classic and poetic plays. It generally requires less scenery.

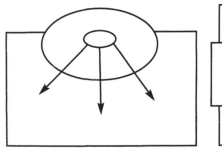

Open Stage

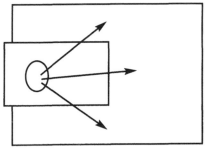

Horseshoe Audience Area

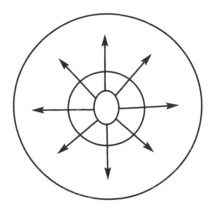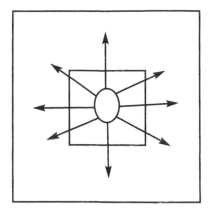

Theatre-in-the-Round, Central Staging or Arena Stages

Theatre-in-the-Round, Central Staging or Arena: This is four-sided. The audience sits on all sides of the stage. The audience may be in a circle, a square, a rectangle or an octagon. The audience is close to the action, and this can work well for intimate and realistic plays and naturalistic acting styles. In terms of walls, most of the scenery is eliminated. There is often some scenery treatment of the floor and sometimes ceiling or half-high walls and door units. Instead of seeing background scenery, the audience mostly sees other members of the audience in the background although they should be in semi-darkness. This type of staging can be a problem to light the performers and not get light in the eyes of the audience members.

Flexible, Black Box or "Experimental" Stage

Flexible, Black Box or "Experimental": This is basically a room with moveable platforms that may be set up in a variety of arrangements or configurations. This might be an end stage, L-shaped, open stage, center stage or some other form. The room is usually smaller than most conventional theatres. This has some advantages in being flexible. However, rearranging all the platforms and chairs can be very labor intensive.

Exercise
Using 4 X 8 platforms test out a variety of seating arrangements.

Preparing to
Perform a Scene

Chapter 9
Improvisation I: An Introduction

Definition, Explanations and Value

When students think about acting they usually think about finding written scripts, analyzing the character's objectives, developing stage business, memorizing lines, planning the blocking and rehearsing the scenes. In a formal, memorized scene the actor knows *what* the other characters are going to say and do and *how* they are going to say and do it. While there may be many creative interpretations by an actor, the basic character is defined by the playwright with guided interpretations and blocking by a director until the play is performed for an audience. The play may be short, from ten to thirty minutes, or up to two hours for full-length.

Improvisation is simply a scene, without a written script, created by actors and based on a loosely generalized structure and framework that involve certain premises. The scenes presented for a classroom audience are generally shorter in length and more concerned with processes than producing a final product. For the actor, it is the spontaneous, instinctive and creative reaction to ever-changing conditions in order to solve a dramatic problem with no written idea how to do it.

Improvisation not only gives the illusion of the first time that something is happening, but it actually is happening for the first time. This "nowness" makes improvisation closer to sports and jazz music where the outcome is uncertain. The scenes can go many directions with many options.

Since there is no written script, you the performer are free from the need to read and memorize a playwright's lines, analyze a playwright's intentions, interpret and perform a playwright's characters or follow a director's interpretation and blocking.

But with this freedom you have new responsibilities. *You* are now the playwright (spontaneously creating your own character, stage business, dialog and plot action) and the director, (blocking the scene in a set arrangement by you). You present the subject matter and solve the dramatic problem of the circumstances given to you.

Since neither you nor any other actors on-stage have any prepared dialog, you only know what to say and how to say it, by listening to what other actors say, and how they say it. With improvisation, as with life, you need to listen, relate and express your thoughts and feelings spontaneously as you communicate with others. Listening focuses on the other person delivering a line and helps you define and express your own personality, feelings and emotions. Listening is one of the most valuable skills learned from improvisation. (For more on listening and relating see Chapter 8.)

Don't be discouraged in early improvisations if they are fragmented or boring or if you "dry up" and don't know what to say next. It's okay to be boring. This will all improve as you continue the process and gain more confidence and trust and begin to relax and "think on your feet." You will learn to explore many topics and relationships and, through associate thinking, expand your dialog about basic subjects. This is creativity though improvisation.

It often takes time, practice and patience to establish and to build trust, confidence and support needed from classmates in order to improvise easily and achieve satisfying results. However, most students, with some practical experience, can improve their improvisational skills and, in the long run, improve their acting skills and communication with others.

Ways to Use Improvisation

Improvisation may be used several ways:

1. As a classroom exercise to further develop acting skills and solve dramatic problems as a process, not a product, for growth. This use is primarily to practice basic skills and develop techniques through listening and relating to other characters in the scene, while focusing on the objectives, developing character traits and creating dialog and stage business. Improvisation makes the actor more equipped to "think on his/her feet" and focus on other characters in the scene.

2. As a method to dramatize a known story or play by creating your own version or interpretation of the play. Examples of this are: fables, folk plays, selected scenes from Shakespeare, Moliere or modern plays; current events from the newspaper or school issues and problems of daily life. (See "Exercise in Using Improvisation Based on Known Plays" at the end of Chapter 17.)

3. As a rehearsal technique for a play being produced. This can help actors focus on the basic text of the play, the characters and their relationships and explore backgrounds that are not in the play.

4. As a means to entertain an audience with short skits using improvisational skills and techniques. In this case, the process is presented as the product. (See people and professional groups who have done this successfully that are noted in Chapter 12.)

5. As a way to create and develop your own totally new play beginning with type or style (comedy, soap opera, melodrama), and/or characters, and/or plot and/or theme. With this approach you need to develop characters and their objectives, relationships and conflicts that are involved in plots or stories with discoveries, reversals and themes within various structures and frameworks that have a beginning, a middle and an end. (See "Structure for Improvisation" in this chapter and more aspects of structure and types of drama in Chapters 17, 18 and 19.)

While a spontaneous improvisation for classroom presentation is usually an end in itself, improvisation can also offer you a chance to create your own longer scenes and short or long plays with story-telling that involves elements of *who, what, why, where, when* and *how*.

Starting Points

Improvisation should have some type of basic structural elements that involve *who* is doing *what* and *where* and a *problem to solve*. In addition, you may add *why* they are doing it, *how* they speak, *how* they move, *when* it happens and the *style*. (For more on the elements and structure of a play, see Chapter 17.)

There are many ways to start a classroom improvisation. Some that follow are: "Contrasting Attitudes" or "Points of View," "Where, Location or Environment," "Lines of Dialog," "Story Words" and "Themes." Most of these situations are gender-neutral situations. (For exercises in "Contrasting Character Traits" and "Contrasting Objectives" see Chapters 13 and 15.)

Exercise: Contrasting Attitudes or Points of View

Form small groups with two or three people each in various parts of the stage. Establish a subject or topic for the improvisation. Using subjects that people often talk about in "daily life" can lend themselves to dialog and stage business. For example, some subjects might be: school, weather, sports, clothes, health and exercise, food and ailments, hobbies, books, entertainment, movies, TV, business or jobs, education, friends, romance, complaints about any number of things or your choice.

One performer in each group starts with a personal statement or comment that involves a definite attitude toward the chosen subject. This might be a statement or opinion of liking or disliking or specific complaint about the subject. Then, another person takes a different or opposite point of view or attitude. This creates a *contrast of attitudes,* or a conflict, and therefore drama. If there are three people then the third person can take sides, change sides or be neutral and negotiate between the two. You can play yourself or create a character that is believable within the context of the subject or scene.

Listen carefully to the other performers and what they are saying. Stay focused on the other character, the situations and what is happening at the moment. React naturally to what happens in the scene. *Show* in what you do rather than *tell* your character traits and objectives. Avoid false emotions or stereotypical characters. Improvise freely for about five minutes. All groups can perform until one or two groups appear to be finished. Or, you may stop earlier if you are finished.

Discussion: What happened in this improvisation? Were the groups able to maintain focus on the subject matter? Were there any surprises? Did you enjoy this process? What could be done to improve future improvisations? Did anyone change attitudes or the basis of the other person's arguments?

Exercise and Discussion: Switch partners or teams and explore another subject with a new partner. No audience. Was the experience different with a different subject and a different partner? What was the difference?

Exercise: Lines Of Dialog

1. Two performers are on-stage. One player draws, chooses or is quietly assigned one line of dialog without either the audience or the other performer knowing what it is. Then, the first person delivers the line and the second listens and reacts and responds to the line while thinking about the situation. (There could be a third person.) Continue until there seems to be a natural end, or the teacher or facilitator stops the performance.

2. Each of two performers is given a separate line of dialog. Neither one knows the other person's line. One just starts and the other performer has to react and be aware of the direction of the scene in order to incorporate his/her line of dialog into the scene.

3. Two or three people draw, choose or are assigned a line of dialog. Together, they build a narrative or short scene around the line without the audience knowing the lines. The lines can appear at the beginning, middle or end of the narrative. After seeing the presentation, the audience tries to determine the line. Possible lines are:

1. You can't imagine what happened.
2. I'd like to tell you, but it's a secret.
3. What are we doing here?
4. Why would you say a thing like that?
5. I'm willing to let bygones be bygones — if you are.
6. Let's do something that's fun.
7. It's not you — it's me.
8. You can't imagine what I've been through today.
9. It's all your fault!
10. Are you listening?
11. I think you're wrong.
12. I have to go to the Dean's office.
13. I didn't know you'd be here.
14. We need to talk about the problem.
15. Situations like this scare me to death.
16. Ha! You make me laugh.
17. Did Shakespeare really say that?
18. Are you still hungry after that?
19. Don't underestimate the power of some people.
20. Are you insulting me?
21. Would you like to get even?
22. Okay, since you're in charge, now what?
23. Are you really going to take credit?
24. It's not me it's you.
25. You can't fool me.
26. Where did you come from?
27. What are we going to do about it?
28. How did you spend the money?
29. I thought we were good friends.
30. Nothing stays the same forever.
31. What kind of party is it?
32. I'm planning a trip.
33. That's a really sad story.
34. That's the truth!
35. I hope you'll forgive me.
36. It's your friend that did it.
37. I deserve an apology.
38. What part of *no* don't you understand?
39. It's not over till it's over.
40. What's makes you so angry?

41. What are we going to eat?
42. We need to do something about this.
43. Your situation is hopeless.
44. What do you know about the accident?
45. This is really embarrassing.
46. It's a misunderstanding.
47. There's nothing to be done.
48. I heard what you did.
49. I promised not to tell.
50. That's the funniest thing I've ever heard.
51. There's something I've wanted to tell you.
52. Either I've got a problem or, you've got a problem.
53. I know it's a bad habit, but I can't give it up.
54. You'd better not say that again, or else …
55. I can't believe I ate the whole thing.
56. Don't tease me
57. I just know you're the right person.
58. We're in big trouble.
59. I think everybody hates me.
60. That's the last time I'll ever help you.
61. You can say that again!
62. Nobody is perfect.
63. You're the luckiest person I know.
64. I never expected that to happen.
65. I hope I never see that person again.
66. I'll never do a thing like that again.
67. Win some lose some.
68. Can't you do anything right?
69. Let's review the plan.
70. Your line.

Discussion: Would you have delivered the first line the same way? Would you have responded in the same way? Did the performers listen and react naturally?

Exercise: Where: Place, Location or Environment

The place or environment may determine, to a large extent, what people are doing. Students go on stage or playing area, and then the place is announced. Don't act. Just listen and react naturally to what you *see, hear, taste, smell* and *touch* and what is happening as you establish your own attitudes or objectives within the environment. Play the scene without stopping for 5–10 minutes.

Then, all stop and discuss what happened.

Possible locations, places or environments might be a(n):

Cafeteria or Hallway: at school

Sporting Event: with your home team playing the big game.

Carnival or Circus

Picnic Grounds: in nature with family or club with games and refreshments

Local Bus Stop, Train Station or Airport: waiting to leave

Local Restaurant such as McDonald's: with families and couples

Children's Playground: with children, parents and friends

Beach and Boardwalk: during holiday

Office of School Newspaper: deadlines approaching

Backstage Area or Green Room: before or after and during production

Waiting Room in Doctor's or Chiropractor's Office

Dog or Cat Show: with owners preparing animals

Emergency Room: on a Saturday night with patients, doctors and nurses

Open House: with real estate person, "looky-loos" and people asking questions about the price, neighborhood, schools, nearby parks, etc.

Zoo, Museum or Theatre: for a field trip to a zoo to see animals, a museum to view art, or a theatre to see a play or musical concert

Furniture Store

Nursery: buying plants and flowers for your garden

For some *where* improvisations, you may need to further establish *who* is doing *what* and *when*. Specific character roles may need to be defined that would perform in that particular environment.

Examples:

Where: Yard for a "yard sale," which is sometimes called a "garage sale" or a "ticket sale". The items usually come from cleaning out storage areas.

Who: There could be two to six sellers for a worthy cause. The rest of the people come and go as lookers and buyers who consider the items for sale.

What: Identify and pantomime the sale items. Then, you can dicker for a price. (It may add a dimension to use items from the prop closet in the drama area for one time. Then, take away the items and do the same improvisation a second time and pantomime those objects.)

Where: Department Store; different departments are designated by being in different areas of the stage or room. Departments might be: men's or women's clothing, sporting goods, shoes, household, etc. Establish offices or area within the store that are not selling merchandise. These could be places such as a window display, ad department, customer service, bookkeeping department and stock room.

Who: Define roles between shoppers and salespeople and store personnel before beginning. Each merchandise department has its own salesperson. Shoppers should define their own specific objectives and attitudes. Store personnel are salesclerks, window decorators, office and security personnel, customer service, advertising, custodian employees, etc.

What: Early holiday shopping. Customers and salespeople are buying and selling merchandise, and store personnel are involved in maintenance.

When: The day after Thanksgiving. Time is 6 a.m. at the beginning of the workday. This continues until the pantomime has a natural ending.

Discussion: What did you see and hear? If you were a customer, what were you shopping for? Are you a frequent shopper there, and does the salesperson know you? Do you have credit? When the sales person describes the merchandise, is it in terms of the senses: how it looks or feels (clothing), smells (perfume department), tastes or offers better health (food), sounds (record or music department)?

Where: In the street at a busy intersection.

When: At sundown or twilight.

What: An accident as people hurried to get home to dinner.

Who: Drivers and victims, observers on sidewalks and in other cars asking questions, police, lawyer and a reporter.

Discussion: What happened? What did the place look like? What did you see and hear? Who were the people involved? Describe the types of characters involved. What were they doing in this place? What did they want? What are the relationships to other people involved? Did the scenes seem natural and realistic? Did you listen and react and stay within the scene the whole time? What did you see, hear, feel, etc. What relationships were established? What were the character traits and attitudes? Describe your character's objectives? What were other people's objectives?

Exercise: Another Way To Create Scenes

Have four large cans, small cardboard boxes or perhaps ice cream containers. They should be labeled "Who," "What," "Where" and "When." A small group of students (two to five) are in each group. Each person chooses or draws one slip from container labeled "who," and the total group draws one slip from each of the "what," "where" and "when" containers. They consult briefly on putting these elements together. Then, they perform their group improvisational scene on the basis of information given.

Exercise: Story Words

With three to five people in a group, choose three of the words below. Or, each member of a small group draws or chooses or is assigned a word. Choosing words that seem to have no connections and making a story out of them often leads to more interesting story lines. The group then quickly confers together for three to five minutes to establish a logical narrative for a story that includes all the words. They then act out the story. The rest of the class members try to figure out what the words are.

Friend	Gossip	Mistake
Apology	Love	Animal
Youth	Message	Accident
Sacrifice	Family	Money
Lie	Rumor	Chase
Tears	Holiday	Brother
Sister	Surprise	Disappear
Missing	Cheater	Fight
Fault	Car	Insurance
Nastiness	Unfair	Food
Mediocre	Bike	Moron
Sweetness	Failure	Stolen
Hunger	Water	Restroom
Dropout	Beautiful	Hate
Fire	Trust	Teacher
Earth	Cigarette	Honesty
Great person	Kindergarten	Sadness
Happiness	Book	Game
Mother	Father	Wound
Partner	Bragging	Shy
Classmate	Dance	Record
Favorite	Sick	Ten minutes late

Compliment	Depressed	Picture
Shoe	Attention	Broken
Scolded	Sand	Lost
Butterfly	Disease	Romance
Bullfight	Stock market	Dancers
Show business	Spaceship	Soapsuds
Message	Ducks	Partner
Compliment	Broken	Holiday
110 Degrees	Hamster	Toothbrush
Monkey	Shakespeare	Money
Compass	Pizza	Boxing gloves
Yo-yo	TV	Postage stamps
Computer	Scissors	Fudge
Lampshade	Ice cube	Comb
Monopoly	Allergy	Thermometer
Shoe	Spinach	Videotape
Flashlight	Thumb	Coffin
Tennis	Ocean	Streetcar
Midnight		

Or, class members can make up improbable combinations from the above and put them into a container. Each group then draws the combination, creates a narrative from those words and acts it out. Don't tell the audience the words.

Discussion: What words did they use? Were they all included in the action? Did the performers build the scene around their words? Did the actors stay involved in their characters and the scene? Did they stick to the subject area?

Exercise: Themes

A Theme/Idea/Moral/Lesson or Title, Slogan or Saying is the underlying idea of the scene. Performing themes can give performers a better understanding of theme and its relationship to plot (what), character (who) and setting (where) in plays and stories. Each group or team of three to seven make up or draw one or more themes, slogans or even titles of known stories, movies or TV shows. Each group is allotted a short period of time to outline a narrative and illustrate the theme in terms of plot and/or character and/or setting. Then, each group improvises dialog to act out the scene to illustrate the theme. Some possible themes are:

1. Money is the root of evil.
2. Ambition brings its own downfall.
3. Crime doesn't pay.
4. Nice guys finish last.
5. Love conquers all.
6. There's a sucker born every minute.
7. Nobody is perfect.
8. A fool and his money are soon parted.
9. An ounce of prevention is worth a pound of cure.
10. Haste makes waste.
11. A penny saved is a penny earned.
12. Waste not, want not.
13. All the world loves a lover.
14. Love is blind.
15. Love makes the world go 'round.
16. Pride goeth before a fall.
17. Early to bed, early to rise, makes a man healthy, wealthy and wise.
18. Giant oaks from little acorns grown.
19. Fools rush in where angels fear to tread.
20. Make hay while the sun shines.
21. Flattery will get you nowhere/everywhere.
22. Power corrupts; and absolute power corrupts absolutely.
23. You can't tell a book by its cover.
24. He who laughs last laughs best.
25. Laugh and the whole world laughs, cry and you cry alone.
26. The only thing you have to fear is fear itself.

Discussion: What was the theme they were dramatizing? Did the characters and the plot dramatize this theme?

Exercise: *Rooms or Areas of a House*
Divide into acting groups of two to five people each. Choose or draw an area of a house.

Dining Room	Kitchen
Activity Room	Porch
Bedroom	Hall
Den	Living or Family Room
Attic	Basement
Garage	Yard

Once the area is decided on, design the specific areas of the room in terms of where furniture and props are logically placed.

Choose or decide on the characters. Determine who they are in terms of character traits and their relationships to each other. Plot the events that could happen in that room, what was happening, where each character came from and what s/he was doing before entering the room or area.

Relationships: These might be parent-child, friends, teacher-student, coach-athlete, boss-worker, relatives, salesperson-customer, etc.

Chapter 10
An Actor's Process

Finding, Creating, Memorizing and Rehearsing

Finding a Character

Whatever you do in theatre, it's important to know plays. Discovering interesting scenes, dialogs or monologs involves a large reading experience in both short and full-length plays. This means an ongoing lifetime of reading scripts, attending play productions and quality movies, reading reviews and discussing plays. To find the optimum scene or character to perform, it's helpful to call upon a backlog of drama experiences and a running list of possibilities.

Plays are usually available in single copies or collections in the school library, the drama office, the English department or at your local public library or bookstore. There may be choices already prepared by your drama department, or your teacher may be able to make some suggestions. The selections range from published plays to cuttings of classic and modern plays, to books of monologs and original material. The selections or cuttings are usually between two to four minutes in length and often ready to perform.

Another source is the newspaper. Articles, editorials and columns material about personal concerns, or domestic problems or humorous observations can all provide interesting source material. Or, you may need to prepare your own scene by cutting or writing an original scene or monolog. The enjoyment of searching and reading for "just the right material" for you to present can often be an exciting experience.

Guidelines for Making Personal Selections

In searching for dialogs and monologs, you may have to reject twenty or more possibilities before you arrive at just the scene or monolog you wish to do. Make sure your monolog is self-contained with an introduction of the subject, an exploration of the subject and a conclusion.

Choose and prepare a character that:
- has a personality that you understand or find challengingly different;

- would be interesting to perform physically and vocally;
- calls for character traits and emotions that you like to perform;
- has a challenging conflict or obstacle that you need to overcome;
- you understand and will be able to analyze if requested;
- calls for a variety of acting skills including dialects or accents;
- does not call for using complicated props (depend on the imagination of the audience to see them); and
- would not be offensive to a casting committee or audience.

You can test out your selections and practice by reading them.

Choosing Material for The Occasion

Most of the time you will be doing scene work for a drama class presentation that involves seeking and preparing dialogs and monologs. But you may also need prepared selections to audition for a play production. If you will read from the actual script for the audition, it is wise to obtain a copy beforehand. Read the script and determine which roles are best for you in order to focus on those characters.

If you are asked to perform your own material, prepare two short monologs, one comedy and one drama or one classical and one modern, that are two to three minutes each. These two selections involve choosing and/or cutting and/or writing your own scene or monolog. But don't get too heavy with emotional selections that call for crying and screaming or hysterics. Remember Hamlet's advice on emotions. And, beware of TV-style scripts that are not easily adaptable to stage presentation or call for special acting talents.

Language for an Audience

In choosing selections from some modern plays, certain types of characters may use strong language that is logical for those characters in these times. Many of these words that some people find offensive are based on an expression of anger, hostility, frustration, aggression or rejection. Some words can alienate members of an audience in such a way that they are unable to hear and appreciate your character and performance. In these cases, you need to decide whether the potentially objectionable language needs to be used as is, or modified or cut, or if you should not even choose the scene or play. Nothing is gained by offending or alienating an audience or casting committee.

But, if the actual words are cut, you can often make the meaning perfectly clear by the emotional tone in the way you express the words. There is often a difference between doing a scene in class as an exercise where everyone knows you and performing the scene in public for a paid audience that includes parents and friends. On the other hand, a truthful creation in writing and performing and freedom of speech in a democratic society should also be weighed. Sometimes the "unsafe" decision offers more truthful insights about people than the "politically correct" and safe material.

Ultimately, you need to be cautiously open-minded when choosing material for yourself while respecting audience sensibilities and other actors' rights to choose material that is meaningful to them. If in doubt, check with your teacher or director.

Language for an Actor

In playing a scene with strong language, actors sometimes have a problem in delivering the words believably out of embarrassment. They might choke on the words or mumble them, or they might punch the words too strongly in an effort to show they don't mind saying those words on-stage.

No one should feel uncomfortable about performing or viewing material that is not appropriate for your group. If you have strong language that is appropriate for your character and not gratuitous in an effort to shock an audience, and you decide to retain the language, then just deliver the words or line naturally as the character would in the context of the scene.

Monologs

A *monolog* is a dramatic presentation performed by one actor, alone on-stage, speaking to self, another character (usually unseen), or to the audience. Unlike the cuttings from plays that frequently need more understanding of what's going on, monologs are usually self-contained and explanatory with a beginning, middle and end. They are like an aside or personal revelation about a problem, relationship, discovery, experience or many other possibilities.

Cutting a Dialog to Create a Monolog

If you find a good script, and your character has a dialog that you want to deliver as a monolog, then you need to cut the script in such a way that it makes sense to you with a smooth continuity for the audience. For example:

1. Cut the other person's lines and/or

2. Incorporate the other person's lines into your own (If the other person asks a question, don't ask the question and answer) and/or

3. Write lines that form bridges to make sense as a monolog.

Writing Your Own Monolog

Take any theme, idea, subject or situation that is of interest to you and write a monolog. You can prepare a monolog based on a(n):

- Personal experience or observed incident or problem.
- Annoyance or complaint of the day. "There's one thing I can't stand ... "
- Relationship with parents, friend, girlfriend or boyfriend, etc.
- Current problem or dilemma in life.
- Description of something that is good for health or experience with food.
- Ethical dilemma that is agonizing.
- Remembrance of people or some event in past.
- Hope, dream or desire. "I had a strange dream last night" or "There's one thing I've always wanted to do."
- Confession or apology to somebody about something.
- Instruction manual: how to build or operate something. For example: computer software, play a sport, drive a car, cook or bake something, drive a car, perform a scene in drama, etc.
- Entry in a diary: "Dear Diary ... You'll never guess what happened today."
- Eulogy honoring someone.
- Most unforgettable character (I ever met).
- Awkward or embarrassing situation: "I don't know how I can explain this to (choose one) my girlfriend/boyfriend, parents/Mom/Dad, teacher."
- Situation that made you really angry and what you did.
- Apology: "I didn't mean to do/say that."
- "Sales pitch," that involves selling some imaginary product. (Don't use a known commercial as a basis.)
- Accident: "Let me tell you what happened."

(For more ideas, see "Lines of Dialog," "Story Lines" and "Themes" in Chapter 9.)

Enhancing Your Monolog

If you've picked a subject for your monolog, you can enhance it in some of the following ways:

- State the problem, personal experience or objective of something that happened
- State what is at risk if you don't solve the problem.
- Describe how the experience affects your senses (if applicable). How does it make you feel? What did you see and/or hear and/or smell and/or taste and/or touch? Give specific images.

112

- Tell a story or joke about a specific instance or example that relates to the subject or theme. This could be a personal example.
- Quote someone, such as an authority, a friend, some supporter or opponent on the subject or theme or a discussion you had with someone.
- State a hypothetical illustration: "I wonder what would have happened if I ... "
- State a factual illustration: what actually happened in a similar situation.
- Give statistics that support the main idea.
- Give an analogy or comparison to support your idea
- Restate the main point or summarize the main point(s). Or, have a discovery and turning point, surprise ending or resolution.

Preparing Your Script

The Stage Directions

The stage directions in your script were probably put in the script by the playwright on the basis of the original writing. Or they are bits of business and stage movement developed by the actors or the director in early productions of the play. The playwright saw these and used them in revisions and publications.

But you, the actor, are the interpreter of your character and the script for your presentation. Those stage directions may or may not apply to your performance because your creative interpretation will probably be different. If you want your interpretation to be yours, then you should feel free to concentrate on your interpretation and not the stage directions in the printed script.

It can be helpful to use the space at the side to write in your own thoughts or notes on character and blocking and a subtext that evolves from your presentation that might enhance your own personal interpretation. Remember, no matter who did the play before you did, it's now your character in your production of the play.

The Set and the Blocking

Design a simple set on the basis of known character relations and stage action that tells the story of your scene. You may do this with pencil and paper or by walking through your dialog or monolog to establish home bases, territories and character relations. (See Chapter 11.)

Plan the blocking in terms of script values that define your character and character relations. Repeat the blocking and refine the movement until this blocking indicates visually what is happening in your script. Getting the blocking right, should help the memory of the lines, because the memory of the blocking should reinforce the memory of the lines.

Technical considerations

For a monolog or short scene, it's best to keep the setting, the props and costumes simple and to a minimum. For example, you may use a table, bench or chairs for a setting. Several chairs together can make a sofa. Props may be real items, pantomimed suggestions or substitutes such as a yardstick for a cane or sword. For costume, a large square cloth folded in a variety of ways may be used as a bandanna, apron or scarf.

It can be helpful when rehearsing a scene to begin early to explore the use of costume or some substitute of costume and props in order to feel as comfortable as you do with your own clothes and personal belongings. Choose those items that might be appropriate in expressing some aspect of your character's personality and are consistent with the costume items that you have chosen. Looking and feeling right is part of getting it right.

However, before you load down the character with costume, props and makeup that may not help establish character, it might be best to start with nothing, and slowly, through experimentation, add items as the need is felt.

Finding and Preparing a Script with Another Actor

If you choose or are assigned a partner to perform a scene, there are several immediate tasks. You need to get to know each other as you search for a scene. You need to find a scene that you both agree has characters you'd like to perform. Once you have found a script, you may need to make changes. Make any necessary changes in the script early before you begin to memorize. It is usually more difficult to "un-memorize" lines than to memorize them. Reasons to make changes might be:

To omit dated and objectionable material.

To omit hard to deliver parts that are not clear.

To make relatively equal parts for both you and your partner.

To take out references to other parts of the play that are not understood in your scene.

To omit the slower moving scenes and maintain the most dramatic moments with the interesting character parts.

To keep the script cuts or additions within the assigned time limits.

Planning with a Partner

Read the script together to analyze characters, clarify objectives and establish some type of stage setting. Then, establish a realistic rehearsal schedule that will prepare you to perform comfortably before the actual deadline of performance. Allow extra time in case any problems arise such as absence due to matters such as health problems. It's easier to cancel rehearsal time than it is to add it.

Memorizing

> *"Memorize the lines, speak them clearly, and don't bump into the furniture."*
> — Anon

Just as there is no one way to act, there is no one way to memorize lines. Even though memorizing the lines should be the least important aspect of acting and playing a character, it's still necessary and can be a problem for some actors. *You don't know what you don't know until you get the script out of your hands.*

If you are holding a script and reading it, you can't use your hands effectively, fully relate to other performers in the cast or fully develop your character. This can be frustrating for everyone. And, you can't be truly creative if you're struggling or "groping" to remember the lines. Just memorizing and speaking the lines of dialog is not in itself creative. Any reader can do that.

In order to be truly creative, you not only need to memorize the lines of dialog thoroughly, but you also need to internalize the dialog and character traits and emotions so that all aspects of your character feel natural, as if you are "living the character" when saying those lines of dialog.

The two main processes of learning are *recency* and *frequency*. Generally speaking, the sooner lines are memorized and scripts are out of your hands, the more opportunity you will have to enjoy working on your character. It's also better for the director, the other actors, the overall production and ultimately, the audience.

Don't get bound to the script. Get the script out of your hands as soon as possible so you can think on your feet.

Changing Lines in the Script

If you are changing lines when preparing a monolog or a dialog with another actor, it is best to make as many of your changes as possible before you start to memorize the lines. It can be harder to "un-memorize," or forget the original lines, than to memorize the lines initially.

Different Methods of Memorizing

Different actors have different methods of memorizing lines, and some memorize more easily than others. Generally, the closer you are to being like your character in personality, the more readily the lines are memorized. Younger performers seem to memorize lines more easily than older performers. By now you may have found your own approach to memorizing lines. However, here are some approaches that might be helpful.

1. *Rote.* Many actors memorize by *rote.* They repeat or "go over" or "run their lines" until they are fully memorized or "internalized" and become part of the subconscious. That is, they repeat them until the lines come naturally and they don't need to think, "What is my next line ... ?"

Some actors feel that memorizing by rote leaves them more flexible and free to react to various subtleties and interpretations of what is happening at any moment and adapt to other actors in the scene and the director's overall vision.

However, if you memorize lines by rote — without feeling, thoughts or interpretation — and delivery of the lines sounds like rote, it defeats the illusion of the lines being said for the first time. In other words, you shouldn't repeat the lines "mindlessly" without thoughts or feelings.

2. *Ideas and Intentions.* Some actors analyze each scene to determine what it's about: the underlying ideas or themes, the character's intentions and what the character wants in relation to others in the scene. Then, they memorize the lines on the basis of the sequence of ideas, intentions or objectives and obstacles and risks if the objective is not achieved. Remembering the character's objectives recalls the lines to express these ideas to the audience. (See Chapter 15.)

3. *Images.* Picturing references of people, places, things or related events can not only reinforce memory of the lines, but also make what you are saying quite clear to the audience. (See Chapter 14.) This is not the same as picturing the words on the page (see "photographic memory" below), although focusing on *key words* may be a start as one way to memorize lines in the process of internalizing lines.

4. *Key Words.* Some actors memorize *phrases* or *key words*, usually nouns and verbs, but sometimes adjectives. They memorize the key words then the smaller, less important words, such as articles and prepositions, fall into place. This can be part of rote memorization.

5. Photographic Memory. Some people have a *photographic memory.* This is a visual approach to memorizing lines. That is, they picture where the lines are on the page. It is like reading a visual image.

However, I know of one instance where a person who used this approach was in the midst of the second act and turned two pages mentally, which caused a strange jump in the logic of the scene. This approach is not highly recommended.

6. Rhythms and Emotional Relationships. By conscientiously rehearsing, you can establish emotional relationships with other performers and capture the rhythms of the scene. This internal rhythm of the scene also helps in calling forth lines more easily. (See Chapter 7 and "Memorizing Dialog with Another Actor" in this chapter.)

7. Personal Movement and Stage Blocking. Memorizing lines and character interpretations generally come more easily and more effectively if you involve gestures, facial expressions, positions on-stage and patterns of movement because *the memory of movement reinforces the memory of lines, and vice versa.* So, don't just sit and "run lines," but instead stay active physically and mentally.

8. Stage Blocking By Director. Some actors say, "I can't remember my lines until I get my blocking, and the director hasn't given me my blocking." There may be an element of truth in this. If you are cast in a production, the director or set designer will plan the set arrangement and the director will block the scenes. Even then you don't have to wait to memorize lines. As soon as you see the ground plan, you can set up a similar arrangement of your own to move around and get a feeling for the set. Blocking is only one element in learning and remembering your lines.

If you are blocking your own scene without a director, you are the person who is primarily responsible for your own blocking. Establish as soon as possible your own home base areas, territories and relationships and move around on "your set." (For more on this see Chapter 11.)

9. Sequence and Problem Areas. Some actors count their lines in each scene to define the scope of the role, where the major part of the role is being played, and what scenes might call for special attention. Determine where you need to memorize long speeches and memorize those first on your own. This can save rehearsal time. Learn lines in a "progressive part" method. That is, work in small sections, move forward, review, review, and move forward again.

Don't avoid the unknown problem areas and only rehearse the easy parts. And, you don't need to start at the beginning each time you rehearse. On the other hand, if the beginning is well known, it can be a warm-up and confidence builder to establish a rhythm to take on unknown sections. Pace yourself to be confident with the whole script.

10. Other Practical Suggestions.

- In dialog, the memory of the line is usually triggered by the other actor's line, which is your cue. Memorize your cues.
- Tape record the cues and rehearse your lines to the recorded material.
- Have the other actor in the scene make an audiotape with pauses. This way you can practice when you are not together.
- Cover your lines, as you read your cues to determine what you know.
- Use flash cards with your cue on one side and your line on the other.
- Note the lines or words of the other actors that call for an emotional response so that you will become emotionally prepared for your delivery.
- Run lines and walk through the role before going to sleep so the lines stay in your subconscious overnight.

Discussion: How do you memorize lines? Is it one of the methods above? Is it a combination? What suggestions can you offer to others to help them memorize lines more easily and more effectively?

Rehearsing

> *"Acting is a conscious preparation for an unconscious result."*
> — Richard Boleslavski

> *"A bad rehearsal always means a good performance."*
> — A myth handed down from generation to generation by bad actors.

Introduction

Just as fine athletes practice the way they plan to play their major games, you need to rehearse the way you plan to perform. Rehearsals are where you do the work. Performance is where you have the fun, but only if you've really worked at rehearsals and you're ready.

General Guidelines for Rehearsal

Rehearsing alone for a monolog or collaborating as a team effort with other people for a scene or play involves a mature responsibility on your part.

- Study your character and memorize your lines as early as possible in order to be as good as possible and as helpful and fair to fellow performers as possible.
- Be on time to rehearsals. Have your script with you. Be prepared to start right away.
- If you need to be late or absent, notify the director and any cast members that are involved because they will be depending on you.
- Just because you are not there doesn't mean that nothing is happening, and therefore you don't need to be ready when you return.
- Breaking character and giggling often indicate a self-consciousness or lack of concentration and focus on the character.
- Every time you break character you destroy the rhythms of the scene and hinder the rehearsal, which affects everyone in the cast.
- Make good use of your rehearsal time. If there are only twelve minutes left in a short rehearsal period, it's not a time to stop and wait for the bell to ring. It's possible to practice twelve pages or fix up a trouble spot in the script.
- Isolate any problems and focus on solving the problems.
- Treat all people working for the good of the production with respect.

In planning a rehearsal schedule, it's wise to allow an additional ten to fifteen percent of time. In case something goes wrong, you're still on schedule without all the anxiety! With proper planning there should be no reason to create chaos by doing everything at the last minute with the feeling that "after this, we die." Don't worry about going stale. If you are still growing, looking for fresh ways to show character and fine-tuning your performance, there should be no final end to your creativity.

For the most valuable use of rehearsal time it is important to get started as quickly as possible. Actors can find all types of delays in getting started. These might include looking for your script, discussing what to rehearse, discussing your character, finding a space to rehearse, arranging the set several different ways, talking about who's going to be at lunch or what you're going to do on the weekend.

Once you have started, it is important that you do not sit and "run lines" and wait for the emotions to come. Instead, get on your feet, plan and rehearse the blocking and rehearse in order to discover the emotions. If there is a suggestion by the teacher or director, don't

119

waste time analyzing it, questioning it, thinking about it. *Just do it!* It may be right. It may be wrong. You rehearse to find out. Once you get started rehearsing and are really involved with emotional intensity, the lines and the characterization will come more quickly, and there can be a lot more personal satisfaction.

While it's important to explore ways to play a scene with other actors, if you try to direct them, it could cause ill feelings, and they could resent it. And you could be wrong, so resist the temptation. On the other hand, if you make your co-performers look good by listening, picking up your cues and reacting honestly, they will not only appreciate it, but it will also make you look good.

Memorize your lines, put the script down, get up on your feet and rehearse. Stay in character, keep your mind and body active — think and feel — rehearse the way you plan to perform for an audience — with emotional intensity!

Interpretations of Character

Generally, it's important and even desirable to be aware of the possibilities of various interpretations in developing your character and decide on some basic interpretations. However, some of the best discoveries about your character and yourself are made in rehearsals. So, to decide on a final, definite reading of lines or interpretation of your character too early may hinder exciting possibilities for creativity, and discovery of new character values may be lost.

In exploring different ways to do a scene you will discover more honest answers by rehearsing than by endless discussion. Frequently, when there is no agreement between two ideas, a third idea may be the best, or at least better, and it will evolve in rehearsing. By doing it, you will find out about it (how it works, what needs changing) and then set about fixing it.

Other factors that shape your performance are the incorporation of the director's interpretation and blocking of the play and discoveries you make in rehearsal as you memorize and rehearse the script and interact with other actors. All these create factors that may promote further modifications to your interpretation.

Even after you begin to perform for an audience you will find new aspects of character based on audience reaction that can further modify and enhance your performance. As you are guided by the circumstances of each production, it's important to stay open and be flexible as you explore and experiment with different interpretations. You may surprise yourself with the results.

Rehearsing and Performing Comedy

A comedy script that you think is very funny when you first read it can become less and less funny to you and other cast members as you rehearse. This is usually because you are familiar with the humor. There may be a point at which you begin to feel stale and unfunny and feel a need to "play it bigger" by punching lines harder or mugging. Resist this temptation. This could be too much and become boring and embarrassingly unfunny. The character that is funny probably doesn't know it, so trust your first instincts about the play and approach your character with a certain, honest innocence, and the humanity and humor of the character should be funny for an audience.

Different audiences may laugh at different places in different performances. It can often be difficult to anticipate where a laugh might come or how loud it might be. You may sometimes get a warm appreciative laugh for something your character says or does. Then, you think, "If I get a little laugh for doing it that way, I can get an even bigger laugh if I play it bigger." If you do, you're liable to get no laugh or an embarrassed laugh. Since comedy also involves an internal rhythm and tempo, resist the temptation to "speed up the action" or "play it bigger." Comedy can be fragile. It comes from playing comic characters honestly and not trying to be funny.

If a laugh comes, allow for the volume to peak and begin declining before you continue with your next line. If it lingers, you can look innocent, do a take, or fill the time with a bit of stage business. Or you may need to repeat the line. You can't know for sure, but you can be prepared.

The Prompter

A *prompter* is a person who holds a script and "feeds a line" to an actor who is in the process of memorizing or forgets in a rehearsal or performance. If you can't remember a line in rehearsal, you might look at the script or you might pause, but stay in character and fill the pause with stage business until you remember the line. Some actors, without breaking character, like to struggle on their own and stay focused on the moment in the script. Others like to get the line right away to maintain the rhythm and flow of the scene. Usually actors just quietly say, "line," and the prompter will quietly give you the line and you continue.

Some actors ask for a line by snapping their fingers. This is not a good habit, since it's possible to momentarily forget a line during performance, and the whole audience knows when you snap your fingers you've forgotten your line.

121

If there is a prompter, this person should know the optimum way to help the actor. However, it is best if actors learn to stay in the scene and work through the lines without a prompter — particularly in the later phases of rehearsal and for the performance.

Staying in the Moment

Stay focused on the moment so that the small individual moments and lines are played honestly one small segment at a time. Even if there is some future part of the script where you have had a problem with such things as lines, emotions, a relationship, stage business, blocking or something else that causes you trouble, don't think ahead because it can cause you to get lost in the present part of the script and drop out of character.

For instance, if you're in Scene One and thinking about Scene Two, you won't be believable in Scene One because your mind is on Scene Two. And, it's very possible you could forget, at least momentarily, the lines in Scene One. Then, you might suddenly realize "Oh, that's my cue! — What's my line?" And, you will probably look and sound distracted.

Stay focused on the moment and play the moment you're on because you can't do anything about the future problem or the lines until you get there. When you get there, the problem will more than likely be solved.

"In the Zone"

In the Zone is a phrase that came into being from a TV show called *The Twilight Zone*. It is a place between the real and the unreal. It is a fine balance, a mental state of awareness between the conscious and subconscious. But it's not "unconscious." It is almost as if you are watching yourself perform. It's somewhat like a dream state where things are both real and unreal at the same time. You are physically relaxed but mentally alert with emotional energy. You are fully in control as you coordinate smoothly, confidently and effortlessly.

When you start rehearsing for a scene or play, the lines and your character traits and emotions are very much on a conscious level. But, as the rehearsal progresses, you memorize lines, develop your character and relations to other performers and everything is internalized and becomes part of the subconscious.

Then, *as in life*, you can act out of your subconscious, and your emotional connection with other performers should be strong, more natural and believable. Eventually, while relating to the other performers, you are projecting a fully developed and truthful performance of a character, and your lines and your emotions flow freely from your subconscious and are projected to the audience in an honest communication. You should feel natural, as if you are living the performance for the first time.

Skilled musicians and trained athletes and actors can all understand this simultaneous state of conscious and sub-conscious awareness because they've "internalized" their performance skills through practice and rehearsal. Aside from arts and sports, you may be closest to this experience when you are driving a car in traffic.

Don't be concerned if you don't capture the emotional essence of the character immediately. Rehearsal is about discovery. So, just relax, stay focused as you rehearse and trust your instincts to produce a performance that is in the zone. It'll come.

Setting the Performance

The big obvious problems should be fixed in early rehearsals. Fewer and smaller problems should be worked on as rehearsals progress. But, it's possible to stop the rehearsal to keep changing things for only so long. There comes a time to stop fixing the little things in your scene and set the performance. At some point you need to step back and trust what's been accomplished in rehearsal, so everyone can have the confidence and experience of an uninterrupted flow of action.

The Class Presentation

Most of the time you will be doing scene work. This may be done as a dialog with another actor or as a solo performance of a monolog. Much of the previous material will apply, but not all.

When you are performing a monolog or dialog for a class presentation, prepare a brief introduction that includes the name of the play, playwright and background to the scene you are going to perform. This may be the essence of the scene, such as the story line, a description of your character, what your character wants and is trying to achieve or your character's major problem. Describe the setting and your relation to it. Then, take a few deep breaths, pause, and begin.

Remember, the audience wants you to succeed. Therefore, you want to give them your best performance. Perform confidently because you are ready. Stay in character. Assume the audience doesn't know the script. Therefore, if for any reason you drop a line or something changes, don't break character. *In acting, as in life,* mistakes happen, so if they happen, treat them as normal.

When you finish, pause to indicate the ending. Resume your own personality as the audience applauds and you return to your seat.

Remember, above all else, it is important to enjoy what you are doing, because acting should be fun.

Chapter 11
Basic Blocking and Showing Relationships

Introduction

Blocking

Blocking is the placement or movement of actors on a stage in order to show the characters' personalities, their relations to other characters and what happens in the scene. Simply stated, blocking is the stage action that tells the story of the play visually by showing ever-changing character relations.

You are interpreting the plot, characters and themes of a play or scene by means of dialog, setting and stage action. Or, in terms of "show and tell," the stage action, or blocking, is the "show," and the dialog is the "tell." In a production situation the director usually plans the overall blocking for the actors, and the technical director usually designs the set in conjunction with the director. For class work you will be directing many of your own scenes.

As an actor you approach the script subjectively and want to get involved in your single character. As a director of your own scene you need to be more objective, to stand back and look at the whole scene or play and make decisions about blocking and how to show the action visually.

Don't think of blocking as just a traffic problem. It is more than that. You are showing the audience the visual story through body position and movement as you deliver the character's lines. There is no absolute right or wrong in blocking, but there is a good, better and best or optimum. While approaches to blocking a scene may change from play to play and scene to scene, there are some basic guidelines.

If you are blocking your own scene, you need to analyze or translate in a sentence or two what is happening in the scene, design a simple setting and plan the basic blocking. Then, the interpretation of your role can go simultaneously with discovery of body positions, areas, territories, home bases and character relations to show the script's values. To begin an understanding of blocking, review some basic principles in Chapter 3.

Territories and Home Bases

Territories

Both territories and home bases often reflect the personalities of the people who control them. *Territories* can show ownership and status or power and control as some seek to protect territory, and others attempt to invade it and take over. Many sports are built on this concept. Which sports come to mind most readily?

At home, the whole house as a territory probably belongs to parents. The kitchen might be your mother's special territory. But, this is not necessarily the case. Dad may regard the family room or shop as his territory, but not necessarily. Your bedroom may be all yours or shared territory, but not necessarily. A character might assume the responsibilities or duties of being in charge of a territory because that person was assigned to do so.

At school, the classroom is generally the teacher's territory, but students have their own home bases for a class period. This may involve being seated alphabetically. This arrangement of teacher and students may vary in different classes. There can be many home bases in one territory.

Home Bases

Home Bases are "personal spaces" that may have been chosen, claimed, assigned or somehow established as "belonging" to a certain type of person on the basis of someone's personality. In originally establishing home bases at home, someone may have been assigned a particular home base. Or, someone sat down in a seat or "home base" sometime in the past. It was assumed that if that person was there first to claim the home base, or territory or area, then it belonged to that person and was designated as his or hers

If someone sits in the seat that you've claimed as "yours," either at home or at school, you're liable to say, "You're sitting in my seat," as if you own it. But there is no legal right because you were there first. It is what they used to call in territorial days "squatter's rights". You, too, probably have a different home base in different places. It can belong to you until someone else takes it over.

In acting, as in life, for the general placement of characters in a family play, each member of the family may have a particular home base. A character can then be identified with a "home base." And when it is not an "actor's scene," that actor can drift to, or stay at, that "home base."

There may also be neutral home bases that are not designated, but instead are used by different people at different times on a first-come, first-serve basis. At home, this might be the sofa, the "guest's chair," the extra dining room chair or a place on the porch or in the yard.

Discussion: Whose territory is the family room in your house? The kitchen? Is your bedroom your territory with a bed and some closet space? Or, is it a shared territory with a sibling? Are you assigned the territory and does someone else own it? Or, is it "your territory," that is expected to be maintained by you to meet somebody else's standards? If so, is this the basis for a dramatic conflict? In the same house, is there a difference between you going into "mom's" kitchen and mom coming into "your" bedroom? How territorial or proprietary are people about different areas? Do you need to maintain a special respect for other people's territory and home bases? How were the territories and home bases established in your home? Describe the home bases in different rooms in your house, on the porch and in the yard. Who has them?

Stage Areas and Placing the Scene

There can be different emotional values for territories and home bases depending on the area of the stage in which they are placed. In exploring the possibilities in terms of the proscenium stage it is helpful to remember that downstage is stronger than upstage because it is closer to the audience and therefore more intense. Stage right is thought to be stronger than stage left because, as viewers, we look toward the left when we begin to read. The side areas are thought to be weaker because they not as readily visual. If there is only one set in a longer play, it is important to use as many areas of the stage as possible for the sake of variety. Sometimes areas, territories or even home bases need to be saved for showing new and/or changing relationships of characters.

Exercise

Using your imagination and subjective evaluation, describe in a general way where you see the optimum area for the following scenes to take place. Should they be close to the audience, far away, in strong areas or weak? To enhance the possibilities, you may suggest the use of levels and furniture. Where might you place scenes that involve the following subjects?

1. Royalty, nobility, judges, executives, etc.

2. Ghosts, sinister intrigue, devious conspiracies, mysterious plans, etc.

3. Romantic scenes
   a. Comic and spirited
   b. Warm and intimate
   c. Forbidden and secretive
4. Scenes with gossip
   a. Secretive
   b. Comic
5. Dying scenes with
   a. A villain
   b. A hero or sympathetic character
6. Major conflicts or showdowns between hero and villain
7. Doors for important entrances
8. People entering quietly and not wanting to be seen

Discussion: Was there creative agreement or consensus or a variety of answers and possibilities?

Simple Settings

On the basis of the script analysis of your character's needs and understanding of home bases and territories, you can begin to visualize the stage space and furniture that would be appropriate for the characters in your scene. For most scenes in a classroom performance, you will need only a couple of chairs, a table, and perhaps a sofa or bench, located someplace between stage right center and stage left center. And, you will enter and exit from the wings.

Even for these scenes, you may be able to get an additional emotional value by using other areas. And you may be able to select furniture and props that are more meaningful.

How are the characters defined? What home territories and home bases are needed? What furniture and props are needed to define your characters? Start with the items that are functionally needed and appropriate for characters in this location. When your characters sit, do they sit on a chair, on the floor, a bench, on a table, steps, window seat, ottoman or some set piece?

If the home bases, furniture and props are arranged properly for the characters in the script, then the blocking of the scene should more clearly show your character and the character relationships. Also, if the set is right and the blocking is meaningful, then the dialog is more easily memorized since you are at the right place doing the right thing when you say it.

A Ground Plan

Below are symbols for some furniture. In designing a ground plan for a set these are some of the symbols that you might use. This way furniture is seen as if you are directly above it, looking down with a "bird's eye" view of the stage.

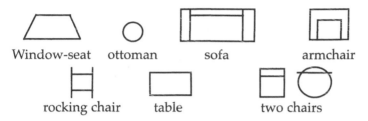

Window-seat   ottoman   sofa   armchair

rocking chair   table   two chairs

Add anything else you might like such as a coffee table or desk.

Exercise and Discussion

Establish a believable-looking "family room" and assign home bases for the following characters: Mom, Dad, Aunt or Grandma, Teenager, Young Child and Visitor. You may arrange home bases on your stage so that they look logical and believable as a family room and a place for the characters in this family. Match up the people with the furniture in the most logical arrangement for the room. While these examples or your choices may in some ways be stereotypical, there can also be a strong element of truth and a basis for blocking.

Plan Furniture Arrangements and Props

Establish your own simple settings in order to block a scene meaningfully. Choose pieces of furniture and props that are believable for the setting and functional for the actors' home bases. Interior areas or territories use furniture, platforms, steps, ramps or doors. Exteriors may have benches or stage pieces such as rocks. Try to establish settings that show a special value in the character's relation to the territory of the room, the home base furniture and the characters' relation to each other.

In arranging furniture it's usually best to arrange the pieces parallel or perpendicular to the stage planes (proscenium arch, curtain line, back wall) and/or set planes (that is, the walls of the set). Try to plan furniture groupings. If one piece of furniture is at an angle that is different, then it is best to establish another piece of furniture in relation to that first piece to make it a grouping.

For example, if a sofa is used, add a coffee table at the same angle. With a single chair, a side table may be added to make it a territory or grouping rather than just one piece of furniture. There is usually an optimum way to establish a setting to show these relationships.

We usually think of people sitting on chairs. They can also sit on the floor, on a table or desk, on the back of a sofa or even on a box if this is in character and fits the relationship that needs to be established. An ottoman or footstool is at a height between the floor level and chair level. Also, an actor can change direction without moving the ottoman or footstool since there is no back. The desk or arm or back of the sofa is a level between the chair's seat and standing. Review once again in Chapter 3 the many ways a single chair can be used.

The placement of props (small hand items that are used by characters) such as clothes, hats (on hat racks or in closets), umbrellas, books (on tables or in bookcases), telephones (on desk or long cord, cordless or cell phone to move around), drinks, glasses, note pad, pencil, pen, etc., might be placed for convenience. Or, they might be placed to facilitate arbitrary movement. For example, a character might cross from a home base across the room to get a glass, then cross back to get a drink and then cross back again to add some ice cubes, etc.

Exploring Stage Positions and Character Relations

Exercise
Review Chapter 3. Using two or three people, test variations of the character relations and the emotional values of the following situations and relationships from the list below.

1. Two people (A and B) standing some distance apart — facing front — DR and DL. Then, turn facing each other. Then, one faces upstage, then one full front. Then, A is slightly downstage and three-quarters back in the direction of B and B one-quarter front in the direction of A.

2. Two people — close together, both facing front. Then, with head only, look at the other person. Then, one facing front and one full back

3. Standing or sitting face to face. Shake or hold hands. Then, change line of vision by looking different directions. Then, one standing facing front and one sitting, facing front.

4. Standing or sitting back-to-back.

5. Two people, one sitting facing front or one-quarter right then, left. Then, sitting or standing with body line of direction toward each other, but one facing front and one facing upstage.

6. Two people sitting on opposite sides of a small table, but one-quarter toward each other.

7. Two people standing on opposite sides of table facing each other (raise fist, angrily, then shake hands.)

8. Two people, one full front, one full back, with shoulders on same plane. Change distance.

9. Two people standing, then sitting back to back.

10. Two people, one sitting on a chair facing front, and one standing directly behind. Then, move the one behind in different directions.

11. Test numbers 1, 2, 3, 4 and 9 of the above in different stage areas: UR, UC, DR, DL, UL.

12. Two people, one sitting on level UC, full front. One sitting RC or LC and facing UC.

13. One person sitting on a chair, one on the floor, one-quarter toward each other. Then one on floor kneels.

14. One person standing full front, one kneeling, facing the other person.

15. Test different body positions using different levels: floor, chair, table, standing on level or chair, chair on level.

16. Change areas, body positions, distance from others, levels, line of vision, line of direction.

17. Continue exploring with your own variations and combinations using other means from Chapter 3 that include lines of direction, size or mass, color, etc.

Discussion: If you saw two or three people in a picture with these different body positions, different levels and different areas, what would it say about their relationship in each of the combinations?

Activity: Analyzing Relationships in Pictures

What are the relationships of the people in the picture illustrations in this book (see pages 149-161)? What principles can you derive from this exploration?

Exercise and Discussion

Once you have a sense about defining character relations visually, note people that you see together at home, on the school grounds, in the cafeteria, in shopping centers, at church and other public places. In other words, if you couldn't hear them and didn't know them, what could be implied from what you see in their relations to each other? (For more on observations see Chapter 14.)

Moving and Speaking

Other things being equal, audience's attention goes to the person *moving*, that is, the blocking or stage action, and also toward the person *speaking*, or the dialog. It may also go to the person who is listening and reacting if that is an important factor. These are important to remember when showing relationships and making decisions about where to direct the emphasis of a scene.

Gaining Emphasis in a Scene

Depending on where you want the emphasis, use this as a general guideline:

1. If Character A is speaking and Character B is listening quietly, the attention will go to A and possibly to B's reaction.

2. If Character A is speaking and moving, the attention will go to A more strongly.

3. If Character A is speaking and B is moving and reacting to what A is saying, the attention will go back and forth.

There are many other factors that may be involved, such as where the action is taking place on the stage. What other ways to gain emphasis can be used?

Exercise

Using a simple setting of chairs at RC and LC with a table in between, test the following by saying different lines and moving at different times. At start, 1 is URC, standing, 2 is LC sitting and 3 is standing DR. All face front to begin.

1. Move to center / stop / speak with the line: "I've been thinking about this."

2. Rise, speak, "I'm not sure I want to hear this." / finish / move DL.

3. Move toward #1 and speak at same time with line: "I'd like to hear what you have to say."

Continue to improvise in the same rotation with speaking and moving.

Discussion: What did you notice about the three different combinations of speech and movement? Is pace of movement, thoughts, line of vision or stage business needed to use any of these?

Repeat the activity. This time, keep the basic location in areas the same, and lines the same. But change the sequence of moving and speaking.

Improvisational Blocking Exercise

Three performers or more. This exercise is basically for proscenium-oriented groups. Each of the performers gets a number. The teacher-director claps and/or counts to ten as if someone were delivering dialog. The performers move freely to new positions. On the count of ten, as everyone stops, the scene is evaluated quickly. Each time this sequence is done, a different person gets to be the emphasis so that each person takes a turn giving and taking a scene.

For instance, if it is #1's turn to take the scene, then #2 and #3 give the scene. Then, #2 takes the scene and #1 and #3 give it. And so forth.

Questions to be asked:

1. Did the performer who should take the scene do so?
2. Did the other actors give the scene to that person?
3. Are they relating to each other? Do they all belong in the same scene? What do their positions say about their relationships?
4. Was there any particular style with which it ended? Was it comedy, classic, melodramatic, etc.?

Movement

Motivated and Arbitrary Movement

Basically, there are two types of movement: motivated and arbitrary. Movement usually involves something in the relationship with other characters or personality traits. In most plays there is "motivated movement," which comes from character motivations or objectives or intentions. In motivated movement there is usually a conflict in the script that gives a reason to move. This conflict may be shown in motivated movement or blocking. For instance, Character A wants something and tries to change, convince, persuade or bully Character B into thinking or doing something his or her way, and B reacts.

Sometimes in blocking a scene there is no reason in the script and, therefore, no motivated reason for the movement. Then, you need to turn to *arbitrary movement*. Information is usually given to the audience about the character, but there is little conflict. For example, A talks to B. Exposition scenes and sentimental dramas (soap operas) usually use arbitrary movement.

But, just placing the actors in chairs and letting them talk may be very boring. While little movement is indicated in the script to show relationships and motivate blocking, there is a feeling that something needs to break up the monotony of people sitting and talking to each other. This calls for arbitrary movement. In these circumstances the director or actors invent reasons to move or motivate the movement and find reasons that involve a character's personality, stage business, intentions or relationships to other characters or the environment.

For example, someone gets up and moves to eat or drink something (tea, coffee, mints, nuts, fruit, etc.) or obtain an article or prop that would support the subject of conversation (a picture of person, a letter) or rearrange clothes, fix hair, warm self by fire, put on scarf or coat, get a fan, prepare a drink or do something that involves a hobby, occupation or sport. (See section on "Stage Business" in Chapter 4.)

Patterns of Movement

Actors often begin the blocking by planning short single movements such as "cross to chair on such and such a line, then cross above table, then … " However, after working on scripts awhile, sometimes with the help of a director, actors can understand and learn *patterns of movement* in order to show personal characteristics and relationships. This is a much more fluid movement and is keeping in the spirit of motivated movement. Sometimes plays that are built around character may be blocked very differently after the actors and director have explored character motivation and found that a new approach is more appropriate than the one first conceived.

Plan your patterns of movement to show the ever-changing relationships of your characters. Begin by blocking or moving within your simple set arrangement to show the character relationships and continue to test the arrangement to see if it feels right in conveying the values of the scene.

a. With a simple setting on-stage you may move around on your set to see if the scene's values feel right.

b. You may draw a ground plan and use small coins or move pieces of paper with characters' names as your read through the script and block the scenes.

c. You can approach blocking by establishing a ground plan and visualizing the blocking in your head. This usually takes some experience.

Exercise

Become familiar with basic blocking and patterns of movement with some gestures. The following is a breakdown of a scene with one small movement at a time. The setting: a table T at C, and chairs at RC and LC. There is a bench at DR. There are entrances at UR and UL.

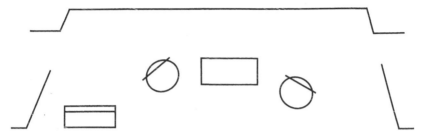

1. #1 is discovered pacing nervously to show tension and anxiety and stops DL.
2. #2 enters UR and X's above Ch. at RC.
3. #1 turns R and faces #2 at RC in three-quarters back position, giving the scene to #2.
4. #2 X's DR in front of bench and faces front.
5. #1 faces front at DL, then #1 and #2 turn and look at each other.
6. #2 turns body and faces toward #1 and then points at #1.
7. #1 X's up in circular motion to LC Ch and sits.
8. #2 X's up and circles behind Ch at RC.
9. #1 faces front.
10. #2 X's to R side of T and points at #1 sitting.
11. #1 rises and X's to L end of T facing #2.
12. #3 enters quietly UL, and looks toward #1 and #2.
13. #1 and #2 point at each other.
14. #3 quickly X's UC above T and raises arms.
15. #1 turns and X's back to Ch at LC, sits and faces front. At the same time #2 X's R to above bench and faces DR.
16. #3 looks at #1, then, points at #1.
17. #1 puts hands over face.
18. #2 glances at #1 and X's DR behind the bench and stands facing front.
19. #3 X's to L end of T and sits on T facing #1. #3 opens palms of hands toward #1 and #1 gives the scene to #3 momentarily as if listening, then turns front.
20. Then, #1 rises and X's DL, facing front.

21. #3 X's below the T, points at #2 and moves toward #2.
22. #2 X's around R end of bench and sits facing front.
23. #3 moves L toward #1 at DL and extends palms or hands in peacemaking motion.
24. #1 turns toward #3 and nods.
25. #1 X's in front of #3 to DRC as #3 slightly counter-X's.
26. #1 stops at DRC turns and faces back to #3.
27. #3 motions for #1 to continue to X toward #2.
28. #1 slowly turns back toward #2 sitting on bench at DR.
29. #2 looks toward #1 and #2 smiles and pats bench for #1 to sit.
30. #3 X's R to behind #1.
31. #1 acknowledges #3 behind and slowly moves forward to DR bench and #2.
32. #1 arrives there, pauses a moment, then sits beside #2.
33. #3 quickly X's above bench and stands behind #1 and #2.
34. #2 extends hand and #1 shakes.
35. All three characters look forward as if they know a crisis has passed.
36. Then, slowly, #1 and #2 look at each other and #3 looks down.

Discussion: What happened in this scene?

Repeat the blocking in smoothly flowing patterns of movement. Reproduce any character values and relationships that came out of those initial movements and the discussion. You may also improvise any dialog that seems to evolve naturally from these movements.

Exercise: Showing Character Relationships Through Stage Positions and Patterns of Movement

Test the following stage relationships to confirm or modify what each position or pattern of movement is showing in terms of relationships. There is no one answer to these situations. Much also depends on actors' attitudes and the way the pattern is executed.

1. Apathy and Indifference

When two characters have no strong feelings toward each other there is a tendency to stay away. If characters are apathetic or indifferent to each other, you may show this by keeping them some distance apart. Their distant positions show that they "don't care about the other person." This may be a scene where two people are just meeting each other or are breaking up and want to "get away," because they no longer have strong feelings.

2. Characters are close, but not "eye to eye." Two people are close but can't see "eye to eye." They are emotionally involved but in some disagreement.

3. A wants something from B, and B stands firm. The boy/girl wants to use the family car or get an advance in allowance, and the parent refuses. Or, the detective tries to get the young person to tell who committed the crime, and s/he stubbornly refuses. Or, the boy wants to marry the girl, but she isn't ready. She refuses and wants nothing to do with him.

4. A wants something from B, and B rejects and wants nothing to do with A. A salesman tries to sell something, and the customer doesn't want to buy and keeps avoiding the salesman. Or, the young man wants to marry the girl, and pursues or "chases" her, but she wants nothing to do with him, ever. She can't stand him and says, "NO!" and moves away to show her rejection.

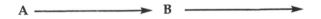

5. A approaches B from several different standpoints but B is firm and resolute in saying "no." As an example of this, Character A has several pleas and arguments, but B still stands or sits "as steady as the Rock of Gibraltar." Character A first approaches from one side then another, as if to say with each new point or position, "But look at it this way." A circles B.

6. *Character A actually pursues B, and B moves away and circles around to avoid A.* The "chase" can be in the form of a "figure 8 chase" as they move line by line around pre-established pieces of furniture placed right center and left center. Match A1 with B1 to begin, then when A1 moves to A2 it forces B1 to move to B2, etc.

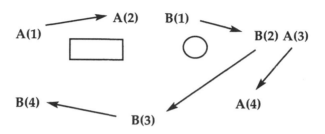

Strong Emotions: When people feel strong emotions toward each other, it means that people are involved with each other emotionally, and therefore close. It might be the positive emotion of love, and they just move together intimately, and there is nothing blocking them being close.

7. *A is close to B, and they face each other positively.*

8. *Or, it may be that A and B are close to each other but they have negative feelings for each other because of some issue or personal thing.* For instance, if there are negative emotions of anger, hate or disagreement, they could be in for a fight, that is shown by placing some object such as a table, chair or even another person between them, holding them apart.

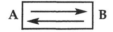

9. *A acts on B and B reacts back negatively.* This might be in the form of a rejection over some issue. For example, a teenager wants the family car, and Mom or Dad is firm in saying "no."

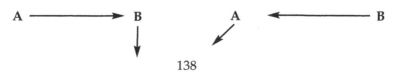

10. *Two strong people who can't get together.* If character A and character B have strong feelings toward each other, but are not acting on each other, they could move in parallel lines and be close but never meet. They may pass and cross but never meet. Or they could stand or sit close together and be facing in the opposite direction.

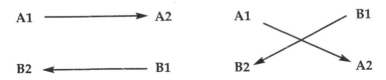

11. *Showing relationships with three people and taking sides.* With three people, the person who is the center of interest or the person who is of the opposite opinion of the other two can be at the apex of the triangle. Or, with more people, you can put all the characters that represent the same point of view on the same side. If any characters switch sides, then they can switch their positions to the other side.

12. *Scene with mediator.* This is an arrangement in which there is a mediator, or some person who represents a point of view in between two people who are strongly opposed to each other.

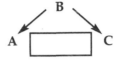

Or, the center person may be the object of the conflict between A and C.

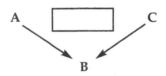

13. *"Invading" Established Territories.* Once home bases and territories are established and an outsider enters the scene, then the outsider doesn't have a home base and, theoretically, is left in limbo. The outsider may feel awkward, as if she or he doesn't belong in this territory. For example: the boy who comes to pick up the girl and the parents check him out. Or, if an outsider is offered a chair or seat, then the territory is for the moment being shared, even though the original owner theoretically still owns the territory.

But, if the outsider attempts to "invade" the owner's established territory and take over more territory than is offered (retrieving a debt, wanting to marry someone's daughter, telling the owner the truth or showing aggressive and hostile feelings) then there is a dramatic conflict. In sports, "outsiders" constantly try to "invade" the other team's home territory and try to take away control and/or power to score points and win the confrontation. On-stage, this can be shown by "the winner" displacing the original opponent and sitting in the other person's chair or at that person's desk or holding a prize possession. That's the nature of sports and *drama ... and life.*

For example, in *The Marriage Proposal*, by Chekhov, the Father could take one side of the stage as a home base, the potential bridegroom the other, with a neutral zone in the middle for the daughter. She is between the two. See Diagram below.

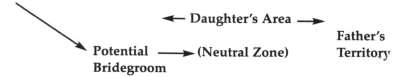

Both, at times, could "invade" the neutral territory and then possibly retreat. It is even possible if the bridegroom becomes strong (with emotion and rational arguments) to pursue the father around the father's territory and even drive him out of the territory and take over. This would be a good demonstration of both the theory of home base, territory and telling the story of the play visually.

14. *Showing inner tension.* Character A has many inner conflicts, tensions or dilemmas and doesn't know which way to turn. The character may move nervously in short intense movements, pacing this way and that. This is not the only answer, however. It depends on the type of inner tensions and how that person will manifest them.

140

Exercise: Translating Lines of Dialog into Blocking Values

Below are lines that might be found in a play. How do you place people and block these scenes to show the relationships of the characters that fit the lines of dialog? Can they be shown with a pattern of movement? Improvise a short scene with blocking that shows relationships using the lines below as a beginning, middle or end of the scene.

1. "Come on in. Let me take your coat. Sit down."
2. "We need to talk about this."
3. "I want to share this with you."
4. "I'm not going to talk about this."
5. "I'd like to tell you a secret."
6. "I can't deal with this."
7. "I don't know what I'm going to do."
8. "I can't go on this way."
9. "Now you listen to me!"
10. "You're still avoiding me. What's wrong?"
11. "You always want to tell me how to live my life and I'm not going to listen to this anymore."
12. "You've got to quit acting like this and face the problem."
13. "I've already said no, and I'm not changing my mind."
14. "I can't face the idea of telling anybody about this."
15. "Please ... one last time. Help me."
16. "I brought you something. Here."
17. "I said no. You're not going to see."
18. "It's not you, it's me."
19. "I only need to borrow it for a little while."
20. "Quit avoiding me and tell me the secret."
21. "This is the most fun I've had in a long time."

Exercise: Show Patterns of Movement

After reading a scene and determining what the scene is saying, what "patterns of movement" would show the audience the following? Establish a setting for the scene, then improvise blocking and lines of dialog to show the characters in this situation.

1. A young boy or girl tries to get a grandparent to loan him/her some money, but the grandparent quietly and stubbornly refuses.

2. Boy tries to convince girl to marry him, but she refuses — doesn't even want to talk about it.

3. The boy tries to get the girl to marry him, but she's unsure and uneasy about her family's reaction. They may enter at any time.

4. Two proud people are in love, but they can't communicate or give in and admit it, even though both would like to.

5. Two bright, witty energetic people are in love, and while they love each other, they snipe at each other.

6. The 19th century villain has the young girl alone and wants the girl in his power.

7. Two or three family members who like each other can't quite communicate.

8. One or more police officers is/are ruthlessly grilling or interrogating an arrested person.

9. Priest or nun is trying to get young rebellious person to give up "evil" ways.

10. Two people are strongly and angrily arguing. They can't agree.

11. Two or three roommates have tried to agree with each other but have finally decided they aren't going to get along and will all go their separate ways. If three people, then one is trying to mediate a dispute.

12. Two people agree on their point of view and are opposed to a third person. As they argue the situation, one of the two people slowly begins to agree with the third person.

13. One person nervously tells or confesses something from the past to another who listens patiently.

    a. The listener wants to hear no more.

    b. The listener wants to help, if possible.

Even though you have established who is where in terms of furniture, there is a way of placing those locations in a place so that the featured character's home base is a featured location.

14. Mother-in-law, mother, daughter (a complainer, a nag, and a whiner) "go at each other" while husband chokes down a cold breakfast. Establish a simple setting and block the scene. So that it is the:

    a. Mother-in-law's play

    b. Mother's play

    c. Daughter's play

    d. Husband's play

15. Husband returns drunk at night and tells them all off — one at a time.

Exercise: Observing and Demonstrating Relations

Watch people in public places such as around campus, at restaurants, shopping malls or an athletic contest. Observe two or three people together or in small groups in a variety of situations and locations.

Note the way they are arranged and look at each other. On the basis of your visual observation and their body and facial attitudes, what are their relations to each other? Is there a leader? Are some people more aggressive, some more passive? Without hearing what they were saying, what can you determine about their relationships to each other? Can you determine their intentions from observing the relations to each other? Make some notes as a reminder.

Demonstration: Explain what you saw and what appeared to be the people's relationship, and demonstrate your conclusion. Then, using fellow students, place them on-stage to show the class what you saw.

Exercise

Read a scene in a play. Put what happened in the scene into a sentence or two. Arrange the needed set and cast the characters and read or improvise the dialog for the scene.

Sample Blocking Approach
Analyze the Script

Read carefully the play or scene that you plan to perform. When reading a script, analyze and define each character's personality traits, their motivations, objectives, intentions and relations to each other. Visualize what areas of the stage, territory, home bases, furniture and props are needed and where they might be placed. Character relations in plays, like relationships in life, are often shown by actors' body positions, lines of direction, lines of sight, stage levels, contrasts and stage movement. (See Chapter 3.)

State in a sentence or two "what happens" in the scene. The playwright probably started with a sentence or two and translated what happens into dramatic dialog. For example, the scene might be described as: "Two neighbors, one owning a dog and one a cat, have a confrontation over the perceived bad behavior of the other person's animal." Then, the playwright wrote the dialog to illustrate that scene. You don't see the playwright's outline but you do see the dialog.

Break down the scene even further and determine the emotional relation of characters and put this relation into sentences of what happens from moment to moment.

Establish a Simple Setting

Establish basic areas, territory and home bases for each character that may be used in their relationships. Within the whole scene there are many different body positions, stage placements and movements of the actors to show the changes in character relations. Show this relation through physical action or blocking.

Plan some general patterns of movement.

1. You may pre-block every move before you start to rehearse;

2. You may pre-block general patterns of movement on paper, and add the details in rehearsal or

3. You may block totally as you rehearse.

If you pre-block, do so in a general way and leave the details of body position and movement for the rehearsal. There needs to be movement for visual variety. But, not all movement should be RC to C to LC. Continuous crossing one way in front of an actor who counter crosses only for the purpose of movement or balancing the stage, without script values, can be really monotonous. And movement for movement sake does not fulfill the basic function of showing visually what is happening in the script. If the blocking is meaningful in terms of the script and the actor is emotionally involved in the character, then patterns of movement should be meaningful and the actor should be able to feel body positions, place on-stage and movement in relation to the lines and the scene.

If the blocking does not match what you see in the character relation on the basis of a line reading or interpretation, you may need to change the blocking. But, movements should be blocked in the script for the characters, not the actors. As you rehearse you can further define and refine the patterns of movement in order to clarify the text and enhance the characters.

Note the blocking for your scenes in your script. Your script is a limited version of a prompt book. A *prompt book* is the master copy of the working script that contains information for a full production. It contains cuts in the script and how each scene of the play is to be staged. It records the actor's entrances and exits, every move and bit of business, notes on speeches and pauses. It also includes light and sound cues and scene shifts.

Finally, ask yourself if you are showing what this dialog is saying and expressing the playwright's values through body positions, stage placement and patterns of movement.

Exercise: Blocking Process of a Simple Script

Read the script, plan a set and then do your own blocking. Then, note the approach to blocking in the scene called "Blocking Cats and Dogs." Compare your set and your approach. Remember there is no one answer. While this example is not the only answer, it does use many of the basic blocking principles that are based on character relations.

"Cats and Dogs" — *The Script*

(At Rise: B is discovered sitting in chair looking at pictures of dog. There's a knock on the door.)

B: Come in.

A: (A enters.) Hi.

B: Oh, it's you. Hi, neighbor. Have a seat.

A: No. I came over to say your barking dog keeps me awake. And you've got to do something about him.

B: What do you suggest?

A: Put him on a leash or give him a muzzle or something.

B: Well, I'm not planning to do anything about my dog.

A: So, that's your attitude?

B: Yes, my dog is none of your business. So, that's that.

A: No, it isn't. That's no answer to the problem. You've got to put your dog on a leash. He's been threatening my cat. And I have a lawyer.

B: Oh, really. Hmm. I didn't know about that.

A: That's right. And I'm not going to leave till you do something about your terrible dog.

B: My terrible dog! What about your mean cat? She's been chasing my birds.

A: Oh, really? I didn't know that.

B: Yes. That's the truth.

A: No, I don't think so. It can't be my cat. I've never seen her do that. Have you actually seen her threaten your birds?

B: Yes. It's definitely your cat. Are you willing to put your cat on a leash, or muzzle it?

A: No. My cat is very sweet and peaceful and cute. And your dog is ugly and he barks all the time and wakes both me and my cat.

B: No, no. That's not my dog. My dog is beautiful and dignified, and he doesn't bark. My dog is a prizewinner and very quiet. And all you've got is an old alley cat that ate my dickey bird.

A: Oh, no, I feed her the finest cat food. She doesn't need to eat birds. And she'd never eat your dickey bird. She's a purebred cat and has won a lot of cat contests. Look at these pictures.

B: Okay, let's see them. I'll know the bad cat that's been eating my birds when I see it.

A: Then, let me see your dog pictures.

B: Okay here. Oh, no, this isn't the cat that ate my bird.

A: If this is your dog, she looks nice and friendly. And she's not the one that barks all night.

B: I told you so. Maybe we should get together more often. You can get to know my dog.

A: Good idea. And you can meet my cat.

B: It's a deal.

Set for "Cats and Dogs"

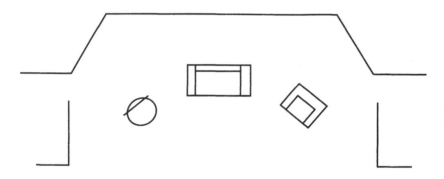

Blocking "Cats and Dogs"

A: Okay, it's time to block our scene.

B: Right. I analyzed the script and designed a simple set. Since it's my house or my territory, I'll start over here at left center sitting in the big comfortable chair as my home base. (B begins to arrange the set.)

A: Then, I'll enter from someplace…maybe up right. Okay?

B: Good. That'll work. Here, I'll put this small chair at right center for you if you decide to sit down.

A: Or, I'll just take a strong stand behind it when I come in while I'm planning how I might approach you. I have no emotional involvement at that time.

B: How's this? I put this sofa here in the center running parallel to the curtain line. It's sort of neutral territory. Then, when we have our big argument we can stand at opposite ends and there's something between us.

A: This looks like a good arrangement. So, let's start.

B: Okay, I'll be sitting in my chair looking at pictures of my dog.

A: I knock on the door. (Knocks: with knocking gesture while stomping shoe on the floor.)

B: "Come in."

A: And I enter. "Hi, neighbor."

B: "Oh, it's you. Hi. Sit down."

A: And I don't sit because I want to stand up for what I believe in. And this is where I tell you that your barking dog keeps me awake. And you've got to do something about it. Put it on a leash or something. And I take a strong position behind the small chair because I don't know how you'll react.

B: That's good. And since I'm not planning to do anything about my dog, I'll just stay seated for those lines.

A: Okay. And that annoys me so I'll move closer by crossing above the sofa to state my case and press the issue. (Moves to above the sofa.)

B: And I figure my dog is none of your business, so I stay seated. I'm firm in my convictions.

A: That annoys me even more so I move even closer. I'm standing above you and behind you looking down on you when I say, "You've got to put your dog on a leash. It's been threatening my cat. And I have a lawyer."

B: And that makes me nervous. So, I'll get up, and cross farther left to get away from you. (Crosses down left.)

A: That leaves me hovering right over your empty chair. I could sit in it since I've driven you out into a defensive position. (Sits in chair.) Then, I say, "I'm not going to leave till you do something about your terrible dog.

B: That'll work. Then, when you do that, I'll start my counterattack. By talking about your mean cat who's been chasing my birds.

A: And that makes me uneasy, so I get up and cross away from you, toward down center ... sort into no-man's land.

B: Then, I can cross back to reclaim my chair, my home base. Or, maybe just stay in the general territory. I'll stand by my chair.

A: And I can proudly defend my black cat at right center.

B: Ah! But then, I cross toward you and take a position at the left end of the sofa. And I say, "Are you willing to put your cat on a leash?"

A: Okay now I'm now on the defensive, so I'll move away to someplace near where I entered. How about here behind my chair at right center which puts a little distance between us?

B: That looks good.

A: And there's some sort of no-man's land between us. But then, I lash out and say your dog is ugly and it barks all the time and wakes both me and my cat. And I'll move to the right end of the sofa.

B: Good. And I say, "My dog is beautiful, and he doesn't bark."

A: Then we're standing at opposite ends of the sofa fighting like cats and dogs.

B: That's good. So I can throw down the pictures of my dog ... throw them onto the sofa ... like throwing down the gauntlet. And I say, "My dog is a prize winner. And "you've got an old alley cat that ate my dickey bird."

A. And I say, "She doesn't eat birds and she'd never eat your dickey bird. She's a purebred cat and has won a lot of cat contests." And that's where I get out my pictures. And I throw my pictures on the sofa.

B. And I say, "Lets' see those pictures. I'll know the bad cat that's been eating my birds when I see it." And I sit on the sofa.

A: And I say, "Let me see those dog pictures." And we both sit on the sofa together looking at the pictures.

B: "Oh, no, this isn't the cat that ate my bird."

A: "If this is your dog, she looks nice and friendly. And she's not the one that barks all night."

B: "Maybe we should get together. You can get to know my dog."

A: And you can meet my cat.

B: "It's a deal." (Then, we'll shake hands.)

The following pictures involve the casts and production staffs of Art Rise Theatre. This was a small community theatre that served north San Mateo County in the Bay Area of California. The pictures were all taken by the author of this textbook during the period in which he served as artistic director of the theatre. They were used for publicity releases and lobby displays.

What can you tell about the characters and their relationships in the pictures?

The Odd Couple (comedy: female version), by Neil Simon. This is the female version of *The Odd Couple* with Florence as the straight talking sports enthusiast and Olive as the meticulous hypochondriac and gourmet cook who is getting a divorce. Florence annoys Olive by interrupting games of Trivial Pursuit to clean. But Olive seeks male company and persuades Florence to invite some men for dinner.

Isn't It Romantic (romantic comedy), by Wendy Wasserstein. This play explores the feminine dilemma between personal independence and romantic fulfillment through the lives and careers of two former college classmates. Both need to deal with their parents.

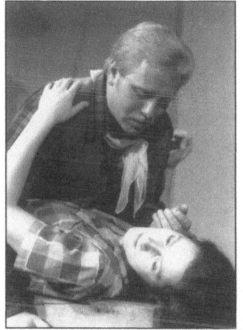

The Rainmaker (romantic folk comedy), by N. Richard Nash. Set during a period of drought in the west, the play involves the fate of Lizzie Curry, a plain, but proud farm girl who lives with her father and two brothers. They worry about Lizzie becoming an old maid. As they attempt to marry her off to the sheriff, a charming, fast-talking "rainmaker" named Starbuck arrives and confronts Lizzie, who thinks he's a conman. But he brings romance into her life ... and ultimately rain to the area.

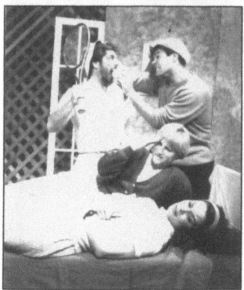

California Suite (four scenes of comedy), by Neil Simon. This tells the stories of four sets of visitors that stay at a California hotel. Each group brings their own problems, chaos and comedy. One woman hates her designer dress because it gives her a hump, and another group can't agree on anything.

Shadow Box (award winning drama), by Michael Cristofer. The play explores with compassion the anxieties of closure to the lives of three terminal cancer patients as friends gather to talk and search for some final meaning in life.

The Dining Room (a theatrical play), by A. R. Gurney Jr. Set in a dining room, the play presents a series of interrelated scenes that shows the changing lifestyle of upper middle class people that live in this dining room at different stages in time. Among those scenes are a real estate salesman, an old man, his nephew and a maid, and two students having a good time.

Taking Steps (Farce) by Alan Ayckbourn. A wealthy tycoon considers buying a Victorian house that is reported to be haunted. His wife, Elizabeth, plans to leave him and leave a note that her brother helps her write. Meantime, a lawyer is asked to stay overnight to complete the deal but finds himself in bed with Elizabeth who has changed her mind. The lawyer thinks she is a ghost.

The Effect of Gamma Rays on Man-in-the-Moon Marigolds (prize-winning drama), by Paul Zindel. In an effort to support herself and her two daughters, a proud but embittered widow takes in a cranky old boarder. One daughter is sickly but the other one, Tillie, while shy, excels in science and proves in an experiment that something beautiful can grow from barren soil.

Lone Star (one-act rural comedy), by James McLure. Roy, a Vietnam vet, and proud owner of a 1959 pink Thunderbird, brags about his military and romantic successes to his younger brother, Ray, as they consume a lot of beer. Cletis arrives to tell Roy that Ray has demolished his car and romanced his wife.

Laundry and Bourbon (one-act rural comedy), by James McLure. Two women, Elizabeth and Hattie, are gossiping about their marriages as they sort laundry and drink bourbon when a third woman, Amy Lee, arrives to tell Elizabeth the truth about her husband. Elizabeth stands by him anyway.

157

The Mousetrap (mystery melodrama), by Agatha Christie. A group of diverse strangers are stranded in a boarding house during a snowstorm. The characters include a newly married couple, a spinster, an architect, a bizarre young man and a retired Army major. Shortly after a policeman arrives on skis someone is murdered. Practically everyone is a suspect. The question is: "Whodunit?"

More *Mousetrap* suspects. Who
do you think dun it?

Stepping Out (comedy), by Richard Harris. Set in a seedy dance studio in north London, an ex-professional dancer attempts to teach a group of bumbling, hopeless amateurs some dance skills in preparation for a recital. The diverse comic personalities quarrel amongst themselves but ultimately succeed in their public performance.

Theatre Staff and Set for *All My Sons.* The four pictures show (clockwise from top): the final set construction for *All My Sons*, a picture of the stage manager and set designer, a consultation for a season of plays by the planning group that include a producer and two directors, and two people establishing a lighting plot.

161

Part C

Techniques in Character Development

Chapter 12
A Brief History
of Modern Acting Theories

"Love the art in yourself, not yourself in the art."
— Constantin Stanislavski

Theatricalism and Realism
Theatricality

Theatricality comes from the idea that something is more like theatre, or putting on a show, than it is like life. There has been a long tradition of theatricality which goes way back into the history of Greek and Roman plays, Shakespeare, commedia del'arte and Moliere and the eighteenth century plays.

In the nineteenth century, there were no radios, no movies, no television, no VCR's, no computers and no e-mail or worldwide web. Many of the plays of the nineteenth century were melodramas, with stereotyped villains, heroes and heroines. There were also romantic dramas with flamboyant heroes in romantic, idealized settings that called for such characters as kings and queens and swashbuckling knights. Or, there were fantasies with witches, fairies, elves and dwarfs. By today's standards, these characters are non-realistic. Classic plays, poetic plays, musical comedies and farces, which are exaggerated comedies, all fall within this category. (See definitions of romanticism, fantasy and melodrama in Chapter 18.)

Acting the characters in these plays in large theatres for a middle- and upper-class audience called for a more flamboyant style of acting. These performances were larger than life, or more exaggerated or stylized physically, vocally and emotionally than real life. Physically, this meant performances were slightly larger or more exaggerated in gestures and movement and a greater flamboyance. Vocally, it meant being louder and using more projection and often calls for elongation of vowel sounds, and more range of pitch and perhaps a richer vocal quality and a slightly slower delivery to make it more dramatic. Emotionally, there needed to be a greater intensity to support the larger than life character.

Acting styles and theories of acting change with the changing of times and social conventions.

Naturalism and Realism

At the end of the nineteenth century and the first half of the twentieth century, there was a change in society and the way society looked at human beings. Beginning with Emile Zola, the novelist, and his theories of naturalism in art, the major influence and style slowly shifted toward Naturalism and Realism. Naturalism is more "like nature" or "like life," and Realism is more "real."

The birth of the "box set" and "theatre of the fourth wall" basically pretends that it is presenting "a slice of life" as though there is no audience. Characters in the plays spoke more like human beings and were concerned about social and domestic problems. (See further definition of Naturalism in Chapter 18.)

Naturalism paralleled the interest in the scientific method that sought to understand, predict and control human behavior. It also paralleled Sigmund Freud's studies on the subconscious and basic motivation of human beings that were the beginnings of psychiatry and psychotherapy. John Watson's studies in behaviorism, which looked for answers to people's behavior from their past environment, were also part of the social climate. These theories became the dominant psychology during the 1920s, 1930s and beyond. So, it was only natural that these explorations in human behavior were paralleled in major acting and writing for the theatre.

The major changes in theatre began in Russia, with Constantin Stanislavski, who was disenchanted with the superficial acting styles of the nineteenth century. The story goes that Stanislavski met with Vladimir Nemirovitch Dantchenko at a sidewalk cafe, and for eighteen hours they discussed the need for a changing style of theatre. Stanislavski sought something with more truthful emotion and life-like presentations of character that paralleled Emile Zola's theories of naturalism. In the spirit of those changing times, Stanislavski and Dantchenko carried these theories into the beginnings of the Moscow Art Theatre, which was founded in 1898. Anton Chekhov, a Russian doctor, wrote plays for the Moscow Art Theatre. In Norway, Henrik Ibsen wrote realistic plays about domestic and social problems that involved such issues as the status of women.

Some New York actors brought Stanislavski's theories into the United States in the 1920s and '30s. They first learned of Stanislavski's techniques at Richard Boleslavsky's American Laboratory Theatre. Then, in the 1930s, these American actors formed what they called the Group Theatre and promoted ensemble acting.

The Group Theatre

The principle people in the Group Theatre were Harold Clurman (a director), Cheryl Crawford (a producer), Elia Kazan (actor, stage and film director), Clifford Odets (playwright), John Garfield (actor), Robert Lewis (actor, director, and teacher), Lee J. Cobb (actor), Stella Adler (actress and teacher), Luther Adler (actor), Morris Carnovsky (actor) and Lee Strasberg (teacher).

They set up classes, taught their version of the Stanislavski method and put on plays using these techniques, as best they understood them in translations from the Russian. Because of social differences, an ever-changing society and the continual evolution of theories, these may not have been exactly the same. But, some of the plays of the depression era 1930s began to deal more realistically with everyday people and everyday personal and social problems.

The Actors' Studio and The Method

After World War II ended in 1945, Elia Kazan and Robert Lewis, who had been members of the Group Theatre, formed the Actors' Studio in New York to further develop their acting theories. In 1947, Lee Strasberg became the primary teacher and continued to teach his version of these theories of acting until his death in 1982. His approach to acting calls for an intellectual and emotional honesty and truth and believability of the character. Many of these theories deal with drawing upon personal emotions and feelings from the subconscious memory to find a deeper emotional truth when acting a character.

The main elements of study involved relaxation, concentration, sense memory, affective or emotional memory (also called emotional recall) and substitution emotions. They also taught the personalization of emotions, and exercises involving imagination of what you would do if you were that character in that situation. Conclusions were based on given circumstances and imaginary circumstances. (For more on this subject see Chapters 13 and 16.)

While Stanislavski never quit investigating and was always looking for more truth, Strasberg froze the lessons into a dogma, where the principal goal was an inner personal emotional truth, which was then called The Method.

The Method

The Method endeavors to present the real or natural in life and portray characters honestly and truthfully. Physically, this might call for restraint in terms of size and frequency of gesture with more personal types of gestures. Vocally and emotionally, the performance must appear to be delivered in an intimate, honest, conversational tone. Emotionally, it could be very low key or even underplayed with a quiet intensity.

The Method, as taught:

- Encourages actors to use their own personalities and emotions to create a truthful character.
- Explores the deeper emotions of the subconscious and teaches techniques of "sense memory," "emotional or affective memory," "emotional recall" or "substitution" to discover deeper more truthful emotions when needed. (See Chapter 13 for further explanation of these techniques.)
- Analyzes the script for a major or "super-objective" which is the "spine" of the character being played or "through-line" of action or overall "arc." Then, each scene is broken down into motivations, objectives or intentions, the subtext, actions, beats or bits. This becomes the justification for all actions. (See Chapter 15 for further explanation.)
- May also use improvisation to discover a scene's intentions, explore a character's background, search for inner personal truth and emotions and create spontaneity in playing a scene.
- Seeks to establish emotional and intellectual relationships with other performers. This can enhance ensemble performances and therefore unify the play's production. (See Chapter 8.)
- Emphasizes the use of props, costume and makeup to enhance the real or naturalistic world. (See Chapter 4 for stage business and Chapter 14 for use of props and costume.)

The Actors' Studio has had notable success. Method techniques have worked well in depicting characters in realistic dramas, and particularly well in dramatic roles in film where the cameras are close and can see the inner thoughts and emotions of the character. (See Chapter 20.)

For over fifty years of the twentieth century, realism and naturalism in theatre have also been the predominant style in playwriting. Playwrights have endeavored to represent a realistic or natural truth about life by portraying real people in middle class or lower class settings. This type or style has sometimes been referred to as "kitchen sink" drama. One of the earliest American playwrights to explore realism in theatre was Eugene O'Neill. With the depression as a background, playwrights Clifford Odets, Arthur Miller and, later, Tennessee Williams, with his poetic realism, established realism as a dominant force in theatre.

Since Method acting works well in film and TV, it is not surprising that while some actors are noted for their stage work, many more have been made famous for their work in TV and motion pictures. From the 1950s until today, many of the top actors have come out of the Actors' Studio. Some of the best known are Marlon Brando, Paul Newman, Joanne Woodward, Montgomery Clift, James Dean, Dustin Hoffman, Karl Malden, Kim Hunter, Julie Harris, Rod Steiger, Eva Marie Saint, Shelly Winters, Blythe Danner, Estelle Parsons, Sandy Dennis and Marilyn Monroe.

From the beginning, the Actors' Studio has been able to choose talented actors and actresses for their training program. While most of these people have claimed that training at the Actors' Studio under Lee Strasberg gave them valuable acting tools, it is thought that many of these talented people might have been successful no matter what methods they were taught or might have used.

Teaching of The Method, or variations of The Method, has been the focus of many, but not all, teachers and teaching techniques in this country. As society has changed over the years, there have also been many teachers who have modified their teaching techniques and branched out. And, there have also been — from the beginning — some detractors.

Among those who differed in various ways and degrees with Strasberg's narrowly defined interpretations of Stanislavski and the controversial "personal feelings and emotions approach" when playing a character, have been Stella Adler, Robert Lewis and Sanford Meisner, to mention only a few. More recently, David Mamet has spoken out against The Method and its teachings.

Some Criticisms of The Method

While The Method and variations are widely accepted and widely practiced, there are some criticisms worth noting:

1. The Method teaches the actor to use his/her own "personal feelings and emotions" in playing the character. These are not always the same emotions and feelings as the character, nor are they always applicable to the play. In other words, this may be a truth about the actor but not about the character. The playwright created the characters. The actor and director are interpreters of these characters.

2. The Method teaches the actor to use his or her own personal emotions from past experiences, and dredging up past emotional experiences often does not fit or is not appropriate for responding spontaneously to present circumstances.

3. The Method teaches the actor to prepare an emotional reaction, which ignores the dynamics of interrelating with other

performers. To prepare an emotional reaction ignores the possibilities of responding spontaneously to what other actors are doing in the present moment and, therefore, may not be truthful.

4. The Method teaches *realistic acting,* but it doesn't prepare a performer for more theatrical roles. While it may be rare, there are some fine actors who are both real in the sense of being personally truthful to the character's inner personality themselves and theatrically truthful to the style of the play.

Searching for Truth

Truth means your physical (body, voice) and psychological (mental, emotional) energy and belief in what you are saying and doing. In addition, it means your emotional and sense response to looking, listening, relating and interacting to the mental and emotional life that surrounds you on-stage.

Personal Truth and Theatrical Truth

There have been long-standing discussions and debates among drama teachers that involve "truth" in playing characters. One group rooted in The Method as taught by Lee Strasberg, believes that truth comes from the individual actor's own personal inner emotional and intellectual personality. Therefore, a *personal truth* in acting is an inner intellectual and emotional truth that you personally feel about the character. It is truthful to your own personality. That's why you should personalize your work. The *Magic IF* asks the question, what would you do if you were that person? (For more on this subject see Chapter 16.)

Many of today's drama teachers say that there is no place for an actor's personal psyche and emotions when playing a character, and if your personal truth is only true to your own personality, then it may or may not be truthful to the character. These teachers argue that truth should come from honestly playing the character that was created by the playwright. Performing a playwright's character should not be about who the actor is. It should be about the actor giving the audience an honest interpretation of the playwright's character.

Theatrical Truth is used in two ways:

1. It can mean that you give the performance a theatricality or style that is "bigger" in body, voice and emotion when projecting your character to the audience.

2. It also means that you are truthful to the character, the life and world of the character and the theme that is presented in the

170

play by the playwright. It is your first obligation as the actor to accommodate the script and the playwright's characters as interpreted by you. Don't try to make the script accommodate you. It can be said that an actor changes to fit the character in the script. Many actors on stage and in film find it more interesting to accept the challenges because that's how you grow.

Discussion: So, what's right? Who's right? What is the truth about truth? When portraying a character, should the portrayal be real and personally truthful to your self, or should it be theatrically truthful to the play, or both? Whose truth should it be, the playwright's or your personal truth, or both?

Other Influences

"Acting is living truthfully under an imaginary set of circumstances,"
— Sanford Meisner

The Neighborhood Playhouse

Sanford Meisner was first a member of the Group Theatre, but he also began teaching at the Neighborhood Playhouse in New York City in the early 1930s. He taught for almost sixty years. Meisner's teaching at the Neighborhood Playhouse was based on many of his theories on truth in relationships. What happens on-stage depends not only on you but on the other performers as well. Many fine actors have been students of Meisner. Some of these people are Paul Newman, Joanne Woodward and Sidney Pollack (director, producer), to mention only a few.

Three of Meisner's fundamental exercises include:

1. Repetition to establish a relationship with others. (See Chapter 8.)

2. Independent physical activities and being specific in actions. As Aristotle said in *The Poetics* over two thousand years ago, "Acting is an imitation of an action." To act is to do.

3. Emotional preparation to perform is a condition of being alive emotionally. This is not the same as the emotional memory of the Actors' Studio. (See Chapter 13.)

Improvisational Theatre

Also gaining credibility were the teachings of Viola Spolin through the publication of her book, *Improvisation For the Theatre,* in

1963. Beginning in the 1950s, Paul Sills (Viola Spolin's son) started The Compass (1955) and The Second City (1959), which were improvisational companies in Chicago. Paul Sills created *Story Theatre*, which was a group of stories based on Grimm's Fairly Tales presented with modern references. (See *Something Wonderful Right Away*, an oral history by Jeffery Sweet that chronicles the Second City and The Compass.)

Improvisational groups were launched with the idea of being a *commedia del'arte* type of theatre, a popular form of improvisational theatre that flourished in Europe from the sixteenth to the early eighteenth century, particularly in Italy. They had stock characters and worked from outlines of plots with no formal scripts.

These companies from the 1950s and 1960s performed modern characters with up-to-the-minute topics. By the mid-to-late 1960s, with the Vietnam War escalating, there was a climate of change and youthful rebellion in the air. The desire to gain more social freedoms and more spontaneous living was just the right background to promote improvisational theatre.

Some of the people associated with the early days of this type of theatre were Alan Alda, Ed Asner, Mike Nichols and Elaine May. Others who have launched careers with these groups are Valerie Harper, Paul Mazursky (actor, writer, director), Joan Rivers, Barbara Harris, Robert Klein, Alan Arkin, Peter Boyle and Anne Meara and Jerry Stiller (parents of Ben Stiller). The Toronto company had Linda Lavin and Gilda Radner.

An improvisational theatre called The Premise opened in New York in 1960. Some of those who worked with this group were Gene Hackman, Buck Henry and even Dustin Hoffman for a while. Robin Williams was with an improvisational group called The Wall in Los Angeles.

Joseph Chaikin founded the Open Theatre in order to create original scripts by using improvisation and working together cooperatively with playwrights, actors and a director to create original scripts.

Paralleling the interest in improvisation in America was the work of Keith Johnstone at the Royal Court Theatre in London. Artistic directors George Devine and Tony Richardson put Johnstone in charge of the writer's group, where he developed his own techniques. He discontinued discussion and acted out the scenes because he thought, "plays were about relationships — not about characters and actor's problems." He developed a touring improvisational group, which he called The Theatre Machine.

In more recent years, Johnstone moved to western Canada as a teacher in Calgary. From that base he created "Theatre Sports," which combines the spontaneity of improvisation with the enthusiasm of a competitive sports event to create a theatrical presentation. Teams oppose each other. There are referees and an Olympic-style group of judges. The audience cheers its favorite teams and boos the judges for bad decisions, and ultimately there are winning and losing teams.

There are teams in Calgary, Vancouver, British Columbia, Toronto and other Canadian cities. In the United States there are teams in Seattle, San Francisco, Salt Lake City, New York, Los Angeles and Washington D.C. The movement is spreading to Australia, England, Europe and Scandinavia. Many of Johnstone's theories and techniques can be discovered in *Impro*, which he published in 1979.

Charna Halpern, along with Del Close and Kim "Howard" Johnson, created another competitive improv technique known as the "Harold". The "Harold" is a form of competitive improv involving six or seven players who take a theme suggestion from the audience and free-associate on the theme into a series of rapid-fire one-liners that build into totally unpredictable skits with hilarious results. This innovative improvisational tool helped *Saturday Night Live's* Mike Myers and Chris Farley, George Wendt ("Norm" on *Cheers*) and many other actors.

Improvisation gives drama a sense of "now-ness," of people relating to each other spontaneously. Improvisation can also be used as a helpful tool for actors in exploring characters and scenes in formal scripts. It is most helpful in film where a fresh spontaneity is important. (See Chapters 9 and 19.)

Leaders of groups in America and England that have used improvisation to create whole plays successfully are Joan Littlewood (*Oh, What a Lovely War*), Caryl Churchill (*Mad Forest* and *Cloud Nine*) and Brian Clark (*Whose Life Is It, Anyway?*). They all began in England, while Paul Sills and the Second City Company started in Chicago (*Story Theatre*) and Joseph Chaikin and the Open Theatre began in New York. While most of these groups do not exist today, their legacy lives on.

Training in The Method and Improvisation

Many actors who have studied The Method approach and work *inside/out* with emotionally intense acting have found success in serious drama both on-stage and in film. At the same time,

In more recent years, Johnstone moved to western Canada as a teacher in Calgary. From that base he created "Theatre Sports," which combines the spontaneity of improvisation with the enthusiasm of a competitive sports event to create a theatrical presentation. Teams oppose each other. There are referees and an Olympic-style group of judges. The audience cheers its favorite teams and boos the judges for bad decisions, and ultimately there are winning and losing teams.

There are teams in Calgary, Vancouver, British Columbia, Toronto and other Canadian cities. In the United States there are teams in Seattle, San Francisco, Salt Lake City, New York, Los Angeles and Washington D.C. The movement is spreading to Australia, England, Europe and Scandinavia. Many of Johnstone's theories and techniques can be discovered in *Impro*, which he published in 1979.

Charna Halpern, along with Del Close and Kim "Howard" Johnson, created another competitive improv technique known as the "Harold". The "Harold" is a form of competitive improv involving six or seven players who take a theme suggestion from the audience and free-associate on the theme into a series of rapid-fire one-liners that build into totally unpredictable skits with hilarious results. This innovative improvisational tool helped *Saturday Night Live*'s Mike Myers and Chris Farley, George Wendt ("Norm" on *Cheers*) and many other actors.

Improvisation gives drama a sense of "now-ness," of people relating to each other spontaneously. Improvisation can also be used as a helpful tool for actors in exploring characters and scenes in formal scripts. It is most helpful in film where a fresh spontaneity is important. (See Chapters 9 and 19.)

Leaders of groups in America and England that have used improvisation to create whole plays successfully are Joan Littlewood (*Oh, What a Lovely War*), Caryl Churchill (*Mad Forest* and *Cloud Nine*) and Brian Clark (*Whose Life Is It, Anyway?*). They all began in England, while Paul Sills and the Second City Company started in Chicago (*Story Theatre*) and Joseph Chaikin and the Open Theatre began in New York. While most of these groups do not exist today, their legacy lives on.

Training in The Method and Improvisation

Many actors who have studied The Method approach and work *inside/out* with emotionally intense acting have found success in serious drama both on-stage and in film. At the same time,

While almost any technique may be planned, repeated, rehearsed and internalized until it feels instinctive and appears natural, the best techniques are the ones that work for you.

You have already started to learn some basic skills and techniques in the previous chapters. But, it is the view of this book that no one method or technique or approach works for all performers in all plays at all times. And, it is the province of this textbook to explain and practice a variety of approaches and techniques to fit a variety of acting situations.

At the same time, you should not get so involved in showing your techniques that you lose the truth of your character. Technique is important in helping discipline in using body, voice and emotions. But, technique is only valuable on the stage when you forget all about it.

Instinct

Instinct means doing what comes naturally. It happens subconsciously and spontaneously and does not involve reason. In theory, the more you are like the character physically, vocally and psychologically in terms of personality, character traits, emotions and values, the more easily you will be able to perform a character instinctively.

However, this is not necessarily a good reason to choose only characters that are like you. While it's possible to be a very good instinctive actor without using techniques, it's more probable you will be an even better actor and be able to play a wider variety of roles by knowing and developing a whole variety of skills and techniques that involve a different use of the body, the voice and character traits and emotions.

If you have talent and you are depending only on your talent with no technique, sooner or later you will probably have an artistic problem that talent alone will not solve. For instance, if you are not like the character, you may not feel anything.

You still need to portray honestly those aspects of the character that are not like you, aspects that are not natural to you vocally or physically or to your basic personality. On these occasions you will need to use more of your skills and techniques and search further within yourself in order to build your character.

This may involve more exploration of the character traits, emotions, observations and motivations to achieve a truthful character. Since portraying a character is not about you, but instead about the character created by the playwright, you will need to find

175

ways to adapt to the character rather than play the character as a total extension of yourself. Even if you are similar to the character, techniques may be used to enhance an instinctive approach and enrich the depth of the ultimate performance.

If there's a difference between yourself and your character, you may need to use a variety of techniques. You might need to call upon research and observation to change physically and vocally and assume the personality of the character.

Very few performers will approach a role by either pure instinct or pure technique. Instead they work back and forth, letting techniques help instinct. Even though you may learn all kinds of skills and techniques, acting is ultimately a personal process in solving acting problems for creative interpretations of characters.

Accepting the challenge of acting a character that is quite different from you can offer great new insights and understanding of another type of person. Solving the problems can be very satisfying and rewarding. To feel how another person feels and thinks is a valuable life skill.

Inside/Out and Outside/In

Broadly speaking, some performers approach characterization *inside/out* while others work *outside/in*. While it is possible to start to build a character inside/out, with character traits and your personal emotions, inner thoughts and feelings (an approach explored in Chapter 13), it is also possible to start with thoughts, images and observations of your character and build outside/in those physical aspects that use costume, props and makeup. (This approach is explored in Chapter 14.)

Inside/Out

This means searching within yourself to find the truth about your character and then, using your own basic character traits, emotions, instincts and personality to project your performance outward. Inside/out is subjective to objective. It is the usual approach for most people that advocate The Method.

Outside/In

This means approaching your characterization by starting from outside yourself and working in a very technical way to build the character within yourself. Outside/in is objective to subjective. This approach to acting may begin with an image of the way the character looks and sounds. This image may be based on what you think the character should look like, or it may be created from one or more people that you know or have observed, or it may be a personal creation from circumstances in the play.

This often involves the selective use of different costume pieces and/or props and/or makeup. It may also suggest the way your character walks, gestures or sounds vocally. (For exploration of this approach, see Chapter 14.)

Many British actors have a tradition of approaching roles from outside/in. This is probably a carry over from the nineteenth century when there were romantic plays, and performers learned a set of gestures that "looked right" for emotions.

In practice, you will probably need to combine inside/out and outside/in while working on the same role. To know and experience both ways of approaching roles is important in the development of your skills and techniques because you will probably use both ways at different times in different plays for different characters. One approach should creatively enhance the other.

Looking Forward

As we go further into the twenty-first century, we will continue to go through vast social and economic changes that will be reflected in our lives and all of our art forms. What is regarded as the norm or truest style of acting in one period or era may be regarded as false or untrue in another era. Changes in society will no doubt create changes in theatre and filmmaking, and these will call for new plays and new ways to regard acting and theatre arts. However, it won't change immediately.

There is still a vast heritage of plays to be acted in a known style. In the meantime, the skills, techniques and activities presented in this textbook can be helpful in developing actors to perform in almost all occasions. Ultimately each actor will develop his or her own personal methods and techniques. That is the mission of this textbook.

In the following chapters you will learn to develop character traits, emotions and images and understand the motivations and objectives of a character. These are all skills and techniques that should be helpful in developing fully realized characterizations and will serve you well in life.

Study the techniques. Do the exercises. Enjoy the process. But, don't let yourself feel overwhelmed by theories and techniques. They are only a means to an end — not an end in themselves. In other words, enjoyment of acting should not be about showing off your techniques. Learning to act is a never-ending, lifelong process because it also involves human interaction and personal discovery. Those are some of the major goals of this textbook.

As you become more skilled and develop your own techniques and ways of developing characters you may look for other ways to enhance your acting. Come back to these pages and they will perhaps mean something more to you at that time. Meantime, keep it simple, make it truthful and be yourself. Then, relax and, most of all, enjoy the process of acting because it should be fun.

Chapter 13
Character Traits and Emotions

"Katharine Hepburn runs the gamut of human emotions from A to B."
— Dorothy Parker, critical review

*"Mr. Clarke played the king ... as though ... (under constant fear that) ...
someone else was about to play the ace."*
— Eugene Field, reviewing a production of *King Lear*

In acting, as in life, each person has many basic character traits and emotions to call on. All character traits are not emotions, but all emotions are, in a sense, character traits. Drama is a way to act out and test your emotions in a safe environment and gain the experience of communicating and expressing yourself honestly.

Character Traits

In acting, as in life, when you describe someone, it is usually in terms of a physical description or basic character traits, emotional makeup, or general personality. A physical description might be in terms of age, such as mid-twenties, middle-aged, childlike, youthful, elderly, etc., or such words as attractive, tall, short, fat, thin, dark hair. Or, the description might involve character or personality traits such as funny, boring, annoying, lonely, aggressive, dependent, angry, independent, shy, sad, silly, sullen, serious and somewhat of an introvert. Other descriptions might be: thoughtful, talkative, tacky, dumb, happy, friendly, a nervous nerd, etc. Sometimes characters are named for these character traits. For example Hap, Biff and Willy Loman (Low man), Tombs the Butler, Sir Toby Belch, Hotspur, Bottom, the Darling family, Captain Hook or Alfred Doolittle (do little).

Reviews of plays often make note of whether some performer captured the nervous insecurity of the character or the passionate intensity that set the tone for the ultimate showdown.

The playwright is the *creator* of the script, the person who creates the original character and writes the dialog. But you, as the performer, are the *interpreter* of the script, which involves the character and the dialog. So, you are the person who needs to supply the character traits and emotions behind the lines that are distinguishing qualities for your interpretation of the character's personality. Showing and projecting these qualities to an audience is at the basis of your performance as an actor.

By "trying on" or experiencing different character traits and emotions until they are internalized and become an instinctive part of your inner character, you should not only find out more about other people, but you can also find out more about yourself.

Most of the approaches to discovering character traits and emotions in this chapter are through the process of working inside/out. (For further explanation of inside/out and outside/in approaches see Chapter 12.)

Exercise: Reacting Freely to Character Traits

The following list consists of descriptive character traits, qualities of character, feelings or emotions. As you hear the different character traits and emotions read, react freely to each of them in order to discover how they feel. Most of these can be registered instantly. Use the whole body to express the trait. It can be helpful to repeat the character trait to yourself by thinking: "I am _____ (character trait)." Allow ten to fifteen seconds each to establish the feeling for each of these traits. Because people are different, some character traits will be easier for some people than others.

List #1 of Character Traits

1. Bored
2. Angry
3. Innocent
4. Secretive/suspicious
5. Arrogant/haughty
6. Twitchy
7. Aloof/not involved
8. Irritable
9. Whiny/tearful
10. Lazy
11. Dreamy
12. Nervous
13. Sad and lonely
14. Pouting
15. Tired
16. Rigid/formal
17. Irritable
18. Sensitive or hurt
19. Friendly/outgoing
20. Dumb
21. Intelligent
22. Unsure/indecisive
23. Fearful
24. Neat
25. Thoughtful
26. Hateful
27. Shy
28. Worried/frowning
29. Doubtful/puzzled
30. Narcissistic
31. Lovesick
32. Calm/patient
33. Proud/vain
34. Surprised
35. Giggly
36. Childlike
37. Old
38. Mischievous
39. Happy
40. Dopey
41. Grumpy
42. Bashful
43. Sleepy
44. Sneezy
45. Joyful
46. Sarcastic
47. Your Choice

Discussion: After repeating this several times, discuss which character traits felt the easiest or most comfortable and honest. This may be different for different people. This exercise may be repeated, or the list may be broken up on different days.

Defining a Character's Attitudes

Choose a character trait or emotion or state of being from the list above for your interpretation. Then, while playing this character trait, read or memorize the lines below. These are simple statements or sentences without much character or personality. But, as an interpreter you will show attitudes toward what is being said. Depending which emotional quality you choose the total effect is quite different. Note how each actor's interpretation changes the meaning. It is optional whether you move around or not.

Daily Activities

I got up this morning.

I got dressed and combed my hair.

I ate breakfast, then gathered my books and went to school/work.

My activities in the morning included _____.
Then, I had lunch in the cafeteria. I don't know what to say about the food.

After classes I _____, and tonight I'm going to
_____.

And tomorrow ... well, everyday ... it's all the same.

Class in Drama

My counselor signed me up for this class in drama.

There are all kinds of strange people in the class. But some are really nice. We're assigned all types of exercises: pantomime, basic stage movement, stage business, suiting the action to the word, breathing exercises, voice projection, character traits, emotions and thinking ... and lots of other stuff. I like some of the things we do and some I don't.

My teacher says I'm going to get better at_____.
And we may do a play ... sometime...later on ... maybe.

Discussion: For the audience, what character traits, emotions or attitudes was the person showing? For the actor: How would you describe your character?

Exercise

Write your own sentences. These sentences may describe an event that happened, such as a trip, party, hobby, going to the grocery, a sport, a job, cooking, etc. Or, show a physical condition such as time of day or weather. Then, read or perform the sentences to show the specific character traits, attitudes or emotions. Or, select someone else to choose a character trait and read your sentences.

Discussion: Were you able to call forth the mental image or picture of a person, place or event?

List #2 of Character Traits
The following list includes more character traits. Many of these character traits are better observed in playing a scene while delivering the dialog. In this sense it is a character trait that is a general attitude.

1. Energetic or active
2. Relaxed/easygoing
3. Gossipy
4. Sloppy/messy
5. Talkative
6. Practical joker or naughty
7. Fair (weighs both sides)
8. Snappish or snippy
9. Smiling/laughing
10. Changeable/unpredictable
11. Silly
12. Sarcastic/snide
13. Fibber/con man/woman
14. Mischievous/teasing
15. Curious
16. Clumsy
17. Apathetic (don't care)
18. Fault-finding
19. Icky-sweet
20. Sour/bitter
21. Overly polite
22. Disagreeable
23. Greedy
24. Threatening
25. Nasty/mean/vengeful
26. Pushy/aggressive
27. Controlled/reserved
28. Smart aleck
29. Envious
30. Gluttonous/hungry
31. Admiring
32. Critical
33. Complaining
34. Disruptive
35. Your choice

Exercise: Using a Duo Scene
Pair off by number or choose a partner for a two-character scene. Then, each partner chooses one or more character traits from either list #1 or list #2, and uses this as the basis for your character in a memorized or improvised scene. (A suggestion might be "Basic Stage Movement" from Chapter 3.) Without telling anyone what character traits you have chosen, perform the scene.

Exercise: Group Improvisation Using Character Traits
Create groups of five to nine (seven might be optimum). Each member of the group chooses a specific character trait. For example, each person might choose a character trait from the lists above. Then, establish where the improvisation is taking place and the basis for

what is happening in the scene. This may be a field trip to a museum or play, a bus trip, summer camp, picnic, party, audition for a play, etc. Establish a relationship, a situation or problem to solve in the story or a setting. (See Chapter 9 for further ideas.) Then, perform the scene showing your character trait without telling anyone what it is.

Discussion: What were observed to be the chosen traits by the performers? Did the choice of character traits fit the characters in the scene? For the actor: What were you were trying to show? Did you feel anything like that person? Were these traits easy for you? Why would a character behave this way?

Exercise: Contrasting Character Traits

Two or more performers choose opposite character traits. It is important to *show* these character traits through what happens in the story rather than *tell* what they are. If they are presented through the action, the audience should be able to tell.

Situation: Two people need to buy a new product. Possibilities might be: item for kitchen (microwave, coffee maker, etc.), item for bedroom (blanket, lamp, pictures, etc.) or item for entertainment (DVD, TV, records, etc.). You both agree you need this item.

A salesperson has tried to sell it to you.

Performer One: You are a suspicious person who thinks the item is too expensive and may not work very well. You don't trust the salesperson either.

Performer Two: You are a trusting person. You liked the salesperson and you liked the item and want to buy it.

Situation: Two or three people. They are studying at night. They hear a sound, then the lights go out and more sounds.

Performer One: You are a nervous, high-strung person who is fearful of the dark. You want to leave, but not alone.

Performer Two: You are a calm, relaxed person who tries to explain what happened. You would like to leave, but not with Performer One.

Performer Three: You are the one who invited the other two over to your house to study. You don't want them to leave. You have no explanation.

Situation: Two people are in a grocery store buying food for a small party they are having. Performer Two is paying for the food.

Performer One: You are a big eater and very hungry and willing to spend money on food. And so are the friends you've invited.

Performer Two: You are a light eater and vegetarian and don't have much money to spend. You keep suggesting things that Performer One doesn't like.

Situation: Two people, male and female, who would like to go to a party together, but don't know each other very well. They talk all around the subject.

Performer One: You are a flirtatious female who wants to be invited to the party, but can't come out and ask directly. You keep dropping hints.

Performer Two: You are a shy male who would like to ask her but are having a difficult time asking her for a first date.

Situation: Three friends are signing yearbooks and discussing what they are going to do after high school and the value of their choice.

Student One: You don't like school and plan to get a job and get married soon.

Student Two: You are smart and expect a scholarship so you are looking into expensive universities in some other city.

Student Three: You are planning to go to a junior college and save your money.

Situation: One person is trying to teach the other how to do something. This may be how to play a sport, play a musical instrument, act in a scene, make a speech, dress for an occasion, drive a car, sew a costume, go on a diet, build a physique, be popular, meet new people, have fun, make some money, assemble a holiday gift with directions and many parts, go to college, interview for a job or discuss your plans for the weekend or vacation time.

Performer One: You are smart and skilled and try to teach something.

Performer Two: You are dumb or unskilled and don't understand and keep making mistakes. But you want to learn. (You may be only pretending to be dumb.)

Situation: Two or more people are in a car going to a party and have just discovered they don't have the address or a map.

Performer One: You are an angry, excitable person and you are driving. You have a need to be at this party.

Performer Two: You are a calm, relaxed person who was supposed to bring the map and the address. You don't care.

Performer Three: You are nervous and getting carsick.

Performer Four: You are critical of everything.

Emotions

In life, people often tend to hide their thoughts, feelings or emotions because that's what they learn culturally or are taught — mostly indirectly. However, in playing a character on-stage, performers should, when needed, be able to call upon a variety of different emotions for different roles and learn how to show their thoughts and emotions and project them to an audience. To do this effectively takes practice. A performer honestly feeling and projecting emotions in a real scene or story can effectively involve and move an audience emotionally.

Within all of us there are a multitude of emotions, and many of these can be felt by just instinctively knowing what emotion is needed. Most people will be able to perform easily those emotions that are closely akin to their own basic personality. *If you don't feel the emotion, neither will the other actors in your scene and neither will the audience.*

Examples of frequently experienced emotions might be: the joy of meeting someone special (perhaps a love interest), the anguish of breaking up with a love interest, the emptiness of losing a loved one in death, the fear of someone or something that could harm you, the frustration of continued failure in some venture, the suspicion of strange events happening to you or the anger of being ridiculed or humiliated.

For many, anger is one of the easiest emotions because most people have felt anger occasionally. And someone who flares angrily and frequently in life will probably be able to call forth anger for a role more easily than someone who is shy, reticent and emotionally reserved in life.

There are different kinds and degrees of emotions. *Feelings* are partly mental, partly physical responses. *Affection* (liking someone or something) is an example of a feeling. *Emotions* are stronger and tend to lead to excitement or agitation. *Sentiment* is an emotion that is inspired by sympathy or compassion out of proportion to reason. *Passion* is usually a powerful emotion.

To feel and express the exact needed emotion with the right amount of intensity, in terms of the character and the content of the scenes, is a crucial part of the actor's challenge.

Many teaching techniques and methods involve finding the exact emotion for a scene. Some performers, just by focusing and concentrating on the scene and the dialog, are very successful at feeling the needed emotion or character trait naturally and instinctively. For instance, if a scene calls for anger, suspicion, annoyance, fear, pain, sadness or loneliness, some actors will just be able to call forth those emotions easily and truthfully without any special technique.

However, since everyone hasn't experienced all emotions, any particular emotion may not be comfortably within the scope of a performer's experience or personality. Or you may not be able to feel and bring forth the exact emotion at a moment's notice, and/or sustain the emotion for the whole play with the needed intensity. If this is the case, and the emotion is not there, meaning you are not able to feel it, there are several approaches that can be helpful in arriving at the desired character trait or emotion.

Showing Emotions Through Thoughts

"The eyes are the mirror of the soul."
(That is, the eyes, and face, show what the mind is thinking.)
— Constantin Stanislavski

One way to create an emotion is to think a specific thought because thoughts often precede or inspire specific feelings or emotions. Take your time. As a warm-up to "get into the emotions," you might even close your eyes and think the thought that is related to the desired emotion.

For instance, think or say to yourself the thought or emotion you wish to convey. Thoughts might be: "I feel angry." "I feel sad." "I'm really happy." Or, "My friend is in the hospital very sick. I feel terrible. S/He was my best friend." "I love my dog/cat, hamster, etc."

Or, in establishing your relationship to other performers, "You are a terrible person. I hate you." Or, "You are a really nice person and I appreciate everything you have done for me." Repeat the phrase(s) several times or until you begin to feel the emotion. Be specific. For example, to feel annoyance is vague and general. But if you *think* — as you look at the other character — "I am really annoyed and angry with you because of what you've done," it should bring forth the needed emotion. But it will need practice.

Listening and focusing your thoughts on other performers, in terms of what they are "giving you" emotionally in the context of the scene should further help you feel the needed emotions and determine the size and intensity of these emotions. (See Chapter 8.)

Keep your thoughts in the present in relation to the other performers, so the thought relates to what's happening in the scene.

Don't think ahead. Instead, stay in the moment.

These inner thoughts can also be used to show intentions, create a subtext of the dialog for your character and convey underlying ideas to establish an underlying relation with other characters. (See Chapter 15.)

Note that the feelings often are centered in the stomach area, but they will register in your eyes and on your face and general body reaction. The emotions should also show what you are thinking and feeling with your body, and will be heard in the tone of your voice, in the way you deliver lines and how you relate to what's happening in the scene. These skills should be enhanced with practice.

This is a particularly valuable skill for small theatres and extremely valuable for film acting where the camera is so close and the camera registers thoughts so clearly. (See Chapter 20.)

Note: There doesn't need to be a lot of "emotional preparation" for scenes that only require a simple playing of the scene for a sufficiently truthful result.

Showing Character Traits, Emotions or Subtext Through Thoughts

Exercise: What am I thinking and feeling?

In the following exercise, use thoughts to show character traits or emotions. Pair off. Choose a thought from the list or draw a thought from a container to convey to your partner. Think the thought that involves the emotion. Once you have the feelings or emotions just right, look at your partner and see if your partner can detect what the emotion or feeling is that you are thinking. It may not be the exact feeling or emotion, but it should be in the general area of the desired emotion. Don't try to "act out" the thought or make faces, mug or gesture.

Think the thought clearly and consistently to create and project an emotion. Keep repeating the thought until your partner interprets or discovers what the thought is. Then, your partner chooses a thought and repeats the process. Continue the thought until it has been discovered. But, don't watch yourself or listen to yourself. Just relax, concentrate, think and feel!

Continue by changing partners. Try this with someone you do not know very well and note the difference. Note how your own emotions change when you think the thought.

This exercise can be repeated many times with different thoughts and used in many different scenes along with underlying motivations and objectives and intentions. (See particularly Chapter 15.)

Thinking Emotions

1. **Positive, energetic and cheerful:** "I feel great! I like everything. I love life. Doesn't everybody?"

2. **Admiring:** "I admire you. You're a fine person."

3. **Mischievous:** "I heard something funny about you."

4. **Dumb:** I feel dumb. And my mind hurts."

5. **Dreamy and innocent:** "Oh, well. I guess everything will probably be all right. And maybe turn out for the best."

6. **Worried:** "I'm worried sick."

7. **Bored and apathetic:** "This is really boring. So, what difference does it make? I don't care."

8. **Suspicious:** "I don't think I can trust you. I really don't."

9. **Secretive:** "I have a secret."

10. **Sad, lonely:** "Oh! — I'm so sad and lonely I don't know what to do ... about anything."

11. **Sour, bitter:** "Nobody does anything right."

12. **Giggling and silly:** "This is fun. I know it's ridiculous and silly and stupid, but it's fun!"

13. **Shy and bashful:** "I'm just shy and don't like to be noticed."

14. **Proud, arrogant:** "I am a very important person. More important than other people."

15. **Whiny, tearful:** "Nobody likes me. Nobody cares."

16. **Fearful:** "I'm really scared. I know I'm in danger! I don't know what I'll do. I'm scared!"

17. **Nervous:** "I'm soooo nervous. I'm shaking all over."

18. **Irritable, discontent, disgruntled, negative:** "I hate everything. And I'm not going to help you and nobody can make me. People are no good!"

19. **Surprised:** Oh! Wow! I can't believe this!

21. **Angry:** "I hate everything ... and everybody! And I'm mad!"

22. **Lazy:** "I feel tired and lazy. I don't want to do anything."

23. **Narcissistic, smug, self-contented:** "I like myself a lot. I'm a very nice and important person. Totally satisfied!"

24. **Disgusted:** "I can't stand this whole exercise."

Exercise: Passing a Thought

The group sits in a line. The first person thinks a thought and "passes it" to the second person. No one else watches. When the second person feels she or he has received the thought, then the second person turns and faces the third person and thinks the thought. When the third person has received the same thought, the third person turns and passes it to the fourth person, and so on through the group. When the thought arrives at the last person, this person tells what thought s/he has received. This is compared with the thought that started with the first person.

Discussion: What was the thought at the end? Was it the same at the end as it was at the beginning?

Exercise: Matching Body and Voice
with Character Traits and Emotions

Two people go on stage. Each person chooses a basic character trait or an emotion. Each person chooses a thought from "Thinking Emotions" or one of your own. Do not tell the audience what character traits and emotions you are choosing for your character. Perform the following scene.

A: Here we are.
B: Yes, here we are.
A: What do we do now?
B: I don't know. (Pause)
A: Maybe there's nothing to be done.
B: I can't accept that.
A: It's a possibility.
B: Maybe so. But we still have to keep going.
A: Let's sit down and think about it.
B: I don't want to sit down.
A: Why not?
B: I think more clearly when I'm standing.

Discussion: What was the basic emotion or character trait being performed by each person? What other ways might these actors have added to body or voice to enhance these traits and emotions?

Exercise: Showing Emotional Moods in a Mini-Scene

First of all, as a group, determine the basic emotions or feelings of the person in each scene of the following six. Then, each person should choose three to six mini-scenes and perform them one after the other. Sustain the mood, feelings or emotions during the performance of each scene. (Changing emotions is somewhat the same problem for a singer who sings a group of songs, each with a different emotion.) In order to get the new feelings for each emotional mood, you may take a slight pause after each one, if necessary. But, be as honest as possible when delivering the lines.

When going from one scene to another or one emotion to another, there needs to be a smooth transition. For the transition to be smooth in life, it takes time. So, don't rush from one emotion to another. This has always seemed to be a problem for pop singers who make a big emotional transition from one two-minute song about the joy of love to another two-minute song about the loss of love. In order to make this work honestly, take your time and let the thoughts lead the emotional transition.

Emotions in mini-scenes

1. I've never felt so wonderful in my whole life — so absolutely wonderful. I'm ecstatic! It's great — just great to be alive. When you look out and see the trees and flowers in bloom — and sun shining — you just know it's great to be alive.

2. You mean me? Oh, Golly — I don't know. I guess I did if you say I did. Huh ... (Clears throat) Yeah, I suppose so. (Chuckles bashfully) But up till now I'd never think of doing a thing like that. Gosh — kiss a boy (girl) out here — and in the broad daylight, too. Wow!

3. I am sad, lonely, unhappy — at times even miserable. (Pause) Everybody seems against me. (Pause) Nobody — just nobody cares what happens to me. I've never been so lonely in my ... (Pause) I don't see how I can possibly go on any longer. (Pause) Everything seems so helpless, because now ... now ... (Sustain mood a moment)

4. You're nobody. Absolutely nobody. What a miserable excuse for a human being ... stupid, idiotic. That's what you are ... and lazy. No good for nothing ... absolutely worthless. That's what you are ... rotten, miserable, lazy, crazy, no good human being. You are nothing. Zero. Nothing.

5. I beg of you ... on my knees. Please, I didn't mean to do it. I'm sorry. I'll never, never, never do it again. Only give me one more chance. Just one more. I know that what I did was awful and terrible, but I'm sorry. Why can't you forgive me just this once? Please, I beg of you. Please!

6. Get out of here! I want nothing more to do with you! I hate you. You've insulted me and been nasty to me for the last time! Get out! You heard me! Get out! I never want to see your ugly face again in my whole life! Get out!

Return to this exercise after you have finished all of the exercises in this chapter and note the changes.

Exercise: Flirting

Pair off in groups of two or three. One person does the flirting and another person(s), partner or audience is the object of the flirtation. Smile shyly, suspiciously, embarrasseingly, apologetically, frowningly, doubtfully, etc. Then, stare with a variety of different emotions. Then, wink while experiencing the same emotions.

Discussion: When can you smile, stare, wink, touch, raise eyebrows or look away, and when should you not? What is the learned or cultural base of these reactions?

Exercise: Flirting when Changing Body Language

Fold or cross your arms and then do the above exercise. Does it feel different or change the meaning when your arm are crossed? Put hands on hips and do the above.

Discussion: What changes did you note in the relation of body language and emotions?

Ambiguity

Ambiguity means that something is understood in more than one context. In terms of character it means showing more than one dimension or aspect when defining a character's traits and emotions. Showing ambiguity can make your character more believable and interesting as long as the behavior doesn't seem inconsistent in terms of how the character was written by the playwright.

It is sometimes difficult for a playwright to show more than one dimension without seeming inconsistent. But, in life people are more than one dimension and sometimes even contradictory.

You probably act differently and manifest different personality traits with your parents or teachers than you do with your fellow students. In other words, you show more than one dimension of yourself in different relationships. All these aspects are essentially you.

Exercise: Creating an Ambiguity

Choose several mini scenes, and for a totally different emotional effect, choose an emotion that is contradictory to the basic text. For example, if delivering No. 1, you might deliver the lines with boredom. Or, if acting No. 6, which is an angry script, deliver the lines while laughing.

Discussion: What effects were achieved or totally wrong? Is it possible, on some occasions, to use this approach to create more depth and nuance of character?

y performers may be able to give intelligent readings of lines with generally believable emotional qualities either by instinct or from thoughts. But, if your character's emotions are out of your instinctive emotional range, and you've tried using "thoughts," and you still don't feel the exact truthful emotion for your character, then it's possible to use some techniques of The Method. These approaches include sense memory or affective or emotional memory, recall or a substitute emotion.

Aspects of The Method Explained
Sense Memory

Sense memory is used to recreate from memory sensory experiences (sight, sound, touch, smell, taste) and show the effects of the senses on you without the actual presence of the stimulus. (Some of these senses were introduced in Chapter 2.)

Your sense memory is called upon if your character needs to smell some plastic flowers and say how nice they smell. Or if your character needs to react to some bitter smell when there is no smell at all. Or, you may be tasting some food that is supposed to be delicious, but instead of being prepared by some gourmet chef, it is prepared by a busy prop crew. Or, you may need to describe something you saw on a trip to a place you've never been.

Affective or Emotional Memory or Recall

To use the personal, intellectual memories from past emotional experiences from your own life that match or are parallel to the emotional experiences of the character you are playing is to use affective or emotional memory or recall.

This is a process used to bring forth or recreate the emotion by recalling, in detail, an emotional experience from your past that made an impression on you in order to regenerate that emotion in the present and achieve a truthful emotional feeling or response in the current scene. And your experienced emotion should be as close as possible to the emotion needed for the character. For example: "What did I do that day? What was I feeling? What was I thinking? What did I see, hear, and smell?"

Examples:

1. Your character needs to show sympathy or compassion for another character that has had something bad happen, and you feel

192

none. You may recall a friend or family member who had a similar problem with health, money, a job or some type of loss that affected you emotionally. Or, your character tells about a loss of a good friend, relation or romance — from moving, rejection or death — that changed your life. Recall something that is similar in your life that made you feel the emotion that your character would feel.

2. Your character needs to show frustration or disappointment over losing an athletic contest. Even if it is not the same sport, you can probably remember a frustrating situation where your team lost and how depressed everyone felt. Or, you may need to substitute the frustration of working hard for something, such as a good grade or role in a play, that meant something to you and being disappointed when you didn't get it.

3. Your character needs to show fear of a villain. You may need to remember the fear of being in some unfamiliar place on a dark night where there was fear of the unknown, and you didn't know what to expect. Or recall or substitute the memory of fear with needing to perform in front of a large audience, and you can't remember any of your lines. Or, you have fear of being caught doing something you shouldn't be doing.

Substitution

This means that the emotion is not parallel or matching exactly the emotional experience of your character. But it is similar. For example, a friend of your character dies, and this hasn't happened to you. But you know what it felt like when your dog or cat or pet hamster died. Or, your character needs to show affection for another character in the play, and you don't feel this affection. Think of someone in life for whom you do have affection. You might even think of a personal pet. (Don't tell the other performer that it's a cat or dog or hamster.) Or, your character needs to show joy from inheriting some money. You haven't inherited any money, and for you, joy doesn't come naturally over money. But you may have felt joy when you won an athletic contest or were cast in a choice role in a play, or fell in love for the first time, or there may be some other event in your life that you could use to create the emotion of joy for your character.

For instance, your character is describing the sights and sounds of a wartime battle, and you have never been in wartime battle. But you have probably seen someone hurt from a fall or accident who cried in pain. And you've heard jackhammers working on street repair that sound like machine guns. Put the two together, and you might imagine a wartime battle.

193

The value or advantages of using sense memory, emotional memory or substitution are in having a technique to use to add depth of emotions when your own emotional resources fail to produce the proper emotion. This approach may be used to give the character a "sense of truth." But it might be best when strong emotions are needed to avoid using some situation of recent origin with the concern that it might be too personal.

Discussion: What are some frequently experienced situations in your life that might cause emotions such as joy, sorrow, frustration, anger, sympathy and suspicion? Discuss some situations in your life that might call forth the needed emotions in the exercise, "Showing Emotion Through Thoughts" in this chapter.

Exercise: Using Emotional Memory or Recall in Scenes

First of all, relax. You can close your eyes and *recall* emotional events from your past that are similar to those that might be needed for a scene or exercise called "Showing an Emotional Mood in a Mini-Scene" in the play.

Keep your mind on the events, and your memory of these events should let the emotions evolve and help to lead to the emotions needed in the scenes. This becomes a transfer of past emotional experiences to the present scene. (Perform several of the mini-scenes you have performed in the past and compare.)

If your emotional responses in the scene feel truthful and honest without using any of these techniques, you probably won't need to use them.

If your approach to "finding and feeling the emotion" by either affective or emotional memory, or by substitution, it is important to a truthful performance that your personalized emotions are also applicable to the character's emotions.

Be careful not to choose emotions out of your personal life that are bigger, smaller or different from the emotions that are normal for the character. Then, once you find the exact emotion, you may need to adjust the size and intensity to fit the scene being played.

Things to remember:

1. While these are the personal emotional memories from the past and may be a personal truth, you need to be sure they are the same as the character's emotions and the play's truth.

2. Since these emotions and memories are called up from your past, you need to make sure they still have a current "now-ness" or spontaneous emotional quality needed for the present situation of the character and the current script.

3. While these emotions may be rooted in your personal realistic truth, they also need to have stylized aspects to give your character a theatrical truth.

Exercise: A Director's Critique

This exercise involves suiting the action to the word and the word to the action with emotions. This can be presented as a rehearsed reading as the director demonstrates and critiques the actors. The Director enters from the audience area.

Director: Okay, okay, (with clipboard checking watch) that run-through lasted one hour and thirty-seven minutes. It's way too long for a one-act. Some parts were exciting and wonderful, but ... I must say, other parts were dreadful and boring. Now, let's see ... (Checks notes.)

1. First of all, Cindy. Patty Jo is a happy child. When you enter you need to skip in smiling and laughing. You looked as if you had just been attending a funeral the way you came moping in the door. Then, Jimmy, jump up and look surprised and react when Patty Jo tells you she's won a beauty contest.

2. Oh, and Tom played Augie as if he was being beaten. You were cringing and cowering every time you spoke. No, no, no, Augie is in charge. Augie is a proud man. He has status! Carry yourself with pride and dignity. Lead from the chin.

3. I liked the way Marvin registered greed as he counted out the golden coins ... one by one. That was deliciously evil.

4. But Doug, you need to be tense and angry. Very angry. So furious you can spit ... particularly after being bitten by Wanda's ferocious dog. But, the next time you throw the dog's dish at Wanda, try to miss her. A band- aid on her nose is not part of her character.

5. Oh, and Donald playing Dennis. No, no, no, Dennis is not dumb. Donald played Dennis as really dumb ... with dead eyes and mouth hanging open and he even talked dumb. Duhhh. Nobody's that dumb, Donald.

6. Harry, Harry! You need to sneak in and tiptoe up to Alice who is sleeping, admire her, and then whisper, "I'm leaving you." And when Alice wakes up surprised, just wave goodbye as you back out of the room.

7. Oh, and, Fred, when you hesitated with your lines, I thought that was good. Very good (thumbs up) ... till I realized, from that vacant expression on your face, you couldn't remember your lines. You forgot your lines! That was bad, Fred, bad. (thumbs down) Learn your lines!

8. But, I liked the way Boris looked at Frank ... suspicious and envious — like when you were looking for ways to get even. Then, when you clenched your teeth as you pulled out your knife ... Wow! — great stuff!

9. And Bobby! How many times do I need to tell you, "Do not eat the food?" You gobbled all the candy like a ravenous glutton. And, the poor prop crew is very angry.

10. Petunia ... I know it's an itsy bitsy part but you standing there in the middle of the stage stealing the scene by shaking nervously, scratching yourself, and chewing gum ruins the whole scene.

Okay we open tomorrow night. In the meantime, get some rest and don't break a leg!

Exercise: Repeat Phone Conversation

Repeat the telephone conversation exercise in Chapter 8. This time, apply specific character traits and emotions as you deliver the monolog.

Chapter 14
Images and Observations

"On your imaginary forces work ... .
Think, when we talk of horses, that you see them
Printing their proud hoofs i' the receiving earth;
For 'tis your thoughts that now must deck our kings,
Carry them here and there; jumping o'er times,
Turning the accomplishment of many years
Into an hour-glass: for the which supply,
Admit me Chorus to this history;
Who prologue-like your humble patience pray,
Gently to hear, kindly to judge, our play."
— Chorus from *Henry V*, by Shakespeare

"Imagination is more important that knowledge."
— Albert Einstein

"Hope exists only in the imagination. We cannot survive without hope,
therefore, we cannot survive without the imagination,"
— *Life in the Theatre*, by Julian Beck

"People look, but they do not see."
— Robert Hartman, artist

The actor's approach in Chapter 13 emphasized inside/out by using your own personal feelings and emotions to create a character. In this chapter, most of the approaches to creating a character use the process of working outside/in by observing people, places and things outside your self. In practice, actors need to work both ways as one approach usually enhances the other. (For further explanation of outside/in and inside/out see Chapter 12.)

Picturing Images

An *image* is a reproduction or imitation of a person, place or event. It can be an exact likeness, a visible representation, a mental picture of something not actually present or something introduced to represent something that it suggests.

In Chapter 6 there was a beginning to picturing images in "Suiting the Word to the Action." But that was only an introduction

197

by saying one word at a time. In this chapter the images are created to visualize a whole character, place or total scene.

An actor needs to have a clear and specific image of what is being said to make it believable to an audience. Remember, if you, the performer, don't have a strong, clear image or picture of what you're saying, then the audience won't have an image either, and therefore, won't believe it.

In other words, if you don't see it, the audience won't see it. But, if you do picture a clear image, it should translate to the audience and show in your body, particularly your face, voice and emotions.

Exercise: Picturing Images

Read each sentence, one after another, to project the people, places and events mentioned. Be specific in picturing the image for yourself so that the sentences are clear and specific to the audience. To be more detailed is to be more universal. Because if it's more real, it is therefore more believable and more widely acceptable.

"My brother (or sister, friend, mom, dad, uncle, aunt) and I went to a wonderful restaurant, and I had _____, my favorite food."

"You should see my house and the way I take care of my room. My pet sleeps there."

"I need to go to the shopping center and buy some new clothes at my favorite store. I particularly need something new for a place I'm going next week."

"When I went on my vacation last summer the weather was unbelievable. And you should have seen the place and some of the people I met."

"A good friend of mine has a birthday next week, and I already know what I'm taking to the party. I can just picture him/her opening the gift."

"I saw the strangest looking person in the cafeteria last Tuesday when I was eating lunch with my friends. I couldn't believe what s/he was eating and wearing."

Discussion: Did you see the person, place or things mentioned? How does the performer feel about the person mentioned? Describe the person, place, and/or things mentioned. For instance, what was the favorite food?

Picturing and Projecting Images

Choose one of the following selections from the four below. Carefully practice picturing in detail the images of the descriptive material. Take time to get this image. Be very specific. Don't think ahead. Then, while focusing on a strong, clear picture of what you're saying, read the following descriptive material. Remember: If you don't see it, the audience doesn't see it.

Exercise: Listening

The audience members need to listen carefully while the actor describes the images to see if they can picture the images. After the lines are delivered, members of the group can discuss what they heard or "saw." Or, a variation might include the audience listening carefully, and if the images are not coming through, members may quietly raise a hand to note this. At that point the reader can go back over a line or just go ahead. But, the audience needs to be supportive in listening and in no way distractive to the reader.

"From the Hill"

From the top of the hill above the town I can see the junkyard with piles of old cars almost two stories high — heaped in twisted wreckage — some still with colorful fenders, and hoods, and some old and ugly and rusted. A heavy, smelly dense smog hangs over the city. The distant mountains are barely visible. It's as if the picture of the town below has been smeared with a black wash. I can barely see the old graveyard with rows and rows of headstones jutting upward. A hearse just pulled up to an open grave pit. Several figures in black get out slowly and quietly remove the coffin from the car. After they carry the funeral bier to the graveside, pray and sing a hymn, they leave in the drizzling rain. Just at the bottom of the hill there is a river running rapidly. It's picked up mud from the banks and various assorted garbage from the smelter upstream. The sun is setting with brilliant red and orange skies. Twilight comes on and the lights come on all over town. I can no longer see the graveyard.

"Remembering Past Times"

I remember afternoons — weekend afternoons — in the early fall when it just started to get cool, and the trees were losing their leaves. We took a picnic lunch to pine-scented mountains. The light sifted through the sentinel-like pine trees and left spotted patterns on the pine needles on the ground. Squirrels skirted among the bushes gathering nuts. We hiked up hillsides, and in the thin mountain air we were exhausted. Way up high at the top of the pines the wind rustled the treetops. When we spoke there was silence or an echo, but nothing else. We returned to the cement picnic tables and ate quietly and listened to the stillness. Somewhere in the distance we could hear a stream running or an occasional bird chirping or a car pass along the road that was 50 feet above our campsite. We spread a blanket, turned on our transistor radio and read for about 10 minutes. It was very peaceful.

199

"Dreaming of Food"

I'm dreaming about food. I'm really hungry. First, I imagine going to my favorite Italian restaurant with recorded music from an Italian opera. I'm having a large pizza with thin crust, rich tomato sauce, slices of salami, mushrooms and green peppers all covered with gooey yellow cheese. Then, I picture a Chinese restaurant with a courteous waitress wearing a long dress with slits on the side. I'm having hot and sour soup, crispy spring rolls, beef with broccoli and brown rice and a fortune cookie for dessert. My dream shifted to a Mexican restaurant with large calendars and serapes on the walls, paper flowers in big vases and ceramic cats on the floor. And I'm eating chips with salsa and a chicken tostada, then crispy tacos with lettuce and tomato and beans. Ummm. Then, I woke up and had oatmeal, toast and orange juice. It just wasn't the same. Maybe I'll go back to sleep and finish eating.

"My Own Room"

If I could design my own personal room, with all of my favorite things, it would be a big room with a king-size bed covered with a giant rainbow colored bedspread. I'd have fluffy pillows and a backrest for reading in bed. My book would be lighted by a Tiffany lamp on a small table with a fresh glass of water. My cell phone is next to the water. And I'd have my CD music collection with all my favorites carefully organized. Music would play softly in the background. On the walls there'd be large poster size pictures of my favorite TV and movie heroes. A six-foot bookcase would fill another wall with all of my favorite books and magazines. Then, over in one corner, I'd have my desk with a new computer and an executive chair in front. I've always wanted a small refrigerator right in my room beside my desk for afternoon and bedtime snacks. I'd have chocolate ice cream and Coca-Cola. And, there'd be a big picture window that looked out onto a yard with large trees filled with little birds. On spring afternoons I would open the window for fresh air. And then, once I had the perfect room, I'd smile and yawn and take a nap.

Discussion: Did you see the images clearly throughout the reading? What parts were particularly clear? Were there places where the images were not totally clear?

Note: If these images are not immediately projected or clear to members of the audience, don't be discouraged. Just add more details to the mental images. Take your time to picture the images. Stay focused on the images, say the lines again, and note how your voice and expression change when the images are clear.

Exercise: Images from a Poem, Novel, Short Story or Play
Choose a three to five minute selection from poetry or literature. Perform and discuss.

Exercise: Images from a Newspaper Article
Newspaper stories often have many descriptive images that include who, where, when, what and why and, therefore, lend themselves to this exercise. For example, you might read a story about an accident or other event. Choose an article from the newspaper, rehearse, perform and discuss.

Exercise: Images from Observations
of Familiar Sights and Sounds.
Write a short two or three minute observation that involves familiar sights, sounds and touches. These might be places or seasonal changes or sights and sounds of your neighborhood, school, shopping center, grocery store, restaurant, or your kitchen. Or it could be a physical condition such as time of day, weather or scenery. This observation of life can be a valuable tool in creating an offstage environment or background for your character. It is also a valuable skill to be developed for writing short stories.

Exercise: Images Using Persons
Choose or write lines that involve images of a person. This might be a character description, "my most unforgettable character" or description you'd find in a zodiac sign. Perform and discuss the images.

Using Costumes, Props and Makeup

"Clothes oft proclaim the man." (... and woman)
— Part of Polonius' advice to Laertes in *Hamlet*

In acting, as in life, the way you look changes the way you feel. Wearing different kinds of clothes, using different props, and changing appearance through makeup can all change the way you feel about yourself, and/or your feeling about your character. While costumes, props and makeup should compliment and enhance your character, they should also be clothes and personal items that would belong to your character. This is because to your character, they *are* clothes and *are* personal belongings and a natural appearance and not just a costume.

201

Costumes

Exterior additions of costume items might include: all kinds of headgear, hats, hairstyles, wigs, hairnets, curlers, scarves, gloves, athletic caps, coats or helmets. They might include glasses, sunglasses (different styles), jewelry, canes, vests and ties, special looking shoes, etc. Or just the right shirt or pants, shorts, shoes, sandals, can be a good approach in finding the ideal essence and truth about the character.

Exercise: Creating a Costume Piece from a Square Cloth
A simple piece of muslin or broadcloth thirty to thirty-six inch square can be folded in different ways or made into all types of shapes that can become a good costume accessory to enhance character. For example, this cloth could become an apron, scarf, cape, shawl, skirt, belt, kerchief for head or sling for a "broken arm."

Props

Props might include: a fuzzy animal, cane or umbrella, beverage, musical instrument, an office supply item, (pencil, pad, clipboard) jewelry, glasses, clock or watch, kitchen utensil, suitcase, telephone, money, book, briefcase, magazine or newspaper, cleaning utensil, toothbrush, flashlight, flower (plastic), medicine or pills, candy or sucker, cup or glass, fruit or vegetable or athletic equipment.

Exercise: Using Props with Character
Pick a prop and choose an existing scene such as "Basic Stage Movement" or any other scene — including an improvised scene — and use the prop to enhance or make it an integral part of the character. It may be used either as stage business or a subtext.

Exercise: Using Props and Costumes to Create
an Image of Your Personal Character
From some source such as a collection of costumes in the drama wardrobe, or from your own closet, freely try on a variety of clothes to create a character. Simultaneously, explore props from the "prop storage" or from your own personal sources at home or elsewhere. Choose items that "feel comfortable" and seem appropriate and consistent with your clothes to express what you feel about your character and the image you would like to project.

Move around, gesture, walk around, and take on a character that expresses and makes you feel comfortable in those clothes with those props. Look in the mirror to see how you might look to other people. Continue adding and changing items until you have created your character.

Makeup

If makeup is available and needed, then some addition might be done with nose putty, mustache, black tooth enamel or some other item. The costume, prop and makeup additions should not look as if they are "tacked on" to the character, but instead they need to be believable as a part of the creation of your character.

Improvisational Exercise: Showing Character
Through Costume, Props and Makeup

Approach your character by working outside/in and experiment with costumes, props and makeup until you get a "visual effect of your character" or an appearance that looks right or feels right. This should lead to body movement, gestures, and vocal expressions that suggest a particular type of character traits that will eventually be internalized.

Once you have created your character, give a short description of your character with that appearance. You might even give your new character a name that fits the description.

Then, form small groups of five to eight people in an improvisational situation at some everyday event. This could be a party, a shopping trip to a department store, grocery store or lunch in the cafeteria where you mingle with each other to explore and further develop your new character. (See Chapter 9 for more ideas.) Perform and discuss.

Observing Animals and People

"Genius is an actor who sees life, and is able to recreate it on the stage."
— Constantin Stanislavski

Creating a Character with Animal Characteristics

People are sometimes described as being like certain animals or having traits of animals. This ties into a literary reference. Examples of animal traits that apply to people might be: bird-like (fluttery), moves like a cat, chicken (scared), wise as an owl, horsey-looking (big with long face), walks like a duck, slimy as a snake or snake in the grass, a rat who rats on someone, mousy (meek and timid), fat as a pig, angry as a bull, stubborn as a bulldog, crows like a rooster, etc. What descriptive words would apply to a grasshopper, an ant, a turtle or a rabbit? What are some other animal comparisons?

Exercise: Observation of an Animal

Choose an animal to observe. Each performer should choose to represent in sound and motion some animal, bird, fish, reptile or some living being other than a human. The observation may be chosen on the basis of his or her own personality, physical makeup or interest. This animal may be at or around your home, such as a cat, dog, parakeet, hamster, rabbit or lizard. Or, it may be in the neighborhood or zoo. Carefully observe the animal and all its features, expressions, body postures, movement, rhythm of movement and sounds. Watch and note as much detail as possible. Listen carefully to the sound the animal makes. Imitate the animal until you have captured the basic sound and motion.

Exercise: Showing Your Observation and Images of an Animal

Five or seven performers go on stage at one time. Working from the observed images, show us your animal in terms of sound and motion, body and voice. Explore the environment, interact with the "other animals" and react to each naturally in character.

Exercise: Using an Animal as the Basis of a Character Trait

Choose a character. Incorporate the sound and motion of the animal into your character. If your character were an animal, what animal would it be? Using animal characteristics, translate that image of the animal to a person with those characteristics. Choose a scene and act the scene with animal characteristics. Don't act the image literally. That is, when using this technique to play a character, you need to suggest the essence of the animal, and not be the animal.

Discussion: What similarities did this animal have to the original character? Why did you choose the animal you chose? How did you approach the problem of body and voice in presenting your animal? What would you change or expand if you did this exercise again?

Developing Your Character Through Observation

While you can observe and use an animal as the basis for your character, you will probably find it more rewarding to observe people. Many actors develop characters by observing and studying people and collecting a whole portfolio of notes and useful information about people's physical, vocal and character traits. Then, from the memory of visual and auditory images, they can imitate or recreate the physical and vocal aspects and character traits of the person observed.

Imitating, Impersonating and Mimicking

To *imitate* is to copy, to follow as a pattern, to reproduce, to appear like. An imitation is the assumption of the modes of behavior observed in other individuals.

To *impersonate* is to assume or act the character of someone widely known or famous.

To *mimic* is to ridicule or make fun of someone by imitation. Often this focuses on some aspect of their character that is different from what you see to be the norm. It is important to be considerate of other people's differences.

People imitate or impersonate other people all the time. If you have ever imitated someone, you probably did it by starting with a visual image of the way the person looked and an auditory recall of the way the person sounded.

When you tell a story and "act out" what someone did or said with voice and gestures that are like the person, you are probably doing so from a remembered image (the visual and vocal recall) of the way that person moved and sounded. That's what performers do when they imitate, impersonate or mimic people on TV shows and in life.

Observing people and imitating or impersonating these people is a valid approach to creating a character. It can be dramatically interesting for an actor to "borrow mannerisms to create a character," and can be a very creative approach.

Some people who make fun of others frequently do so because those people are different in some way. And, they do not feel as safe or comfortable with people who are different. They only feel comfortable when they are around people like themselves.

But, to mimic someone in order to ridicule or make fun of them can be cruel and hurtful. It may belittle them as a human being. In addition, it often diminishes the person doing the mimicking. The goal in acting is not to ridicule someone simply because they are different in some way.

On the other hand, being aware of, accepting of and understanding of other people's differences can be interesting and can enhance you as a human being by making you a more compassionate person, and more accepting of yourself. The goal of using this approach in acting is to create and portray a character honestly through observation, in order to help you and the audience better understand other people and the diversity in our society.

205

General Exercise: Observing People

Observe people in public places such as on a campus, in the cafeteria, at a restaurant, at work, in a shopping mall, on a bus, at a party, etc. They can be friends or family members or strangers, people whom you do or do not know, someone like yourself or totally different. Choose people on the basis that you would like to find out "how it feels to be like that person and to better understand them."

Focus your attention on their *physical aspects* such as their facial expressions, posture, body movement and the way they walk, their gestures, and most particularly the use of their hands. Hands may show special traits. And, if you can hear their voices, listen carefully to the *vocal aspects* such as quality, pitch, tone, diction, accents, speech rhythms and patterns.

Note the way people move at different ages (childhood, teenage, middle age, elderly), their physical makeup (thin, fat, tall, short, etc.) character traits (happy, worried, tense, etc.) types of clothes, and any special items that you might duplicate as props.

Record your observations in a notebook or use the "Observation Form" on page 207 so they are not forgotten. What conclusions can you draw about these people from your observations?

Exercise: Using Observations of One Person
to Develop Images and Create a Character

Choose, for observation, one person with whom you are in contact. You may or may not know the person. Observe and record all that is relevant about this person in terms of body and voice, character traits and emotions. Then, using the "Observation Form" on page 207, write a description of someone, and note all the details. Note: If you "borrow mannerisms and characteristics" for a character, it is generally safer and more tactful if the model for these characteristics is not known personally by members of your audience or your performing group.

Once you have observed a character and formed a composite image, practice moving and speaking and acting like this person to discover how it feels. The more times you practice and repeat and refine the image, the more it is internalized, and becomes a part of you. And, you should also become more relaxed and honest in the presentation of the character.

Choose a scene such as "Basic Stage Movement" in Chapter 3, "Suiting the Action to the Word" in Chapter 6 or "Using Character Traits and Emotions to Define Character Attitudes," or "Emotional Moods in A Mini-Scene," both from Chapter 13. Then, while you focus on the remembered physical and/or auditory images, or picture the person, play that character in some scene.

Observation Form
(Record this information to see the character in total.)

Gender:_____ Probable age:_____ Appr. ht. and wt.:_____

Possible race, nationality or ethnicity
(only if valuable to understanding):_____

General description of person:_____

_____

Describe clothes (what does this say about the person?):_____

_____

Physical appearance (posture, movement, walk, gesture, facial expression, etc.):

_____

_____

If this person were an animal, what kind of animal would s/he be?
(Don't be cruel.):_____

What appears to be the cultural or economic background?

_____

In what occupation do you see this person?_____

What is the possible wealth of this person?_____

Description of voice if heard (quality, accent, rhythms, traits, etc.):

_____

Possible origins of person on basis of accent:_____

Describe basic character traits or personality (as best you can from your
observation):_____

_____

If seen with someone else, what is that relationship?_____

Is there any clue to what this person wants in life?_____

Give this person a name on basis of observation:_____

Other special notes on character:_____

Write a background of this character on the basis of your observation:_____

_____

Observing and Performing Different Ages

Exercise: Through the Ages Improv and Monologs

Choose one or more ages to observe. This is like research or an advance assignment. These may be observing family or friends or society at large. Note body movement and voice and subject matter of the conversation of the age observed. Get a clear image and practice moving and speaking like the age group you observed. Then, in small groups of similar ages plan the subject matter of a scene and the setting. Choose topics that would be of concern to that age. This may be from one of the suggestions below or one of your own. With an outline, go on stage and freely improvise dialog and movement, with your own character traits, in an effort to capture the essence of the age. Each scene can be performed for three or four minutes. Let it play its own rhythm and cycle.

Improv

Age 4-6: Preschool playground: sand pile, swings, jungle gym using ladder, teeter-totter.

Age 6-11: Childhood elementary school, birthday party with food and opening gifts, looking forward to summer vacation with parents.

Age 12-16: Teenage middle school and high school, cafeteria or summer camp, field trip or club meetings with same age friends, planning dance, newspaper staff meeting.

Age 17-21: College deciding on a major or planning for a career, going steady, breaking up, seeking friends, auditioning for a play or club meeting, or registration for classes or studying in library.

Age 22-34: Young working people in office or elevator, meeting other young people, dating, several getting married, planning office party, or work activities, or learning skills, or applying for job.

Age 35-47: Young married people with children, home and family, home maintenance, house furnishings, children issues: soccer, illness, behavior, money problems, need to buy things: new car, clothes, electronic gadgets.

Age 48-60: Middle-age parents to parents and parents to children, backyard picnic, vacation plans, retirement plans, investment, and home improvement plans.

Age 65 and Older: Elderly health problems, money problems, front porch, senior center, convalescent center, elder hostel, bingo game, learning computers, learning foreign language, remembering bygone days, family pictures.

Monologs

Observe as many ages as possible in advance of performing these monologs. Then, choose any two to four and perform them in character. An additional possibility is to add the quality of an animal.

4-6: Preschool (Discovered in sand pile making roads and playing with cars.)

Brrrruuudddinna. Put, put, put. Chug, chug, chug. Brrrruuudddinna. Honk! Honk! Crash! You need to drive more careful! And put on your seat belt! Hear me? (Stops and looks around.) I don't like to play cars alone. Daddy said I might get a bicycle for Christmas. And Santa Claus is gonna bring it ... if I'm good. Mommy and I wrote him a letter. My Mommy's goin' to the hospital to get a baby. Daddy told me. The new baby is gonna sleep in my room with me ... so I can watch it. (Pause) That'll be fun cause I don't like to play alone. I think everybody's at school with the big kids. I'm going next year. After summer is over. I can hardly wait. (Slight pause or wood blocks clap to show passage of time.)

6-11: Childhood (Holding a soccer ball)

I love soccer. I get to play goalie and that isn't easy. But when I get a save, the whole team congratulates me. All my friends are on the team. And my parents haven't missed a game. We do a lot of things together when my dad can get off work. That's a lot of fun except sometimes my little brother/sister can be a pest. We're going on a camping trip this summer and maybe to Disneyland. I can hardly wait till summer. And my parents said I could bring a friend. I think I'll choose Chris. S/He's my best friend right now. We're in the same homeroom. And, when we're older we're going to the same middle school together, cause we live in the same neighborhood. That sounds like fun. I can hardly wait. (Slight pause or wood blocks.)

12-16: Teenage (Getting out cell phone)

I know it's crazy, but a couple of years ago somebody was baby-sitting me and now I'm the babysitter. (Dialing the cell phone.) I mean, like everything goes so fast anymore. Sometimes I want to be older and sometimes I think it was a lot easier when I was in elementary school. Sometimes life is so hard. I just don't know anymore. It's just a matter of getting through it. (Someone answers on other end.) Hi. It's me. (Beat) I'm baby-sitting. He just went to bed. What are you doing? (Beat) You mean you're with somebody? Who? (Beat) Okay, don't tell me. I just called to see what you thought of the new kid in class. (Beat) Uh-huh. S/He looks okay to me, too. But not exactly like one of us, maybe, but ... Oh! That's who you're with. Listen, I think I just heard the kid cry or something. Gotta go. (Hangs up.) Wait'll the gang hears about this! (Slight pause or wood blocks.)

17-21: College Years (With pencil or pen and a clipboard or catalogue in hands.)

Now let's see … if I major in Humanities, then I'll have to take a science and a foreign language. But I'm not good at either one. Scheduling is really difficult with all these course requirements. It's hard to make decisions in such a short time that affect my whole life. I feel like everybody's rushing me. I hate all this stress. And, it didn't help any to break up a romance with somebody I'd been going with for six months. But, I just wanted to be friends. I mean I'm not ready to make a long-term commitment about anything right now. I don't want anything that's permanent. I mean, what if I'm wrong, and there's nobody else out there? Or, maybe there's a better choice of occupations or careers? I hate to make all these big decisions in such a short amount of time. It all happens so fast. I wish I was already twenty-one or twenty-two and out of college. Then things would be a lot easier. (Slight pause or wood blocks.)

22-32: Young Working Person

Here I am — right in the middle of my twenties. I have a job. The job isn't so bad. It's not the beginning of a career, and I don't make much money. (Checking appointment calendar.) But I meet all kinds of wonderful new people from all kinds of different places. We sometimes meet for lunch. Like today I'm meeting someone at the deli at twelve thirty. Then there's the group that meets after work. I don't know where any of these relationships are going but some of them are a lot of fun while they last. Some of the group are even engaged and planning to get married, settle down and have a family. Not me. Not yet. But sometime. I just broke up with someone after six months. It's hard to meet the perfect person. But I'm looking. Still this is an exciting time. I'm always on the go. (Checking watch) Ohhh, I'm late for a date. Gotta go. (Slight pause or wood blocks.)

33-45: Young Married with Children (With some type of home repair equipment such as paintbrush or hammer.)

Hard to believe how fast time passes. Both of us are working to make ends meet. We just bought this old house. And we're fixing it up. That takes a lot of time and it's expensive. Oh, it's nice enough, but I'm not sure it's big enough for all the things we've got going. One of the kids is into soccer games. That means a lot of weekends and a lot of driving. But I guess it's worth it. One of the kids will be going to college in a couple of years. And with the price of colleges, I don't see how we can afford it. There always seems to be money problems these days. Or sick kids, or we need to buy something ... clothes and books for school and things. And my parents are getting older. And they've got their problems, too. I don't know. Sometimes everything seems so hectic I can hardly wait till the kids are gone, and there's just the two of us again. No. I'd miss those kids. I know I would. (Slight pause or wood blocks.)

45-60: Middle Age

I never thought I'd be both parents to my children and parents to my parents at the same time. But here I am. My parents are having all kinds of health problems. And we just got the last of the kids out of college. One has a job and one is married and they're expecting their first child. That's exciting. But they moved a long way from here so we don't get to see them as often as we'd like. And the third kid, the baby in the family, doesn't know what he wants to do. He's thinking of going back to college. But that's more expense ... unless he moves back home. And he's talking about it. We wanted to do some traveling before we got too old. And we need to makes some repairs to the house. But we don't need a house this large anymore, now that the kids are gone. So, we're thinking of selling it. But then, if the kids come to visit, we need the room. I don't know. I remember when I was first dating seriously. Those were the days. I was in my twenties. And life didn't seem nearly so complicated. (Slight pause or wood blocks.)

60+: Elderly

(Moans) Ooooohhh. Growing old isn't for sissies. I don't feel good anymore like I used to. Seems like I spend all my time these days going to visit doctors. And they give me all these different tests and all these different pills. Seems like I have a pill for every ailment known to mankind. And, they all upset my stomach. And my back aches and I don't sleep well. I guess I should have taken better care of my health when I was younger. My friend Chris doesn't have any of these problems. S/He's still playing golf and tennis and going to meetings and things. Maybe I need more things to do. But I don't feel like it. Or maybe if the kids would come visit and stay longer that would be nice. I remember all those wonderful holidays with all the kids running around the house. We never had much money, but those were the happy days. I've got pictures here someplace of those days when everything was fun. Oh, dear. Time goes so fast, but some days seem soooo long. (Moans) Ohhh, I don't know what to do next. I hate growing old. Maybe it's time to take a little nap. That sounds good. (Lies down. The wood blocks click.)

Chapter 15
What Does Your Character Want?

Motivations, Intentions, Objectives and Subtext

This section has multiple titles because different teachers use different theories and different words to explain the underlying purpose of a character relationship (what your character wants in a scene). And while these words are not exactly the same, putting them together can be a clarifying guideline.

In acting, as in life, if you know what a person wants, and analyze a person's *motivations, objectives, intentions or subtext*, you will be better able to understand why that person exhibits particular character traits, emotions and attitudes or acts in a certain way. It can explain to a large extent the personality and behavior of a person. Usually the dialog indicates what the character wants, but you as a performer playing the scene also need to be aware of any subtext or underlying meaning that is not readily evident in the dialog.

Motivation is something that causes a person to act in some particular way, a reason to express a need, desire or wish.

Intention is a determination to act in a certain way, a purpose, aim, objective or goal. Intention is what you are doing, on the stage at any given moment, regardless of what you are saying.

Objective is something toward which an effort is directed, that is, a goal, aim or intention, inner action or subtext. There are primary objectives and secondary objectives. Each scene may have its own objective.

Obstacle is something that stands in the way of, opposes or is an obstruction to the objective.

By noting a pattern of objectives or intentions and the basic obstacles in terms of achieving these objectives, you can chart a *through-line of action*, or *spine* for your character that forms an *arc*, or composite picture of your character's actions that build scene by scene throughout the script and culminates in the character's *super-objective*, (the ultimate purpose behind the character's scene-by-scene actions).

The *subtext* is the underlying meaning of the text that is written by the playwright. The words being said in the text may not be the same as the real intention of the character. An example might be a person who is manipulating another person or lying. The subtext may be conveyed through inner thoughts or innuendo that is sometimes called *inner action*. This manifests itself through looks, glances, takes, stage business or just listening and reacting.

Analyzing Motivations, Objectives and Intentions

Motivations and objectives can offer insights to your character and self-awareness for you in playing the role. What are your character's primary and secondary objectives, in each scene? What are the super-objectives? In other words, what motivates your character? What are the major obstacles in achieving these goals?

What does your character want? Why? The questions are: Does your character want love, romance, money, power, control, revenge, respect, a job, a career, an education, a friend, a faith? Or, is it to win something: a man, a woman, a war, a wager or a contest? Does your character want fame? Why? Public approval? Or, is it to achieve something: a deadline, peace or escape. Or, is it to pay allegiance to something: country, organization, club, gang, etc. Or, does your character want fortune? Why? Is it for money to buy possessions? A house? A car? Or, is it to feel happier, healthier and live a more secure life? And what is the motivation for each of these? And what are the obstacles? And what is the risk? What is at stake if your character doesn't get what you want, and fulfill the objective? What is lost?

Your character's motivation, objective or intention may be inherent and obvious in the dialog, in which case you don't need to do anything special. On the other hand, your character's dialog may be one thing, while the true motivation, objective, inner intention or subtext in the scene is about something different. The true motivation, objective or intention can change the way lines are delivered. For example: your character may be complimenting another about something, but what your character really wants is to borrow some money, sell something or establish a romance. Or, if your character is jealous of someone else's good fortune, and has the line, "I'm very happy for your success and good fortune," you could be thinking, "I hate you, because I want what you have."

Or, a villain, whose intention is to harm someone, may need to appear smiling and trustworthy in order to gain the confidence of the victim. For example, Iago in *Othello* is trusted. But this doesn't mean that "evil triumphs over good" just because a charming villain is temporarily succeeding in doing some evil deed.

Or, you may have the line, "I've always envied people who can act." Is this real admiration or envy, which might mean, "I wish I

213

could be as good as you," or is it sarcasm, meaning, "But you aren't one of them"? Or, "I've written a new play, and you'd be wonderful in it." Is the real intention here to be flattering, or to find someone to read the play and admire it, or in hopes that if it gets produced this person will act in it? In other words, what is the real intention?

After defining a character's overall motivations, intentions or objectives and the subtext for each scene, you can further define the subtle changes in your lines of dialog during a scene by writing reminders of your character's particular intentions for each scene in the script.

Since you relate differently to different people for different reasons you may have different objectives with different people. Therefore, your character in any particular scene may also have slightly different motivations, objectives, intentions or subtext with different characters in different scenes.

Actors' and Playwrights' Objectives

An actor's objectives for a character may be slightly different from a playwright's objectives. For the playwright, a single scene is only one of many scenes that are used to organize a play's structure and the major themes in a logical sequence to build dramatic action. The playwright's objectives are illustrated by the action taken by the characters. The super-objective for the playwright is the major theme or the idea underlying the whole play. In other words: what is the play about?

While the actors' or characters' objectives in each scene are smaller and more personal they should relate in some way to the playwright's themes and super-objective. And, in analyzing your character's motivations, objectives, intentions and subtext, you need to be aware of the playwright's thematic goals and objectives and your relation to them in each scene. You need to find a motivation, super-objective, intention or subtext that both creates a purpose for you and serves the intentions of the playwright's objectives.

To take a simple example, in *Goldilocks and the Three Bears*, Goldilocks' objective is to satisfy her curiosity, then her hunger, then her fatigue. Then, when she is awakened, she is in fear and runs out. The actor's objective is to show her innocence and different emotions, and how, if a young person is not careful, she can, step-by-step, get into a dangerous situation. The playwright's super-objective, or theme, is to warn very young people to stay out of other people's houses when they are not at home, because it could be dangerous.

Discussion: Analyze the motivations, and objectives of the major characters in *Little Red Riding Hood, Cinderella, The Three Little Pigs* or *Hansel and Gretel.* What does the wolf want or represent in *Little Red Riding Hood* and *The Three Little Pigs?* What are the obstacles? What are the themes? What is the optimum age level for each story?

Objectives and Obstacles in "Boy Meets Girl"

Primary objective: Boy tries to win girl's affections because he likes her. "Boy and girl fall in love." *New objective:* He wants to marry her. *Obstacle:* The girl's parents object because he doesn't have a good, steady job. So, he drops out of school and seeks a well-paying job. *Secondary objective:* He pursues a job. *Secondary obstacle:* He can't find a good job because he doesn't have many skills or a very significant past employment record. And he can't get the skills unless he gets an education. Crisis! He tries to convince her to get married anyway. They have a fight and break up. Boy loses girl. Now he has no romance, no schooling and no job. Now what? Perhaps they decide to wait until he gets some type of training. He goes back to school, gets an education, a good job and gets married. Boy gets girl. Or, he may find someone else in college. Or, they drift apart for a while...or permanently. So, was his super-objective to get married, specifically to marry this girl or to grow up? The way the playwright ends this story is the underlying idea or theme or the playwright's super-objective in telling the story.

Exercise
Form small groups and outline what happens in any one scene from the plot above. Then, name the characters and improvise the dialog for the scene.

Exercise
Read aloud the "soda fountain scene" between George and Emily in *Our Town,* by Thornton Wilder. Discuss Emily's objectives, George's objectives and the subtext. What does each character want? Did this change during the scene? What is the scene about? What are the playwright's objectives?

Exercise: Determining Objectives
Choose a play from one of the plays listed at the end of the Chapter 17. Or select a play of your own choice. Analyze each scene to determine a character's motivations, objectives or intentions in that scene. Start with the lines of dialog, and the situation in the scene to determine what each character wants, either directly or

indirectly. Then, perform the scene using character traits, emotions and images to make clear the underlying intention or objective of each character.

Discussion: Were you able to determine the true intention and objective of each actor in the scene? Were there changes of intentions during a scene?

Exercise: Choosing Objectives and Intentions

Choose three to four lines from Part I for a variety of interpretations based on an underlying emotion listed in Part II. Then, choose three or four lines from Part I and direct each individual line to a different character relationship in Part III.

For example: Assuming you choose from Part I, "I wouldn't do that if I were you," as your first line of the three or four lines. Then you deliver this line with three to four different emotions chosen from Part II to show how various interpretations can be achieved by changing the underlying emotion. Do the other lines in the same way. Illustration B: Assuming you choose "I think we have a failure to communicate" to deliver to one of the types of people in Part III.

Part I: Lines for Interpretation. Choose one, two or more lines from below:

1. "What time is it now?"
2. "Is this the place we we're going to eat?"
3. "Is that person over there who I think it is?"
4. "I wouldn't do that if I were you."
5. "I've written a new play. You'd be wonderful in it."
6. "I've always envied people who can act."
7. "Oh. You're absolutely unbelievable."
8. "You are looking really nice today."
9. "I didn't know I wasn't supposed to be here."
10. "I don't think you understand the whole problem."
11. "I don't think I know you well enough to do that."
12. "I think we have a failure to communicate."

Part II: Emotions to Use to Change Intentions

1. Admiration
2. Love
3. Disgust or sarcasm
4. Laughter
5. Crying
6. Anger
7. Boredom, possibly a yawn

8. Resignation
9. Threat, revenge or getting even
10. Fear
11. Embarrassment
12. Envy
13. Suspicion
14. Annoyance
15. Sadness
16. Disbelief or surprise

Part III: Changing the Object of the Intention
1. Young child
2. Sibling or friend
3. Parent or teacher
4. Grandparent
5. Boss
6. Coach or someone who is sharing a sports victory
7. Principal or teacher
8. Favorite actor or musician
9. Choice of your own

Discussion: Did the use of different emotions change the intention of the meaning? Did changing the object of the line change the intention?

Exercise: Changing the Objective by
Changing the Person to Whom the Line is Directed

Once again choose three to four lines from Part I and deliver the lines, one at a time to four different people chosen from Part III. You may use the same lines from Part I or different lines. Say the lines in a way that would indicate the person to whom you are talking. Picture this person clearly so that the audience can also see the image. (See Chapter 14.)

Discussion: Were you able to note changes of intention and subtext with change of emotions? Which lines and emotions seemed to be most effective? Could you determine from the delivery the person to whom the speaker was talking, and what their relationship was? Did the listener react in character?

Contrasting Objectives

Two or more characters each want something different. The situation is established and announced. Then each performer is assigned a role and given or chooses a different objective in the situation. One person's objective becomes another person's obstacle, which creates a conflict. One way to contrast objectives is by a difference in status. For example: parent-teenager, teacher-student, salesperson-customer, coach-athlete, older-younger siblings, employer-employee, and doctor-patient.

Situation: Teenager wants to borrow the car to go to the movie.

Parent or Older Sibling's Objective: Doesn't want to loan car and makes excuses. Thinks it isn't safe.

Son/Daughter or Younger Sibling's Objective: You want to impress your friends.

Situation: Three people are at a video store trying to choose a movie for the evening. Three other friends are joining them later to see the movie. All three friends have different objectives.

Friend One: You like war and adventure movies and so does your friend.

Friend Two: You like comedies and romantic and sentimental movies.

Friend Three: You like Sci-Fi and "slasher" movies because your friend does.

Each tries to convince the other person that theirs is the best choice for the evening.

Situation: Backstage where there is a speech contest. The facilitator has just introduced the speaker for the evening then turns for the person to enter, and sees the person cowering in the wings with stage fright.

Facilitator Objective: You need to convince the person s/he's ready to speak on the chosen subject or there's no program.

Speaker of the Evening: You are petrified and want to back out because you suddenly realize that there are a lot of strangers in the audience who want to "judge you," and you can't even remember your first line.

Situation: Boy and Girl have been going together for some time, but he is now going to a summer job in another city for three months.

Girl's Objective: You expect him to say they'll both be free to date while he's gone. You want him to say it's okay. (You may have someone else in mind.)

Boy's Objective: You don't want to lose her and you want her to promise not to date anyone else while you're gone.

Situation: Three people, student roommates are living together near campus. Student One has just heard that a parent, who pays 50 percent on the apartment, is going to arrive to check out living conditions. The apartment is a mess.

Student One's Objective: You need to get the apartment clean by the time your parent arrives to make a good impression and are fearful you might have to drop out if it's not acceptable. But you're allergic to dust.

Student Two's Objective: You are a smart, ambitious student who needs to finish an important research paper as soon as possible, and you don't have time.

Student Three's Objective: You are a lazy student, who causes most of the mess. You don't want to be bothered. You plan to go to a movie.

Situation: The semester final is a two-character scene, and partners have been matched up by the drama teacher. One student has made an appointment to talk to the teacher about the assignment.

Drama Student's Objective: You want to explain to the drama teacher that you don't like the other person and think that person is not a good actor and you would like someone else.

Drama Teacher Objective: You need to explain to the student that in drama … as in life, it's important that you work with and get along with all kinds of people.

Situation: Three actors (either male or female) are all waiting to try out for a senior class play. The play is *Our Town*. They all want to be cast in the lead roles (boys for George and girls for Emily.) Each tries to talk the other person out of auditioning.

Actor One's Objective: You try to convince the others you have the experience, because you have been cast in leads all through high school. And since you're a senior, you think you should also get this role because it's your last chance.

Actor Two's Objective: You are an underclassman, but you think you're right for the role, and you love acting and are planning a career in theatre and need the experience.

Actor Three Objective: You think you should have your turn to be cast in a lead role and have an opportunity to act because you've been working in stagecraft for three years and you're tired of it. (Your talent is in question.)

Situation: Three characters. A thrift store with used clothing, furniture and other items. Two friends are looking for a gift for a friend. A salesman is trying to promote items.

Two Friends' Objectives: You want to buy something cheap in good condition. You are picky and can't agree. Price is negotiable. Want to buy it with a credit card.

Salesperson's Objective: You need to sell something to keep your job. So you do everything possible to make the sale. Doesn't accept credit cards.

Situation: Three or four characters. (One is a temperamental dog.) Two or three people (family members, roommates, friends, etc.), are arguing over keeping a stray dog that is loveable, but dirty. The dog is possibly on a leash.

First Person's Objective: You brought the dog home and want to keep the dog for protection and companionship. You don't have a good record of taking care of anything.

Second Person's Objective: You want to get rid of the dog because it is dirty, unfriendly, expensive, etc. And you don't want to do all the work.

Third Person's Objective: You try to convince them it's a bad idea because it would be expensive and take a lot of work, and someone will have to feed it, bathe it, etc. You know because you work for a veterinarian.

The Dog: You want to stay because you like the first person.

Situation: Five people. One is the principal who needs to save money for the school and has called a meeting to discuss this with heads of different departments, and maybe even staff. The four people are: The Principal, The chair of the athletic department, the Fine Arts chairperson, and chair of the English department, Head of Custodian Services.

Principal's Objective: To save money for the school. The meeting is called to gain information about all programs and their needs: teacher materials, size of departments, class sizes, etc.

Department Chairs and Head Custodian's Objectives: Each person argues for his or her area and tries to make a strong case for more money and support for their particular areas.

Situation: A Boy and Girl are discussing the problems they've had in the past and how they might get together again.

Girl's Objective: Your boyfriend was very hurtful to you when you went to a recent party, and you don't want to go with him anymore.

Boy's Objective: You are aware that you did a couple of things that were insulting and cruel, and you're sorry and want to make up with the girl.

Situation: Two people looking for "pills for better health" (exercise and/or vitamin pills, aromatherapy, etc). The first person thinks she has found a new remedy for feeling better.

Character A's Objective: You want to get Character B to test the pill before you try it. You tell her it's really a "truth" pill that makes people tell the truth.

Character B's Objective: You want to be able to tell the "truth" to Character A about A's personality under the pretense that you are under the influence of the "truth" pill. You take the pill and fake getting dizzy and weave around talking nonsense. The Character A starts to quiz you over some relationship or romance, and the Character B tells the "truth," much to the distress of Character A, who leaves very distraught. Then, we realize Character B was faking it.

Situation: Boy and Girl have been dating for some time. Boy says he needs to talk to her about something important.

Girl's Objective: You think he's going to ask you to go steady. He's your first serious boyfriend and you've told your friends.

Boy's Objective: You want to break up with the girl because you have met several other girls. You don't want to hurt her feelings so you say, "It isn't you, it's me."

Situation: Two or three people are assigned to write a commercial about a new product that shows people can have a better, happier life that involves them spending money (investing, banking, buying), buying a product (food, clothes, cars), a lifestyle (exercise machines, clothes, food, etc.), health (drugs for ailments), leisure time (vacation cruise), etc. They do their own imaginary product rather than a specific product that everyone knows. First of all they have to agree on a product and give it a name. They can't agree on anything. (See "Contrasting Attitudes.")

First Person: You want to do a satire on an existing commercial.

Second Person: You want to do an original, sincere approach to a new product.

Third Person: You've already done one and you want them to accept yours.

Exercise: Showing Objectives and Intentions
Choose an objective or intention and, without telling anyone what it is, perform the following lines. Then, discuss what those objectives or intentions were.

A: What are you doing?

B: Isn't it obvious?

A: I don't think you should do that.

B: Why not?

A: What does it mean?

B: Isn't it obvious?

A: No. (Pause) Yes. But why?

B: It's because of you.

A: I'm sorry. It's my fault. (Pause)

B: Will you help?

A: If you need me.

B: I do. I can't do this alone.

A: Are you sure you want to do this?

B: Yes. Are you?

A: Won't we be sorry?

B: I try not to think about it.

A: Will this take long?

B: Not if we get started fairly soon.

A: Okay, then, let's get started.

Exercise

Choose a scene or improvisation from earlier in this book. Perform the scene without telling your intention. Then discuss what the intention was.

Chapter 16
Types, Analysis and Representation

"Character is fate."
— Anon.

"Know then thyself, presume not God to scan;
The proper study of mankind is man."
(... and womankind is woman or humankind is human.)
— Alexander Pope

"Love the art in yourself, and not yourself in the art."
— Stanislavski

Character Types
Straight Parts

These are parts that often represent the norm in the audience. They are usually leads and played by actors with whom the audience can identify. These are heroes or heroines or romantic leads. Many actors who play these roles are often personality actors who play themselves or variations of themselves. Some performers like to play themselves, where their personality is the character. Some actors actually have a very difficult time playing themselves. Others like to submerge their personality into the character.

Character Parts

These are parts that have some degree of physical, vocal or psychological eccentricity. They may be offbeat, funny, villainous or unusual in some other way. There are character actors who like to take on the challenge of playing these unusual types. Character roles are often more interesting than straight roles even though the straight roles are the leads. But, for a character actor it's possible to enrich a character with slightly offbeat, unusual and even quirky backgrounds.

Stock and Stereotypical Characters

These may be straight or character parts that are based on easily recognizable stereotypes that have a long history. Stock characters include such characters as the hero, the heroine, the funny sidekicks

223

of the hero and heroine, the villain, the ingénue or the juvenile, the spinster aunt and jolly uncle. They may also be based on occupations such as the boastful warrior, the court jester, the saucy maids, stuffy butler, scheming banker, the cowboy, the gangster and the old codger.

Other typically identifiable characters are national, regional, racial types such as the southerner, Texan, New Yorker, Irishman, Englishman, Italian, African American or Mexican American. While these have sometimes been stock characters and stereotypical character types that may have had an element of truth at one time, the stereotype may not be true anymore. Times and realities and attitudes change.

To play a stock character using stereotypical character traits may do a disservice to some group of people either because of religion, nationality or ethnicity. To perform any of these groups in a demeaning way may not only be untruthful, but hurtful, and serves no purpose in the art of drama and human awareness. And it can make your acting seem very clichéd and non-creative.

It is often much better to look for new creative ways to perform a character and seek human traits beyond the stereotype by playing your stock character for the honesty and humanity rather than using clichés and stereotyped approaches.

If you can approach the acting challenge without preconceptions about your character, it can make stock characters more interesting, more honest and more rewarding to you as a performer. You can also learn something new, and the audience will also gain fresh insights and enlightenments.

Analyzing the Character
The Script and the Characters

You may sometimes see a review of a play in which the critic says that "so-and-so actor created a role or character on Broadway." Well, the actor did not *create* the role or character. The playwright is the creator of the characters and the play. The actors, director and technical designers are all interpreters. The actor may have been the initial or first interpreter. And, the actors and others may give a very good creative interpretation. But the playwright is the original creator, the person who created the characters and the play. (See Chapters 17 and 18.)

As an interpreter, you have chosen or been cast as a character in a scene or play. When describing characters in plays the description is often in terms of character types. Characters may be defined in many ways:

Physical Description

This involves such descriptive elements as age, clothing, complexion, glasses, tall, short, fat, thin, etc. Or, walks with limp, uses a cane, looks tired, etc. (See Chapter 14.)

Character Traits and Emotions

These involve such traits as proud, angry, greedy, jealous, arrogant, childlike, dreamy, sensitive, neat, messy, bored, fearful, dumb, sad, lonely, etc. (See Chapter 13.)

Intentions, Objectives and Motivations

This is what a character wants and why. It defines his or her goals and is the driving force behind the action. (See Chapter 15.)

Relationships

This involves family, friends, siblings, romantic couples, relatives, roommates, opponents, business associates, parent-child, student-teacher, coach-athlete, etc.

Social, Cultural and Educational Background

The social or cultural or financial class often establishes attitudes, wealth, education, manners, speech and dress. It may also indicate occupations and hobbies.

Occupations and Hobbies

The occupation or hobbies may define what the character is doing in terms of stage business. Examples might be: doctor, lawyer, carpenter, teacher, home decorator, golfer, custodian, writer, cook, etc. (See Chapter 13 and Chapter 4 for "Stage Business.")

When people meet each other at parties for the first time, they often like to ask, "What do you do for a living?" Or, "What school do you go to?" Or "What is your major?" All of these questions are a quick, but not always accurate way to get an idea about another person and try to evaluate if you have anything in common with the other person. On another level it might be "What kind of car do you

225

have?" or "What movies have you seen?" or "What books have you read recently?" Or "Where do you like to eat?" "Are you interested in sports?" "Did you see the game the other night?"

Discussion: Does it make a difference if a person is an architect or engineer or used car salesman or teacher or stockbroker? What can you tell about them? How do you describe people? If you go to a party, what do you notice first? Do you note gender or age or race or look for people like you and friends? Do you ask where they go to school or what is their favorite music? Do you notice what people are wearing or the food being served?

Defining the Character

In choosing a character from a one-act or full-length play, you will have a great deal more information than you would with only a short cutting. To define a character from a whole play, start with a careful study of the script. Read the whole play several times to determine the "facts" established by the playwright about your character. On the second or third reading, note and list those facts and references that are meaningful in defining and forming a composite picture of your character. These basic facts found in the script are the *given circumstances.*

Given Circumstances

Basic Description of Your Character
Basic information about the character usually appears in the cast list or in the stage directions on your character's first entrance. This often includes: name, age, general physical description, family relationships, personality, character traits, occupation, hobbies of your character, general relationships to other characters, and romantic or marital status.

The Background Conditions
Note and list the time and place of the action and the social, cultural, economic and political background of the play. These elements can establish the mood, atmosphere and environment. On the basis of all this you can write a background or antecedent action to create a past history of events that took place before the play begins.

Your Character's Function in the Script
Establish your character's function in the play in terms of the type of character you are playing: the protagonist, antagonist, lead, support, comic relief, friend of lead, villain, hero, heroine, etc. Also,

note the cast balance, the parallels and contrasts pertaining to your character's role and other characters in play. In other words, why did the playwright write your character into this play? (See Chapter 10.)

Your Character's Motivations and Objectives

Since people play different roles with different people, analyze your character's basic motivations or primary objectives for each scene. Then, note and list what character traits and attitudes are shown in different situations and their changing relationships.

For instance, if you are Character A, and you have a scene with B, then C, then D, then B again, you need to determine what objectives and character traits are exhibited in each scene because A to B are different than A to C or A to D. And you need to determine if A to B might have changed in their relationship when they meet the second time.

What Other Characters Say and
Do in Relation to Your Character

Note and list what other characters say and do in relation to your character and how they act toward your character. Note most particularly what they say about your character, both when you are present and to other characters when you are not present. *In drama ... as in life*, this is often the way you find out about your friends and other people in your life.

Research

If you are cast in a role, for which you have no background that is familiar to you, you may need to use some type of research to prepare yourself to play a fully rounded character. This could be in terms of history or social or economic background or customs of another time and place or different accent.

Or, it may be your character's occupation or hobby or some type of ailment or disability. Doing the research should be prepared for in the context of the play, focusing on your character in that situation. For example, if he were a young miner in Wales in the 1890s (Morgan Evans in *The Corn is Green*), you would need to do many types of research: Welch accent, working conditions of miners, educational opportunities, culture of the region, etc.

Exercise

Choose a character from a full-length play or well-developed character from a short play, and then do a character analysis of the "given circumstances" using the following forms as a guideline.

Character Analysis Form #1: Given Circumstances

1. My name: _____

2. Name of play: _____

3. Name of playwright: _____

4. Name of character: _____

5. What is the type or style of play (comedy, drama, etc.)? _____

6. What is the time and location of the play (present, past and place)? ____

_____

7. Write a brief summary of the plot. _____

_____

8. What is the theme or main issue of the play? _____

_____

9. What is your character's function in relation to the plot, other characters and theme? (That is, why is your character in the play?) What are your key scenes, with whom, and what happens in those scenes? _____

_____

10. What is the playwright's description of your character (gender, age, basic personality or character traits and emotions, physical appearance, posture, movement, ethnicity, if applicable)? _____

_____

11. What is your character's background (social, economic, vocational, hobbies, sports, arts, etc. and, origins: south, New England, west or foreign) and what influences have shaped the character? _____

_____

12. What does your character say and do to show character traits? (Write down actual lines and who says what and when.) _____

_____

13. What does your character want/need/hope for or fear? What are your character's primary motivations/objectives/intentions (love, money, revenge, ambition, religion, safety, escape, etc.)? _____

_____

14. What are the obstacles in the way of achieving these objectives or overcoming fears or problems? What is your character's main personal problem or secret? _____

_____

15. What do other characters say about your character and how do they act toward your character? Who are the characters on the same side of the issue, and who are characters on the other side? _____

_____

_____

Similarities and Differences: You and Your Character

Once you have established the given circumstances, you need to compare and list similarities and differences between you and your character. For instance, if you are playing a character not already part of your physical and psychological makeup, a character that is quite different from your personality, you may need to turn to a variety of acting techniques to further realize, enhance and perform your character honestly.

1. How am I like the character (physically, vocally, psychologically, emotionally, etc.)?

2. How am I different from the character the playwright created?

3. What changes do I need to make to best interpret this character creatively (in terms of body, voice, and character traits)?

4. What special research do I need to do to truthfully play this character?

This list should help you understand and clarify what might come naturally from instinct, as an aspect of character development and what parts you will need techniques.

Imaginary Circumstances

"Acting is living truthfully under an imaginary set of circumstances."
— Sanford Meisner

The Magic IF

Based on the given circumstances, the *imaginary circumstances* should help you feel free to explore and enhance your character by adding your own special creative interpretation. Imaginary circumstances might be questions asked, hypotheses raised, and inferences drawn about your character that are not actually in the script. They lead to the *Magic IF,* which poses the hypothetical question, "What would you do "IF" you were that character in that situation, from that period in that play, by that playwright?

This is not what you would think and feel and do if you were in the situation. But instead this is what you might imagine you would feel and think and do IF you were in the character's place.

Posing and answering these questions should help to give you an image and emotional perspective, and psychological understanding

229

of your character, that suggests more ideas for body and voice and character development. Fill in other details and draw inferences that might be true.

Exercise

From a composite description of detailed characteristics in given circumstances, and a comparison with your own attributes, what can you add to the whole character analysis by imaginary circumstances? (See form on page 231.)

Putting It All Together

After noting and listing the given circumstances from the playwright's words, you should have a well-rounded composite picture and understanding of your character. Then analyzing how you are the same or different from the character should offer a basis to make honest and believable decisions about how to create your own interpretation.

Think through the possibilities and imaginary circumstances that are available to you. In making choices for your character, many things are possible. Decide what you would like to show the audience in terms of your character. Then, experiment and practice to internalize these character traits, emotions and images, and see which body movements and voice qualities seem to feel most right to convey your character truthfully.

Even though you've been careful about analyzing your character, don't just perform the results. Instead you need to internalize the character and let your character evolve truthfully.

1. Analyze and learn the given circumstances about your character.

2. List the inferences you can make about the character's behavior and the research that will be needed. Begin research.

3. Create a group of character traits based on imaginary circumstances or the "Magic IF."

4. Mark your script into workable units or bits.

5. Choose emotions and senses involved in your character.

6. Create images of your character.

7. Define your objectives and obstacles in each scene and the super objective for your character.

8. Note the connections between the objectives and chart a through-line of action that forms an arc.

9. Alter your physical and vocal personality traits to match those of your character.

10. Wear a costume, use props or substitutes from early rehearsals to get a feel for the character.

Character Analysis Form #2:
Imaginary Circumstances

1. What conclusions or inferences can I draw from the given circumstances?
_____
_____
_____

2. What immediate images do I get of my character? _____
_____
_____

3. What character traits, emotions, props, costumes and makeup would be appropriate in creating my character? _____
_____
_____

4. What is the past history, the political, social, economic, educational, and religious background of my character that is not in the play directly?
_____
_____
_____

5. What, in my character's past history, in terms of family or friends or events, has influenced my character and can explain the actions of my character.
_____
_____
_____

6. How do I show my character through body and voice? What vocal qualities or accents do I need? _____
_____
_____

7. What possible stage business can be used to enhance my character? (What am I doing? Why am I doing it? And how am I doing it?) _____
_____
_____

8. What is my character doing when not on stage or at other times in his or her life? _____
_____

9. What are the details of my character's love life? _____
_____

10. What research do I need to do? (This can involve background, occupation, hobbies, lifestyle, etc.) _____
_____
_____

Representation

Accepting Your Character

Characters in plays, like people in life, are sometimes dumb, lazy, greedy, arrogant, envious, angry or gluttonous. While the audience may have negative judgments about these characters, you must remember, the character probably doesn't think of herself or himself as a terrible, despicable person. In fact, whatever bad acts this character has done, they are probably — in the mind of the character — justified. And, if the character doesn't think in these negative terms, then you shouldn't dislike or reject or judge the characters negatively either. But instead it's important to accept the playwright's character with those character traits in order to represent an honest, well-rounded characterization.

It is no reflection on your personal work ethic to play a lazy character honestly. Nor is it a reflection on your personal intelligence to play a dumb character honestly. You are not that character. You're an actor representing that character. In a sense you are an advocate for your character. And the more convincing you are the more the audience may think you are actually like your character. But that's an excellent compliment to your acting — not a reflection on you. So, it is important not to judge your character negatively.

The playwright is not on-stage. No one is sure what the director did. But your performance is the one seen by the audience. So take the point of view of the character and let the audience make the value judgments about the character.

Empathizing

To empathize is to connect with another person's feelings or ideas. For an actor it means you will understand human justification for the character's actions. If you empathize, it means you are truly compassionate and non-judgmental. This is not the same as sympathy or pity, which may distance you from the person. To empathize with your character you need to immerse yourself with deep feelings in the character so that appropriate and involuntary actions appear.

Personalizing

This is not the same as personality acting. And this is not part of The Method. It is you personalizing your interpretation of the playwright's character. Memorize and internalize your lines and the given circumstances of the play.

When rehearsing, relax and focus on your character in the here and now and make instinctive personally emotional character decisions. Enjoy the process of personal discovery as you respond to:

- Your environment: interior, exterior, time of day, weather.
- Your senses: the sights, sounds, smells, and touch, etc.
- Your own physical condition: aches, pains, stiffness, a cold or allergy.
- Your character traits and emotions and intentions.
- Your emotional reaction to what is happening around you in the scene.

Let the other actor share the emotional life with you. Acknowledge the feelings and thoughts you are receiving from the other actors. Don't plan your emotions. Don't force anything. Just be yourself playing your character but still within the framework of the character and the script. Show how your character would feel under the circumstances in the play.

Being More Specific is More Universal

The more specific or more detailed the interpretation of your character is, the more universal your character is. While this seems a contradiction of terms, it's true because if your character is very detailed then your character is more believable and accepted as a real person, a character with whom the audience can identify. On the other hand, when a character is generic — "the bad guy" or "good guy" — it is only two-dimensional, and not as believable as a real human being.

> *"All good art is derived from specific observation;*
> *all bad art from generalizations."*
> — Sir Richard Eyre

Part D

The Playscript

Chapter 17
Elements and Structure of the Play

"The play's the thing ... "
— *Hamlet,* by William Shakespeare

Introduction

In simple terms, a play is a story told in dialog performed by actors on a stage for an audience. Playwriting is a very demanding form to use for telling stories. Unlike novels, every line of dialog needs to add something to the character and/or the plot and/or theme, because there is a time limitation of approximately two hours for most full-length plays. And there is often a financial limitation on settings and cast size.

The playwright is the creator of the script or play. The actors, director and technical staff are all interpreters of the script. While they offer a creative interpretation of the play, they are not the creators of the script. The same relation applies in music to the composer, conductor and musicians.

Formal Elements of Drama

Over 2,300 years ago, the Greek philosopher, Aristotle (b. 384 B.C. d. 322 B.C.) wrote *The Poetics* in which he defined dramatic structure. His analysis of the main elements in drama, which includes discussions of plot, character, theme, dialog, setting and stage action, is still valid today.

Plot/Story (What Happens)

The plot is the dramatic action of what happens to the principal characters and their interaction with other characters in many sequential scenes that make up the total play. Structurally, the plot is a series of related events starting with the background and establishing the major dramatic question or problem, followed by the initial incident, leading through rising action to the crisis, climax and ending with the falling action and conclusion.

During the course of the action there can be many discoveries and reversals or turning points that cause a change in the direction of the plot.

The Premise

The premise is a brief preliminary description of the subject matter or basis of the story. When people ask, "What's it about?" they are usually referring to the premise. For example: A young prince is going to school in Germany when he hears his father died. He returns home to Denmark to find that his mother has married his uncle. The ghost of the young man's father appears and tells the young prince that he must seek revenge by killing his uncle who is now king.

Probability of Action

There are many levels of probability in the plot action. Of course, anything is possible, but the action is more believable if the events that happen are probable. And it's artistically best and most believable if the action is necessary because all other choices have been ruled out. (See *Julius Caesar* and *Hamlet* for examples of necessary actions.)

Sub Plot

While the protagonist is involved in a major plot line or series of dramatic events, s/he also may be involved in another or secondary plot line, or subplot that is interwoven with the major plot line. (For example: A character has a problem balancing or being successful in both a career and home life.)

Parallel Plots

This involves two separate plot lines.

Story line A is the major plot.

Story line B involves the minor or subordinate characters in a minor plot.

Classic examples of parallel plots involve Story Line A with the hero and heroine, and Story Line B with their comic friends or sidekicks.

Character(s)/People (Who Is Involved)

Protagonist(s)

In life you have wants, desires, goals and objectives. So, too, the protagonist(s) or main character(s) in a play is the person with whom we identify and who is presented with a problem that must be solved. The protagonist usually wants something or has a goal, or objective or intention, and therefore initiates the action. (For more on objectives see Chapter 15.)

One or more obstacles are put in the way of the protagonist in achieving this objective or solving the problem. This creates a conflict, which is a dramatic action that causes a momentary crisis between the characters. The problem for the protagonist may be a flaw or weakness within a character, such as too much ego or hubris, false values or some personal problem to overcome such as a physical disability or some obstacle in nature such as a river, mountain, or storm.

Antagonist(s)

The person(s) who opposes the protagonist and puts up obstacles in the way of the protagonist getting what s/he wants. In a melodrama the villain initiates the action. The most dramatic scenes are those between two opposing and fairly equal forces whose conflicts are most logically arranged with ever increasing emotional impact until the ultimate showdown and maximum emotional impact at the climax.

The problem or obstacles may be a conflicting desire of the protagonist and antagonist, such as winning an athletic event or some other type of contest, making money, competing over the affections of a woman or many other things.

Compare the problems created by characters that have opposite or conflicting character traits, such as good vs. evil, or contrasting emotional qualities, which may be drama or comedy. For example, in *The Odd Couple*, Felix is neat and prissy in contrast to Oscar who is tough talking and messy.

Risk. There must also be a risk for the protagonist if the objective is not achieved. The stakes need to be significant and high enough in order for us to care what happens to the protagonist.

Ensemble

A group of mutually unified, supporting characters (or actors) who are relatively equal in importance and balance. This is compared with one or two lead characters such as a protagonist and an antagonist. It has a supporting cast of lesser importance. It is the difference between a concerto and a string quartet.

Theme/Idea/Moral/Lesson/Message (Why Play Is Written)

This is the underlying meaning or essence of the play, the message communicated by the characters and plot action. The basic theme, idea, moral or lesson is a reason behind the character's character traits and the way a character acts. The way the story ends often reveals the underlying theme, idea, moral, lesson or message and tells us how the author feels about the characters and life. The theme should not be confused with the premise.

Each small scene should be part of the whole theme, and all of the small scenes add up to one major theme of the play. The theme is illustrated by what happens to the characters and why. For the actor analyzing the play it may be thought of as the spine of the play.

Simple illustrations of the difference between subject matter, plot and theme may be illustrated by children's stories. For example, the theme of *Goldilocks and the Three Bears* might be, "stay out of other people's houses when they're not home, and don't touch their possessions." This lesson is aimed at pre-school children. Or, the theme of *Little Red Riding Hood* might be, "be careful when walking in strange places, and don't talk to strangers." Or, *Cinderella*'s theme might be "if you're a good person and work hard, you will eventually be rewarded even if you come from difficult circumstances or a broken home." These same themes could be stated with different subject matter and different plots.

When the formal elements of the play: Plot, Character and Theme — or what happens, to whom and why — are determined, much of the basic planning is done. However, these three formal elements need to use the means of Dialog (how we know about characters), Setting (where it takes place) and Stage Action (to show the story of the play visually) to be conveyed to the audience.

Means to Convey Formal Elements

Dialog/Talk (how we know about characters)

A conversation among the characters shows their feelings about themselves and others, what happens to them and what it all means. The dialog may be written, or it may be improvised with given circumstances, created orally on the basis of actors exploring the characters, plot and theme.

Any dialog for the characters should sound like normal speech used by real people, unless it's a classic or poetic play. People usually speak in short, even fragmented speeches, rather than long uninterrupted speeches. At the same time, different characters will speak differently on the basis of their basic personalities and their accent or region of origin.

Setting/Place/Location (where/when the action takes place)

The setting can often show the background or environment of the characters or the mood and feeling of the play. Broadly speaking, settings are either Interiors (Int. in play catalogs) or Exteriors (Ext. in play catalogs).

Examples of interiors might be the family room, the kitchen, office or store, a schoolroom or bedroom. Exterior examples might be backyard, park, beach, woods, etc. If you are creating your own script, try to limit the settings to one place, since it can be very expensive and labor intensive to plan and build a set.

Stage Action/Movement
(when and how of physical movement of actors)
The script tells when the characters enter, exit, have a fight, etc. The director plans the blocking of the scenes, which is the placement and movement of actors on-stage to show character relationships in order to tell the story of the play visually. (See Chapter 11.)

The Unities: Time, Place and Action

In the Neo-Classic Period of the late eighteenth century, there was an attempt to recreate the greatness of Classic Greece and Rome. The French critics proclaimed that all plays should abide by the three unities of *Time, Place and Action.*

Unity of Time calls for the story to take place within one twenty-four-hour period.

Unity of Place calls for the action to take place in one location.

Unity of Action states that the story should happen in one continuous flow of time or within one day.

In *The Poetics*, Aristotle only defined or called for unity of action, meaning that every event should have a cause-effect relationship. But, he barely mentioned unity of time and said nothing about unity of place. The Greek Chorus usually set the place.

While these unities can focus attention and intensify the play by honoring the unities, it can also stifle creativity by forcing them into a structure that is unnatural for many stories.

However, while unity of place is not required artistically, many of today's plays are written for one set because of the expense of set building. When plays are made into movies they are frequently "opened out" to use many locations and many more images.

Structure of Drama
Length of Plays

Plays are often categorized according to length. They are usually either full-length or short plays, which are often called one-acts. Shakespeare's plays were often five acts and took many hours to perform.

Plays in the twentieth century up until the 1960s were often three or four acts with several intermissions. During the 1960s and '70s, plays became two acts with one intermission. Most full-length plays today are two acts with Act I being slightly longer than Act II. They run between ninety minutes and two hours ten minutes and have one intermission.

One-acts are between ten and fifty minutes with the average being in the twenty to thirty-five minute range. Sometimes two to eight short plays are combined to make up an evening's entertainment. In recent times there have been many ten-minute play contests that have produced a large body of interesting work in this short form.

Elements of Structure

1. Exposition
2. Initial Incident
3. Rising Action
4/5. Crisis: Minor and Major
6. Climax
7. Falling Action
8. Denouement

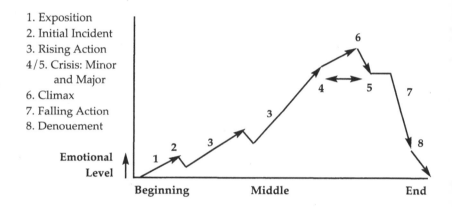

Scenes and French Scene

The word *scene* may be used to designate a part of an act such as Act I, Scene 1 and Scene 2. These are usually unified time sequences. A *French scene* further defines a scene as beginning and ending with the entrance or exit of a character. It may have several subjects, several emotional moods and changes of intensity within a time period. It may be a mini scene on its own with an introduction rising to a crisis and climax with a turning point and a denouement.

For actors, a scene is sometimes referred to as a "beat." The word "beat" is derived from the Russian teachers in the 1920's who explained that they broke the whole play into scenes, segments or small bits. But the Russian teachers enunciated "bit" as "beat." The term "beat" is still used by the Actors' Studio to define a segment of a scene and also applies to the play's rhythms.

Exposition

The exposition scene takes place early in the play and establishes the background conditions and preliminary action of the play. It introduces the where (place), when (time), who (major characters) and what (plot or story or major premise). This scene establishes the "major dramatic question of the play," the major character's wants or problems and/or who is going to do what to solve the problems or overcome the obstacles.

The opening scenes may also establish the social, political, economic and personal realities that surround the characters. The exposition also indicates the type of play, comedy, farce, mystery, or sentimental drama, which includes the mood and atmosphere.

For example, the background conditions of *The Rainmaker* establish there is a summer drought on a western farm during the depression years, and the daughter is also having a dry desolate life. In *The Diary of Anne Frank*, the Nazis are arresting the Jews in Amsterdam in WWII to send them to concentration camps, so Anne and her family need to hide to survive.

Antecedent Action

The exposition also includes the antecedent action or information that happened in the past before the play began. The antecedent action also reveals details from the past lives of the characters that explain their immediate situation and the major dramatic problems of the play. While past history is usually near the beginning of the play, new information or discoveries may come throughout the whole play. In recent years, the term "back story" has been borrowed from the film industry and writers of screenplays.

This opening information — the exposition and antecedent action — may be established by the major characters or less important characters. In many of the plays of the nineteenth century, the servants, who were cleaning the house, established the information, and it was therefore called "dusting maid exposition." Aside from being an obvious and clichéd way to present this material, very few people of today have maids who live on the premises.

Initial Incident

This is the first emotional conflict or event to take place between the protagonist and antagonist forces. It is the first of many emotional confrontations and crises to dramatize the major dramatic question.

Most of today's plays with smaller casts have the major characters immediately involved in some dramatic problem or crisis that creates or establishes bigger problems and major dramatic questions. Many of today's movies open with some dramatic scene or initial incident to capture the audience's attention, and then goes back to establish the background information.

Rising Action

With each scene there is an increasing and more intense emotional involvement with the characters and their problems.

Crisis, Major Crisis and Climax

A crisis is an emotional turning point. There are many small crises during the action. These are related to the major problem facing the lead character in which there is a major turning point or added conflict and the protagonist has to make a decision. The major crisis, or major decision or turning point may come before or after a climax. That is, the major character can make a discovery or make a decision that brings about a reversal that then leads to a climax. Or, some dramatic climax will cause the major characters to have a crisis or turning point.

The major climax is the highest point in the dramatic action or the most dramatic moment of the play. There are small crises and climaxes along the way, but the major climax should involve the greatest emotional involvement for the audience. After the major climax, the falling action and the denouement follow.

Denouement or Falling Action

The denouement is a French word that means a "winding down" or "untying" of the action. It is part of the "falling action" or conclusion. And the basis of the way the story is resolved or ends determines what the playwright is saying about these people, which is the theme or meaning of the play.

Discoveries, Reversals or Turning Points

Discoveries and reversals can appear throughout the play to make the plots and characters more interesting. Discoveries involve new information about some character or event that brings about a change or reversal in the story. Example: It is discovered that Character A is related to Character B. Or Character X owns a gun in a murder mystery. The discovery may be personal for the character or a new plot development. Reversals usually happen on the basis of a discovery that can bring about a change. Things may be going well, or badly, for the protagonist, and then comes a discovery, which produces a crisis, turning point or change of fortune.

Exercise: Analyzing Selected Plays

Below is a short, subjective list of full-length plays to read, analyze and discuss in terms of types and styles and elements and structure.

Our Town (1938), by Thornton Wilder

The Glass Menagerie (1944), by Tennessee Williams

Death of a Salesman (1949), by Arthur Miller

The Rainmaker (1954), by N. Richard Nash

The Diary of Anne Frank (1955), by Albert and Frances Goodrich

Inherit the Wind (1955), by Jerome Lawrence and Robert E. Lee

A Raisin in the Sun (1959), by Lorraine Hansberry

Discussion:

1. What is established in the exposition in each?

2. What is the antecedent action or background in *The Rainmaker, The Glass Menagerie, The Diary of Anne Frank* and *Inherit the Wind*?

3. What is the initial incident in *Inherit the Wind, The Rainmaker, The Diary of Anne Frank* and *Death of a Salesman*?

4. What do the major characters want (motivation, objective, etc.) in *The Glass Menagerie, The Rainmaker, Inherit the Wind, A Raisin in the Sun* and *The Diary of Anne Frank*?

5. What are the obstacles in the way of the characters getting what they want?

6. What is at risk if they don't get what they want?

7. What character traits or values show a contrast in the major characters in *Inherit the Wind, The Diary of Anne Frank, Death of a Salesman, The Rainmaker* and *A Raisin in the Sun*?

8. Compare and contrast the dialog of the characters in each of the plays above and discuss why they talk the way they do.

9. What character relationships are shown between parents, children and siblings in *The Glass Menagerie, Death of a Salesman, A Raisin in the Sun, The Diary of Anne Frank* and *Our Town*?

10. At what points are there discoveries and reversals in the plot?

11. At what points are there major crises and/or climaxes in all of the above?

12. What happens after the climax in the falling action and denouement? Does it follow believably from the preceding plot, characters, crisis and climax?

13. What are the major themes of *Our Town, The Rainmaker* and *Inherit the Wind*?

14. How does the playwright handle the unities of time, place and action in *Death of a Salesman, The Glass Menagerie, The Diary of Anne Frank* and *Our Town*?

15. What are the technical requirements of each play: the set lighting, costumes, makeup?

Exercise

Explore character by using improvisation from known plays. Choose one play from the list above. Read the whole play. Choose one scene. Read the scene once again, then put down the script and improvise. Then, read it again and improvise again. Do not carry the script. Just focus on what you know about the scene and the characters and concentrate on listening and relating to the other actors. If you create new material that is in the context of the original scene, then you are using this exercise in the way it is intended. Continue this process until you feel comfortable with the scene. If you were to actually do the play, you would need to use the playwright's dialog. Consider this approach in rehearsing. (See Chapter 10.)

Chapter 18
Types and Styles of Drama

Introduction
Types of Drama

These are generic forms that have been with us all throughout the history of drama. Historically, the two broad categories or main types of drama are comedy and tragedy with the twin masks used as symbols.

However, there are different types and degrees of comedy and tragedy within these broad categories. These types are based on natural human responses to human beings in situations that create laughter, tears and fear. Because people like to see other people laugh, cry and be scared explains the basis and longevity of realistic comedy, farce or satire, sentimental comedy or drama, melodrama, musical comedy or musical drama and tragedy.

Styles of Drama

There are forms of drama that pertain more closely to and reflect periods in history, or in other words, "the style of the times." Examples of this might include allegory, symbolism or fantasy, particularly in the medieval period under the influence of religion. Comedy of manners, which depicted the upper class society that patronized theatre and the romanticism that depicted royalty, might be associated more closely with the plays from the seventeenth through the nineteenth centuries. These gave way to realism and naturalism as the predominant style in the 20th century. During the depression years of the 1930s, naturalism sometimes became social drama, a style of play about the social and political protest during those times. Other minor styles that have come into being during the twentieth century also include the highly theatrical forms of expressionism, which dealt with a character's subconscious thoughts and paralleled the growth of psychoanalysis, and theatre of the absurd, as an outgrowth of a cynical view of society that was rooted in the philosophy of existentialism that followed both world wars.

Types of Drama
Comedy

Comedy is a type of drama that has been with us since the Greeks. The original symbol of comedy was Bacchus, the Greek God of wine and revelry. Broadly speaking, this is a type of drama that is intended to "entertain" by provoking laughter. But there are many types and gradations of comedy. Most will have humorous characters in funny situations that produce laughter and end successfully for the main characters. Many situation comedies on TV, known as sitcoms, are based on elements of different types of comedy.

Realistic Comedy

In realistic comedies, the characters and plots are based on real life situations that are plausible and believable. Romantic comedies often end in a male and female getting together and perhaps planning a wedding.

Farce

Farce is an exaggerated comedy with exaggerated characters and situations to produce laughter through the eccentricity or foibles of the characters who are involved in funny situations. Farce is often built around plot situation and stage action. It is usually exuberant and lively with a life and spirit of comedy. Farce is often based on doing the forbidden, the unexpected or the bizarre. The characters are often sub-normal, strange or bizarre, immature, dumb or fearful. They could fear loss of money, friends, death, etc. Disguise, mistaken identity and mistaken intention are some of the comic elements used in farce. Sometimes, comic elements are based on one person's inhumanity to another person.

Satire

Satire ridicules or makes fun of something that is taken seriously or accepted in popular culture. Satires need to be timely or else they have no meaning. In a sense, satire is built around a theme with stereotyped characters and known situations. On a TV comedy show, you may frequently see a "takeoff" or satire of a soap opera, situation comedy or commercials. Because of the timeliness needed, satires work best as a TV comedy show production or cabaret revue.

A. Plot elements in comedy, farce and satire are built around situations or stage action. These might be:

1. Messiness: pie in the face, soaked with water, dust, mud, gum, etc.
2. Chase: without real threat.
3. Mistaken identity: identifying a person as the wrong person.
4. Mistaken intention or misunderstanding of what someone wants.
5. Disguise: hiding behind a mask, or it might be male and female characters cross dressing which results in speaking at cross purposes.
6. Teasing, tickling, pinching, slapping, spanking or romantic playfulness. These usually produce embarrassment and/or discomfort, but no real pain.
7. Loss of control: dizziness or drunkenness.
8. Pomposity: such as someone acting like a "big deal."
9. Blackmail: may be comic or melodramatic.
10. Repeated interruptions of a rendezvous.
11. Mimicking or making fun of someone and being caught in the act.
12. Eavesdropping for secret information.
13. Fears: loss of money, loss of friends or fear of death.

B. Characters in comedies can be realistic or have exaggerated character traits or be stock characters. While there is a semblance of being real in realistic comedies, the acting style is usually more exaggerated than normal life, more emotionally intense in farce and more ironic in satire. The characters may be built around contrasting character traits that can produce or result in humorous conflict. For example: neat vs. messy, dumb vs. smart, naughty vs. nice, clumsy vs. well coordinated, etc. The subject matter may be based on frustration and insult or doing the forbidden.

Exercise

Write or improvise a short scene with the elements of a farce comedy. For example: The scene has one girl, her younger brother/sister, and a boyfriend of older girl. The girl and her boyfriend have been eating a custard or blueberry pie she made, but the boyfriend hates it and doesn't want to eat it. He has just left, and the younger brother/sister comes out of hiding where s/he's been eavesdropping. S/He mimics the older sister and the boyfriend blackmails her. The older sister chases and throws pie at younger brother/sister and misses, hitting the boyfriend who has returned. (If you do this scene, pantomime the pie.)

Sentimental Drama

This is a serious type of drama that appeals to feelings and emotions rather than reason or thought. Sentimental dramas are built around character relationships to produce sympathy, empathy and tears. The characters are often family members of close friends who are involved in concerns of deep human feelings such as love, hate, joy, sadness, suffering and grief that intensify their relationships. The characters often do the wrong thing for the right reason. From empathy with the suffering characters, the audience reaction is often sadness and tears. Sometimes sentiment is used in an unfavorable sense, denoting mawkishness, weepy emotional weakness or the tendency to be swayed by emotion rather than thought. This is exaggerated sentiment or sentimentality.

Because present day sentimental dramas on TV often sell soap products and are sponsored by these companies, the programs are called "soap operas." Typical plots involve concerns about birth, death, accident, illness, love, marriage, divorce, hopes, fears, misunderstandings, etc. The plots are often built around misunderstandings, mistakes, money, broken romances, illness, accidents, suffering, etc. There is rarely any humor in the characters of soap operas.

Examples of sentimental plays in this style are: *Our Town, Little Women* and *I Remember Mama*. Many straight dramas or comedies also have elements of sentiment.

A. Plot elements or common subjects in sentimental plays might include:

1. Birth, youthful romance, marriage and death
2. Mother love, father love
3. Self-sacrifice: love, cause or duty, ambition or honor
4. Defeat, a losing struggle turned to victory
5. Women past middle age seeking and/or finding romance
6. Sickness and suffering
7. Dreams, hopes, illusions and nostalgia
8. Tyrannical or stern, unbending person quietly reforming (For example: acceptance of person previously rejected)
9. Loss of romance or affection, breaking up
10. Reuniting of friends, lovers or relations
11. Patriotism
12. Disappointments faced nobly (For example: being rejected or stood up)
13. Babies and cute or ugly-cute children

14. Animals: cute or ugly dogs and horses or sick animals
15. Special occasions: birthdays, picnics and marriage
16. Feeling proud of someone and showing it
17. Prayer or Pledge of Allegiance
18. Loneliness
19. Lies and gossip
20. Jealousy and revenge
21. A person changing from mean-spirited to compassionate

B. Types of characters or character traits in sentiment are often overly serious, anxious, worried, sad, shy, lonely, suffering, pitiful, fearful, tearful, sensitive, dreamy, etc. The acting style is usually super-real and exaggerated. Watch soap operas for an example.

Exercise

Write or improvise a short scene in the type of sentimental drama. For example: Two girls, friends. The first girl says that her boyfriend is returning home from seeing his sick mother in the East. The second girl reluctantly says that her boyfriend joined the Army because of his patriotism. He was ill-suited for the life and died in boot camp. She reads his last letter and cries.

Melodrama

A melodrama is an exaggerated comedy in the sense that it has exaggerated characters and stock types and ends successfully for the hero and heroine. It has a seeming seriousness, but at times it is close to farce, even using some of the same elements such as grotesque comedy.

The genre of melodrama includes mysteries, suspense, action-adventure and westerns. The "suspense mystery," which is also known as "whodunit" because we don't know who committed the crime, is also called a "thriller." In suspense, we may or may not know who the villain or killer is, but our heroine — or possibly hero — is in great danger. "A woman in danger" is a frequent plot component.

Mysteries and westerns are often stories built around plot and stage action and what happens. Mysteries should arouse fear and hate: fear for the hero and heroine and hate of the villain. Then, we feel relieved when the hero finally triumphs.

All forms of melodrama have always been with us, and they've been very popular particularly on the nineteenth century stage before the advent of the motion picture. "Old style" nineteenth-century melodramas are now often satirized, but they were serious,

251

or seemingly serious, then. As a form, melodramas are often more successful as written stories or as movies. Note the whole mystery section at your local library or bookstore. In movies, they may also take the form of "action-adventure" or science fiction stories.

A. Some of the prevalent plot elements for melodramas are:
   1. Crimes: stealing or robbery, murder, kidnapping, arson, counterfeiting, assault, etc.
   2. Chases: villain pursuing heroine and/or hero pursuing villain in cars, on horses, in airplanes, on foot, etc.
   3. Fights or shoot-outs: usually the climactic showdown between the hero and villain. This might be a fight with guns, fists, knives or swords.
   4. Courtroom trials, usually for murder.
   5. Hiding: out of fear or ambush to create suspense, such as stalkers.
   6. Races: good guy vs. bad guy, against time to save heroine, a whole city, the whole universe or humanity from foreign or space invaders.
   7. Danger: walking on railroad tracks, rooftops, edge of ledge, deserted parking garages, warehouse. Or, it might be a danger from some dread disease, monsters or invading forces of unearthly creatures.
   8. Rescue: policeman, firefighter or hero rescues heroine from danger.
   9. Blackmail: threat or extortion.
   10. Torture: lashing, tied to railroad tracks, whipping, sleep deprivation.
   11. Revenge or getting even for real or imagined wrongs.

B. Types of characters in melodrama might include:
   1. Exaggerated or stock types: hero, heroine, villain, funny friend of hero or heroine, detective, cowboy, spies, counter spies, drug pushers, low-life characters, crazy possessed people, etc.
   2. Grotesque characters: mad or crazy scientists, world power controllers such as evil invaders from other planets or monsters.

Examples of melodramas, mysteries or thrillers: *The Mousetrap* (Agatha Christie), *Dial "M" For Murder* and *Wait Until Dark* (Frederick Knott), Alfred Hitchcock and James Bond movies and the *Friday the 13th* genre. Acting style is usually seemingly serious, melodramatic, exaggerated, and intense.

Exercise

Write or improvise a short melodramatic scene. For example: A murder has been committed in the lonely house at the end of town. We suddenly discover the quiet sister has murdered her sister's husband with her scissors.

Or, two friends alone in an isolated cabin prepare for bed when the lights go out and noises suddenly come from off-stage in the kitchen.

Musical Comedy or Drama and Opera

This popular form has a long history, and the United States has led the way in defining the form for modern times. Many of the early scripts had implausible plots, people often sang without motivation, and dancers were chosen because of their looks rather than their dancing ability.

Then, *Oklahoma!* integrated the script, songs and dance into the musical's plot, which started a whole new era of musicals. *West Side Story*, loosely based on *Romeo and Juliet*, dealt with gang life in New York in the late 1950s. *The Music Man* dealt with a man selling musical instruments to young people and the effect it had on small town Midwestern life. One of the longest running musicals was a small charming musical called *The Fantasticks*. Based on *The Romancers* by Edmund Rostand, this simple musical adaptation tells the story of a young couple that seeks romance, but must experience pain and grow up before they can discover true love. In more recent years the musical has turned to classic stories such as *Les Miserables*, *Phantom of the Opera* and Disney-like stories based on myths with the spectacle of costumes and sets, such as *The Lion King*.

Tragedy

Tragedy needs to have a worthy protagonist of stature such as a king, son of a king or nobility fighting against an antagonist for some noble and meaningful cause. Because of a tragic flaw in his or her character (often hubris, or pride), the protagonist loses or dies at the end, which produces fear and pity in the audience with a catharsis, or cleansing.

It has been difficult in our times to identify with a hero of stature. Arthur Miller attempted to write the "tragedy of the common man" when he wrote *Death of a Salesman*.

Examples of classic tragedies: *Oedipus the King* and *Antigone*, by Sophocles, or *Hamlet*, *MacBeth* and *Romeo and Juliet*, by Shakespeare.

Emotions of Different Types of Drama

The very nature of drama is meant to create certain emotional reactions in the audience. A melodrama (western, mystery, suspense, thriller) uses fear (usually for the heroine) and hate (for the villain). Sentimental drama (soap operas) produces tears (crying for lost love, death, etc.) for the hero or heroine. Comedy and farce are intended to produce laughter as the basic emotion. Tragedy deals with pride of a great person and his/her downfall, which produces a catharsis.

Exercise

Divide into small groups and choose one type of drama. Then, create your own short scene, using plot and character elements that are given for that type of drama. Rehearse the short play in the acting style called for and perform it. (For more on this activity, see Chapter 19.)

Styles of Drama

Romantic Drama or Romanticism

Romantic drama has the spirit of idealism and revolution. This is not romance in the sense of love. Prevalent in the nineteenth century, romantic characters are usually of nobility or high station, such as kings, queens and knights. They often speak in stylized, grandiose and sometimes poetic language.

The time period for these dramas was often during the medieval period and the settings are faraway places such as castles and forests. The plots frequently included daredevil adventures to rescue princesses or maidens in distress. The romantic drama of the nineteenth century is a prototype for the modern action-adventure movie.

A. Plot elements in romanticism include sacrifice, miracles, dangerous threats, kidnapping, suicide, conniving and sinister plots, revenge, honor, nobility, evil menace, adoption, etc.

B. Character types involve kings, queens, lords, ladies and both good and evil knights, maidens, servants, wise fools or court jesters, grounds and hounds keepers, blacksmiths, evil knights, nannies, nurses, teachers and doctors.

C. Themes involve nobility, honor, self-sacrifice, allegiances and heroism.

D. Set elements might be a kitchen or castle, king's chambers or throne room, tower room, stable, tent (at jousting tournament), forest, servants' quarters, battlements, etc.

Examples of Romantic plays are *Cinderella, Sleeping Beauty, The Three Musketeers* and *Robin Hood*. A later example for the stage is *Cyrano de Bergerac*, which also has sentimental elements.

Exercise

Write or improvise a short scene in the style of romantic drama. For example: A beautiful scullery maid is asked to sacrifice her love for the Prince so he can marry the Royal Princess in a nearby kingdom. For the honor of the future king and the kingdom, she nobly practices her speech of rejection, but realizing she won't be able to go through with it, she considers committing suicide by leaping from the balcony. The language should be ornate and flowery.

The romantic drama of the nineteenth century was often combined with fantasy. Both were popular in their day.

Fantasy

Fantasies are plays that have imaginative, make-believe characters and stories. They are often built around character and settings that are in a forest.

A. Plot elements for fantasy might include magic, spells, transformations, evil menace, miracles, sacrifice, etc.

B. Character types might include a dwarf, giant, elf (mischievous fairy), sorcerer, ghost, Satan or the devil, gnome (misshapen dwarf), beast (dragon), witch or warlock, saint, etc.

C. Settings are generally unrealistic with magic forests, fairyland or even heaven and hell.

Examples of fantasies: *Snow White and the Seven Dwarfs*, (which are also has elements of Romanticism), *Rumplestiltskin*, parts of *The Wizard of Oz* and elements of the *Harry Potter* stories.

Exercise

Write or improvise a short scene. Two elves, dwarfs or gnomes are arguing over whether to grant a third wish to a foolish prince who is heir to the throne and has already used up two wishes foolishly.

Allegory

An allegory is a symbolic play that is built around a theme (a morality tale) with characters being symbols and a plot that serves the theme. An example of an allegory is *Everyman*. Written in the late fifteenth century, *Everyman* is a morality play with abstract characters such as Wisdom, Faith, Hope and Charity whom Everyman meets on the way to the grave. In the end, Everyman is abandoned by everyone except Good Deeds.

Exercise

Write or improvise a short scene on the basis of the following outline or one of your own. Everygirl or Everyboy is tempted by one of the seven deadly sins: anger, sloth, envy, lust, gluttony, greed or pride. Each character personifies a sin and offers a temptation. In the end, Everyboy or Everygirl rejects all the temptations to perform good deeds and states the lesson learned.

Comedy of Manners

A Comedy of Manners portrays upper class characters having witty conversations about the manners of the day, which are mostly built around character, dialog and plot situation. They sometimes speak in epigrams, which are witty, ingenious, clever sayings that are briefly expressed. These plays are usually associated with the seventeenth, eighteenth and nineteenth centuries when the plays were written for wealthy upper classes audiences. Examples of Comedy of Manners are *The Way of the World*, by William Congreve, *The Rivals* and *School for Scandal*, by Richard Brinsley Sheridan, and *The Importance of Being Earnest*, by Oscar Wilde.

In more modern times, these would be considered romantic comedies. Examples can be found in the 1920s, '30s and '40s: *Philadelphia Story*, by Philip Barry, *Hay Fever* and *Private Lives*, by Noel Coward and *Sabrina Fair*, by Samuel Taylor. Also, many movies of the 1930s depicted an upper class society.

The plays that catered to an upper class audience have diminished since the mid-1950s. In recent times, A.R. Gurney, Jr. has been one of the few modern practitioners of this type of comedy of manners. He wrote such plays as *The Dining Room* and *Love Letters*.

However, romantic comedies that deal with middle class foibles and culture could be classified as realistic comedies. Middle class characters and culture are prevalent in the writings of Neil Simon, author of *The Odd Couple*, *Lost in Yonkers* and *Rumors*. Alan Ayckbourn of England is equally prolific in writing such plays as *The Norman Conquests*, *Absurd Person Singular*, *How the Other Half Loves* and *Joking Apart*. A well-known example in the movies is *When Harry Met Sally*.

Exercise

Write or improvise a scene in the style of Comedy of Manners.

This might be early style or modern. Lord or Lady _____
discusses with Lord or Lady _____ the secret meeting and love
match that will lead to an inheritance. Or, they are planning to give
a party and are making a guest list and making comments on the
absurdity of the guests who are their friends.

Or using some of the ideas from the elements of realistic
comedy, write or improvise a short scene with today's characters.

Folk Play

Origins of a folk play come from sections of the country that use
folk tales to define the people in their past and present lives. Folk
plays may involve myths and history of folk tales of the region. The
stories are usually built around rural characters in rustic settings.

Some examples of folk plays are: *Playboy of the Western World*, by
Irish playwright John Millington Synge, Lady Gregory's *Spreading
the News*, the story of Barbara Allen called *Dark of the Moon*, or the
musical *Oklahoma!* by Richard Rodgers and Oscar Hammerstein.
Some of these elements are also in *The Rainmaker*, by N. Richard
Nash. There are also localized historical pageant plays around the
country such as *Ramona* in Hemet, California.

Exercise

Write or improvise a short scene in the style of a folk play. For
example: A schoolteacher comes to a rural farm community and
organizes the school system, finds resistance to education, almost
gives up. Then with the discovery of a bright young student, who
wins a scholarship, the community realizes the value of education
and builds a new school.

Modern Styles

Realism and Naturalism

Charles Darwin's *Origin of the Species* in 1859, which
scientifically attempted to show the evolution of man to his present
form, shook traditional religious faith and was one factor that
helped to produce the beginnings of a realistic movement in drama
in Europe around the 1880s through the 1900s. It came later in the
United States with the social protest plays in the depression years of
the 1930s. With the rise of the middle class in the nineteenth century,
the romantic plays with their "well-made" plots, that involve
unnatural and unmotivated events with stories of lords and ladies
became less meaningful for the new audience.

257

Emile Zola set forth his theories about realism and naturalism in the forward to his novel, *Therese Raquin,* which he adapted for the stage in 1873. These theories sprang from the natural sciences, and he felt art should be like nature or life. By taking a slice of life (*tranche de vie*) or life as it is, without rearranging it — almost photographic realism — was an attempt to find more truth.

Realism and naturalism have come to us in two ways. One is that both words mean the same thing, but naturalism is more used in Europe, and realism is more common in the United States. The other way is the matter of degree in which naturalism is just like life (like taking a tape recorder into a kitchen or supermarket), and realism is slightly ordered and arranged in terms of plot and character.

Realism has been the most popular form from the 1930s through the end of the century. But this style has been almost fully explored, and audiences are often able to anticipate the plot. Because society changes, there will ultimately be a new prevalent style. But this often happens slowly and needs a leader.

A. Plot elements in realism and naturalism are, in theory, based on life experiences and are, therefore, not arranged and organized. But, in practice there is a carryover from the structure of the "well-made play" and the general nature of story telling, that calls for some arrangement of plot elements. The emphasis, however, goes to realistic characters because of an interest in the psychology of human beings.

B. Characters are drawn from everyday, average, normal people and show the inner life and depth of character. The characters in these plays are more middle class and lower middle class than in the plays of the past. This is partly to coincide with the economic status of the people who attend today's theatre.

C. Themes often involve domestic relations, home problems or romances that are of concern to the audience.

D. Dialog is usually believable as everyday speech with pauses, repetitions, interruptions, and short speeches.

E. Settings and props often show us life in living rooms or sitting rooms, which are filled with details of daily life such as coffee cups, books, telephones, etc.

F. Stage action usually shows, or is involved with small, natural, detailed business.

There are hundreds of fine examples among the early pioneers. Some playwrights who had an early influence were Anton Chekhov in Russia who wrote *The Seagull, The Three Sisters* and *The Cherry Orchard.* Henrik Ibsen in Norway wrote *A Doll's House, Hedda Gabler* and *Enemy of the People,* and Swedish playwright August Strindberg wrote *Miss Julie*. These plays are still performed today by resident theatres, colleges and universities.

Social Drama

This is a style that springs from social unrest and depicts social problems and institutional failings and seeks political answers. It is often based in elements of realism or naturalism, but it also may be highly theatrical. It is built around theme: a realistic play with a message or a social conscience, which is sometimes called "agit-prop" or agitation for propaganda. The issues involved need to be timely, or they will seem dated, since social problems change or get solved while problems of poverty, crime and corruption still exist. We have fewer of these today because many current theatergoers do not find these plays "entertaining." Today's documentary filmmakers often explore social and cultural problems.

Examples of social drama are: *Waiting for Lefty*, by Clifford Odets, *All My Sons*, by Arthur Miller, and possibly *West Side Story* (book by Arthur Laurents, music by Leonard Bernstein and Stephen Sondheim, and choreography by Jerome Robbins). The acting style is realistic, honest, and has perhaps a greater than normal underlying emotional intensity.

Exercise

Write or improvise a short scene in the style of social drama. For example: The setting is a dingy kitchen. One character in a family with small children has lost a job, and the family has little or no money and not enough to eat. They discuss fighting the cruel boss or the corporation and decide to join a union or protest rally.

Expressionism

The term "expressionism" comes from the fine arts. It was coined in 1901 to serve as an explanation of the features in art such as exaggeration, distortion and grotesqueness and revolt against authority and "common sense" that defied objective or realistic presentation of everyday life. It portrayed a more surrealistic or dreamlike view of life with incongruous images and unnatural juxtapositions and combinations. Expressionism is in some ways dramatized fantasy or daydreams and in other ways night dreams with all of the Freudian symbolism. The expressionists also opposed the revival of nineteenth century romanticism and eighteenth century neoclassicism. They wanted an ethical, social and even political revolt.

Expressionism in drama is built around theme rather than plot and characters. The themes are based on grim views of modern society with somewhat dehumanized or robot-like characters that often portray modern mankind's isolation and victimization in a modern worker's world. The characters are often symbols that have conflicts when trying to change society into a utopian world. The acting style in expressionism is exaggerated, grotesque, intense, and somewhat abstract. Sometimes masks are used, along with monologs, choral chants and non-realistic sets. The characters often deliver lines directly to the audience in a stream-of-consciousness way as an external projection of an inner emotional state.

Examples of expressionism can be found in the art of Picasso and the cubists, Jean Cocteau and the novels of James Joyce. In drama, Jean Paul Sartre, the expressionist philosopher, wrote *No Exit*. Other expressionist plays include *Morn Till Midnight*, by Georg Kaiser, *R.U.R. (Rossums Universal Robots)*, by Karol Capek, *The Adding Machine* and *Dream Girl*, by Elmer Rice and *The Hairy Ape*, by Eugene O'Neill. The later avant-garde writings of Berthold Brecht also used elements of expressionism. Expressionism was the forerunner of Theatre of the Absurd. This style is very theatrical.

We have also seen this point of view in many science fiction-type movies that involve robots, grotesque monsters, invasions from outer space and catastrophic views of the world. An example might be *Star Wars*.

Exercise

Write or improvise a short scene in the style of expressionism. For example: Two office workers with abstract names: Office Worker No. 1 and 2 or Typist and Clerk. They plot the overthrow of the Corporation and/or the Boss — violently. They "express" their inner personal, inner psychological frustrations: home life, and/or little cog in a big wheel feelings that result in a loss of personal identity ... directly to the audience. There is use of symbolism.

Theatre of the Absurd

This style originated as an outgrowth of cynicism in Germany after World War I, and the philosophy of existentialism in France with Jean Paul Sartre as one of the chief exponents. Existentialism dealt with disorientation, disenchantment and despair with the western world and the lack of meaning in existence. This negative philosophy was built around character types and themes that stem from the assumption that the world is an absurdity.

Characters are pure theatre types: tramps and clowns with opposite or conflicting character traits: generous and greedy, master and slave, sadist and masochist. They discuss universal values abstractly or universally. They use one- or two-word sentences with repetition or long speeches. There is more use of pauses, or rapid-fire delivery or long monologs. The acting style is more theatrical with exaggerated, possibly unreal movement and speech rhythms.

Examples of theatre of the absurd plays: *Waiting for Godot*, by Samuel Beckett, *The Sandbox*, by Edward Albee and *Rhinoceros*, by Eugene Ionesco.

Chapter 19
Improvisation II: Creating Your Own Scenes

Different Objectives

Situations Involving People with Different Objectives

Two people choose a situation in which they have contrasting or opposing objectives or intentions. Each person tries to persuade the other one to do what s/he wants. Plan the scene so that the opposing objectives are clear, reasons are valid and stage action adds to personal intentions. Examples of situations:

1. "How to spend an evening." One person wants to study for an exam and the other person wants to go to a movie, watch TV or visit friends. Each can give a reason for the other to do what s/he wants. For instance, if Character A needs to study to pass a test in a course to get a better grade, or can't go out on school nights, etc., and Character B wants to see the movie because of a favorite movie star in it, and it's going to close, etc. As each tries to convince and persuade the other person, A may even do such things as continue to study or turn on music and B may read good reviews of the movie or offer to pay for the ticket.

2. "Buying and fixing food." Two people are talking about making a grocery list to buy food or planning to fix food, possibly for a small party. One loves food and eats everything including junk food. The other person is health conscious and on a diet and reads the labels on boxes to see how many calories and how much fat content is in everything.

3. "Cleaning a house." Two people are put in charge of cleaning a whole house. They will be paid. One is task-oriented and wants to finish. The other one is lazy and messy. They can't agree who cleans what room and how.

4. "Decorating a room." Two people are going to decorate a room. One wants to paint it one color and use pop culture and posters, and the other one wants it to look like an office or bed and breakfast with antiques. This can also include furniture arrangements.

5. "College bound." Two people are deciding what and where to go to college. They want to go to the same college, but each is choosing a different college because of strength in particular subject

areas and interest in future career opportunities. There is also a difference in college tuition at the two colleges.

6. "Angry and getting even." Character A is angry about not getting cast in a play or not making a sports team or getting a bad grade in a course and wants to get even. Character B is trying to keep A calm to protect the person who made this decision and convince A it was his/her own fault. Or, they both want to get even and can't agree on a plan of how to do it.

7. "Allergies." Character A is allergic to something that Character B is doing, and B won't quit. B could be dusting, smoking, building a fire, using perfume or paint thinner, arranging flowers or even wanting to let a stray cat into the house.

8. "Sports enthusiasts." Character A wants to play golf, and Character B wants to play tennis. Arguments can be on the basis of time, money, equipment or skills, health and enjoyment of the sport.

9. "Fun seeker." It's late at night and Character A wants to do something that's "fun," before going home. But it could be risky. Character B wants to get home right away and is fearful parents will already be angry.

10. "Packing for vacation together." Two people will be traveling to many places on their planned trip. Character A wants to take clothes that are appropriate for sports and beaches, and Character B wants to go to a city and take clothes for going to plays, museums and musical concerts.

11. "Confidence and insecurity." Character A is totally unsure of himself or herself and doesn't think s/he will ever get a role in a play, get a good job, go to a good college or pass a test. (Pick one.) Character B is fully confident and plans to try out, interview or apply for one of the above.

12. "Possessions." Two people who have been sharing an apartment for some time are now going different directions and need to move. They bought some things together and gave each other gifts. Now they are moving out and have to divide everything. Since every item has a history they can't agree on who gets what.

13. "Dressing for a costume party." The theme of the party is "famous people in history," "poverty," "comic book characters," "funky" or some other theme. Both look through closets and collection of costumes and props, try things on and look at themselves in the mirror. Both want some of the same items and give reasons why a particular item is more right for them.

14. "Inheritance." A relative and two people are going through boxes of leftover items in the attic. They have to clear the house for sale, so they have to take everything or give it away. They both want some items and both reject some items. Neither one wants to be responsible for the rejected items. This could involve old pictures, records and personal clothes.

While all of these scenes are primarily for two people, it is possible to include Character C with another objective or as a negotiator between the opposing objectives. (For more improvisational possibilities look again at Chapters 9 and 15.)

Make a Story
1. Divide into groups of five to eight.

2. Using all the words in the group write a scenario or outline of a story from these words. These words lend themselves to:

Group 1: Melodrama	Group 2: Farce	Group 3: Sentiment
1. Gold	1. Hiding	1. Love
2. Townspeople	2. Mistake	2. Animal
3. Daisies	3. Chase	3. Youth
4. Villains	4. Disguise	4. Message
5. Teardrops	5. Money	5. Accident
6. Gossip	6. Suitcase	6. Sacrifice
7. Fortune-telling	7. Jokers	7. Family
8. Your choice	8. Your choice	8. Your choice

3. Allow ten to thirty minutes to prepare.

4. Read the story to the class. Everybody listens and helps to "fix up" the story.

5. Then, each group returns to the original group and fixes it up. Each member of the group adds a character s/he wants to be in the story and writes a description of the character. (See my "Made-Up Character" in this chapter for a possibility, but not a requirement.)

6. Then, improvise all the stories. After that, put all the stories together into one big story. Choose one major plot or story line and let all the others become sub-plots in the story. Work out the major plot and minor plots and decide how they can be combined and keep your characters. Write dialog or improvise from characters and plot outlines.

Performing: Your Made-Up Character

On the form on page 266, "My Made-Up Character," create your own character. This is an opportunity to play a character of your own creation, some type of secret person you've always wanted to perform.

Once you have created a personal character, perform this character in a variety of improvised scenes. It is possible to come to class in character and react to events that happen.

Join with others in creating a scene. This might be a group scene or something in the vein of a class reunion. (See Chapter 9.)

Improvising Types of Drama

Creating Your Own "Western" or Melodrama

A "Western" is one type of melodrama that often has the cowboy as the hero, and is set in the western part of the United States in the latter part of the 19th century, when the country was moving westward and being settled.

1. Divide the class into groups of six to twelve students each.

2. Tell them to make a story of the old west — a "Western." Typical elements of this type of play are:

Characters (Who):

Hero (the cowboy)	Heroine
Funny friend of hero	Funny friend of heroine
Father of heroine	Villain
Sheriff	Practical jokers
Townspeople	Fortune teller
Undertaker	Town banker
Gossips or old maids	Dance hall girls
The schoolteacher	Old prospector

Story (What):

Secret	Rumor
Money or gold	Disguise
Map	Love
Patent medicine	Law and order
Treasure	Revenge
Chase	Hiding
Coffin	Showdown

My Made-up Character

(Create a character you would like to perform.
Read the whole form before beginning, then complete.)

Your Name: _____

Name of Your Character (Make it sound like the character. Go by sounds and ideas and suggested character traits. The newspaper and phone book are good sources for ideas.): _____

Age:_____ Gender:_____ Where Born: _____

Brief Description of Character's Personality and Emotional Traits (See Chapters 13–16): _____
_____
_____

Physical/Vocal Description — Body and Voice (general appearance, posture, walk, gestures, voice quality, accents and diction, etc.): _____
_____
_____
_____
_____

Character's Occupation/Career/Job (Other than student):_____

Social, Cultural, Educational, Financial Background: _____
_____

Character's Wants, Needs, Hopes, Desires, Goals and Objectives: _____
_____

Problems, Worries, Fears, Flaws and Secrets: _____
_____
_____

Relationships (Describe friends/opposing forces or obstacles): _____
_____
_____

Hobbies (Use of leisure time): _____
_____
_____

Stage Business (That expresses character): _____
_____

Other Details of Character: _____
_____
_____
_____

266

Contest	Hate
Mortgage	Stolen
Fight	Gun
Drink	Funeral
Fear	Discovery
Murder	Counterfeit
Arson	Ambush
Blackmail	Torture
Kidnap	Cards

Settings (Where):

Saloon	Street of town
In parlor of heroine's house	Bank
Town Square	Other

3. Each student should develop a character that includes the character's name, age, occupation, personality, physical traits, possible animal that character is like, prop that is used by character (such as a cane, umbrella, hat, glasses) and the wishes and fears of the character which include the goals or main objective in the play. (See "My Made-up Character" in this chapter.) After starting with a general choice, be as specific as possible.

4. Each group chooses as many words from the "Story" category as they have characters. Then, by combining the words they make a story. All words have to be used. Note: If you decide who the villain is, what he or she did to whom (and why), and how the play ends, then much of the playwriting (or plotting) is solved. If the story is set in motion, then sub-plots can be explored and the play will still hold interest.

5. Each group is allowed enough time to work on a satisfying outline. As long as you are working on the story, you may continue. Then, each group reads its story to the whole class and everyone listens and helps "fix up" the story. (This is product improvement. Remember, it's the story of the group who wrote it, so don't let someone do something to the story that is not approved by the group who originally created the story.)

6. When everyone in your group seems ready, perform your play by improvising the dialog. Then, fix it up. (It is possible to put all the stories together and make one story. Choose one major plot or story line and let all of the other story lines become sub-plots in the story. Work out the major plot and minor plots and decide how they can be combined while still keeping your characters. Then,

write the dialog or improvise dialog on the basis of character and plot outlines.)

7. Then, working from the description of the character and improvising dialog on the basis of character and story outline of the play, rehearse your group's play until it feels polished, and it is finally "ready." Perform it for the group and possibly students in other classes.

The Mystery
"The Case of the Backstage Robbery"

A western is one type of melodrama. A mystery is another. It is an exaggerated comedy in the sense that it has exaggerated or stock type characters. It is built around an exciting suspenseful plot with a fear for everyone's welfare. There's the villain (the persecutor or murderer), the victim or victims (often a heroine) and the detective (the hero or rescuer of other potential victims).

The Situation. A group of community citizens are involved in a local theatre production. Choose seven or more students to be actors in the cast and seven students to be members of the theatre staff working on the production. Something of value is stolen from backstage, and everyone plays detective in determining who did it.

Sequence. Everyone stands or sits in a circle facing inward with eyes closed. The facilitator circles behind the group and quietly taps once on the back of the person designated to be "The Thief" and twice on the back of the person who is robbed. Everyone opens his or her eyes. No one should know who the thief is.

At this point, either the facilitator announces what was stolen, or the person who was robbed chooses what was stolen. Either way, the person who was robbed says, "I was robbed."

Suggestions of possible items stolen:

    A wallet or purse (with credit cards)

    Cash

    Jewelry: ring, watch, pearls or diamonds

    A piece of clothing or a costume

    A valuable prop that was loaned to the cast

    A controversial book

    A prescription medicine

Everyone a Detective. If any members of the group want to know about the item stolen or the circumstances, they may investigate the robbery by asking the person who was robbed one question about the robbery to define exactly what is missing and the circumstances surrounding the robbery. This might include the value of the item stolen, the time of the robbery, where everyone was, or why someone might want the missing item.

Once the situation of the theft is clear, everyone introduces his or her character one at a time. This includes theatre staff and the actors who are in the play being presented. The actors in the play tell who they are in "real life". These characters may be based on "My Made-up Character," or they may be chosen from the following list.

Doctor	Actor
Maid/Butler	Cowboy/Cowgirl
Interior decorator	Pharmacist
Artist	Architect
Writer	Librarian
Teacher	Flight attendant
Taxi driver	Computer specialist
Business person	Athlete
Banker	Stockbroker
Realtor	Mechanic

Students who are part of the theatre staff might choose any of the following positions:

Director	Stage manager
Artistic director	Prompter
Light/Sound person	Prop manager
Set designer/Builder	Stage crew

If two people want to be the same position on the theatre staff, then the first person who chooses the role gets to be that position.

Everyone tells a few key facts about his/her character: name, age, occupation, important relationships, hobbies, sports, goals and personal faults. This needs to be brief.

The Thief. The thief needs to include something in his or her character sketch that might give some special clue as to how and why he or she committed the robbery. Some possible motives might be:

Needs money
Was rejected in romance
Wants revenge for an insult
Dislikes a cast member
Is envious of something
Is a frustrated actor
Is a kleptomaniac

For example: An expensive piece of clothing is missing and the thief runs a thrift store or goes to costume parties. Or, money is missing, and it turns out the thief's hobby is gambling in Las Vegas.

The Questioning. Each person is a detective and gets to question one person with one to two questions. Anyone can pass on questioning if s/he desires. Actors must answer truthfully, and no "detective" can ask directly or indirectly, "Did you do it?" The detectives need to remember possible motives, the relationship to the stolen item and the relationship to the person from whom it was stolen. If the thief is asked a question that is too revealing, he or she may need to come up with an alibi.

Finding the Thief. After all of the detectives have asked their questions, they write out whom they think committed the robbery. One by one, they announce who they think did it and explain their reasons for voting the way they did. The thief pretends it was someone else and only tells the truth after everyone has discussed his or her choice. Then the thief says, "My name is _____, and I did it."

Final discussion includes ways the game could be improved.

Dial a Story

For the following four activities, make a dial like the face of a clock with a spinner. Spin the hand of the dial four or five times, recording each number. Check the corresponding lists for two or three **Characters**, the **Setting/Place**, the **Scene/Situation** and the **Styles and Types** of plays or stories. (Only the first three or four numbers may be needed in some cases.) Example (first activity): Dialed numbers 3–2–10–12–4. Story elements are: Characters: 3 — Cowboy/Cowgirl and 2 — Fortuneteller; Setting: 10 — Sewer; Scene: 12 — Running away; and Style: 4 — Musical play.

#1 Character (Who)
1. Custodian
2. Teacher
3. Cowboy or cowgirl
4. Taxi driver
5. Waiter or waitress
6. Hobo or clown
7. Police officer
8. Doctor
9. Burglar
10. Librarian
11. Soldier
12. Interior decorator

#2 Character (Who)
1. Actor or actress
2. Fortuneteller
3. Beautician or barber
4. School principal
5. Maid or butler
6. Flight attendant
7. Car salesman
8. Golfer
9. Witch or devil
10. Secretary
11. Babysitter
12. Lawyer

#3 *Setting/Place* (Where)	#4 *Scene/Situation* (What)	#5 *Styles/Types* (How)
1. Amusement park	1. Surgery	1. Mystery
2. Airplane	2. Flood	2. Farce
3. Cave	3. Strange guests	3. Western
4. Library	4. Rumor	4. Musical play
5. Desert	5. Murder	5. Soap opera
6. Car	6. Illness	6. Fantasy
7. Zoo	7. Prison break	7. Tragedy
8. Movie	8. Thunderstorm	8. Make-believe
9. Department store	9. Surprise	9. Folk play
10. Sewer	10. Accident	10. Sitcom
11. Prison	11. Stolen	11. Romance
12. Moon	12. Running away	12. Sci-fi

A. Write a scenario or outline that uses these story elements.

B. Improvise or create your own dialog to act out a scene of the story line.

C. Make your own list of words to use. Or make up lists of words for another group to act out. Exchange lists.

Dial a Farce

A farce is an exaggerated comedy with exaggerated characters and situations to produce laughter and, in the case of satire, ridicule. The characters are often sub-normal, strange, bizarre, immature or fearful. They could fear loss of money, friends, death, etc. Farce is often based on mistaken identity or doing the forbidden, the unexpected or the strange. Comedy can result from conflict of opposites.

Spin the dial to select character traits and story elements (listed on the following page). A team could choose opposites by spinning one number for two characters. For example: If you dial 7, one character will be healthy, and the other will be sickly.

#1 *Character Traits*
1. Dumb
2. Neat, fussy
3. Always hungry
4. Negative, complaining, rude
5. Nasty, angry
6. Naughty, mischievous
7. Healthy
8. Childish
9. Clumsy
10. Does crazy things
11. Practical, rational
12. Sweet

#2 *Opposite Character Traits*
1. Smart
2. Sloppy, messy
3. Rarely eats
4. Positive, polite
5. Calm, polite
6. Proper, righteous
7. Sickly
8. Mature
9. Well-coordinated
10. Cautious in behavior
11. Creative, imaginative
12. Sour, bitter

Add your own opposites: innocent/know-it-all; bored with everything/interested in everything; happy-go-lucky/grouchy-complaining; quiet/noisy; angry/calm; suspicious/trusting; talkative. Characters could start a problem, add to the problem or try to resolve the problem and only make matters worse. For example: Offer food to Character #3, suggest an athletic contest for Character #9 or ask about a financial investment with Character #4.

#3 *Story/Plot (Subject of scene)*
1. Blackmail
2. Hiding
3. Messiness
4. Eavesdropping
5. Secret meeting
6. Money
7. Mistaken identity
8. Danger
9. Chase
10. Fibbing
11. Teasing/mimicking
12. Disguise

#4 *Setting/Place (Where)*
1. Zoo
2. Office
3. School
4. Living room
5. Beach
6. Hospital
7. Car
8. Hotel
9. Department store
10. Restaurant
11. Basement/attic
12. Playground

Write an outline that uses the story elements you dialed.

Improvise or create your own dialog to act out the scene of the outline.

Dial a Soap Opera

A soap opera (or sentimental drama) is a serious type of drama that appeals to the feelings and emotions rather than reasons and thought. The characters are often family members or close friends or loved ones who are involved in concerns of deep human feelings (love, hate, joy, sadness, suffering) that intensify their relationships. Some of these concerns are birth, marriage, death, accident, illness, love, hopes, fears, misunderstandings, etc.

#1 Character Trait	#2 Character Trait
1. Worried	1. Fault-finding
2. Whiny	2. Fearful
3. Sad/lonely	3. Tearful
4. Threatening	4. Hateful/nasty
5. Nervous	5. Shy
6. Irritable	6. Sensitive/hurt
7. Innocent	7. Arrogant/haughty
8. Icky sweet	8. Sympathetic/consoling
9. Proud/vain	9. Pouting
10. Sloppy/messy	10. Unsure/indecisive
11. Sarcastic	11. Dreamy
12. Secretive/suspicious	12. Dumb

If a third character is desired, dial again from list #1 or #2 to choose a trait for the third character or simply choose your own trait.

Establish relationships to give an added dimension: family — brother, sister, mother, father, aunt, uncle, grandparent; school — teacher, principal, counselor, coach; hospital — doctor, nurse, etc.; other — classmate, friend, co-worker, enemy, boss.

#3 Story/Plot (Subject of Scene)	#4 Setting/Place (Where)
1. Accident/injury	1. Hospital
2. Blackmail	2. Park
3. Special occasion (birthday, etc.)	3. Living room
4. Disappointment	4. Kitchen
5. Gossip/rumor	5. Car
6. Missing person	6. Porch
7. Apology	7. School
8. Illness/suffering	8. Office
9. Lie	9. Café or drugstore
10. Love/romance (lost)	10. Movie theatre
11. Sacrifice/failure (pick one)	11. Garage or carport
12. Death	12. Funeral parlor

Optional choices: mistake, money, revenge, stolen item, reuniting with an old friend.

Dial a Romantic Drama/Fantasy

Romantic drama has a spirit of idealism and revolution. (Not romance in the sense of love.) The characters are usually of nobility or high station, characters such as kings and queens and knights. They often speak in stylized, grandiose and sometimes poetic language. The settings are in far away, idealized places such as castles, and forests. For example: *Sleeping Beauty, The Three Musketeers,* and *Robin Hood.*

Fantasy has imaginative make-believe characters such as angels, fairies, ghosts, giants, elves, spirits, dwarfs and gnomes. The settings are generally unrealistic: magic forests, fairyland — even heaven and hell. Both of these types were popular in the Medieval Period and while they never fully faded, gained new stature in the late eighteenth century up to the beginning of the twentieth century.

Romantic Drama and Fantasy are often combined. For example: *Snow White and the Seven Dwarfs* and *A Midsummer Night's Dream.*

In dialing characters, the performers may choose two or three solely from Romantic Drama or solely from Fantasy, or they may mix them up — choosing one or more from each.

#1 Romantic Drama Characters	*#2 Fantasy Characters*
1. Magician	1. Dwarf
2. Personal servant	2. Giant
3. Wise fool	3. Robot
4. Lord or lady	4. Ghost
5. Good knight or good maiden	5. Sorcerer
6. Blacksmith or hounds keeper	6. Angel
7. Court jester	7. Satan or devil
8. Stable keeper	8. Marionette
9. Cook or scullery maid	9. Vampire
10. Evil knight or evil maiden	10. Beast
11. Queen or king	(for example: werewolf)
12. Governess, nanny or nurse, teacher or doctor	11. Witch or warlock
	12. Saint

Other possibilities, choices or substitutes might be: god or goddess, elf (mischievous fairy), troll (fabled dwarf, giant, demon or monster that lives in caves or hills) gnome (misshapen dwarf), evil spirits or android.

#3 Place/Settings (Where)
1. Kitchen of castle
2. King's chambers
3. Tent (at jousting tournament)
4. Drawbridge by moat
5. Forest
6. Weaver's room
7. Throne room
8. Tower room
9. Armor room
10. Stable
11. Servants' quarters
12. Battlements

#4 Plot/Story (What)
1. Sacrifice
2. Miracle
3. Power
4. Dangerous threat
5. Kidnapping
6. Suicide
7. Magic spell
8. Conniving, sinister plot
9. Revenge
10. Honor
11. Evil menace
12. Adoption

Create Your Own Play

Now that you have explored types and styles of drama, elements and structure of the play and techniques of character development, you are ready to create your own play. You can also become the playwright, the actors, the directors and even the set planners.

There are many possible starting points: choosing a type or style of play, key characters (protagonist and antagonists or an ensemble) or a premise or theme as the basis of what the play is about. You can use "My Made-up Character" to create your own character within the chosen framework. Or you can build a story or plot line and then determine what characters are needed to be part of this plot.

This can all be worked out through group efforts. It is possible that your large class group may need to break down into several smaller groups that create their own shorter plays. This may take time to get started on the central project, but once you make some basic decisions, it should go more smoothly. So as you become playwrights, directors and actors for your own longer plays, good luck. I mean, "Break a leg!"

Film Acting

Chapter 20
Acting On-stage for an Audience Versus Behaving for the Camera

In one sense, acting is acting or playing a character is playing a character, whether it's for stage or film. And there are similarities between acting on-stage for an audience and behaving for the camera. In another sense, there are definite differences for the actor in each medium in terms of size of performance, relation to audience and camera, rehearsal preparation, continuity and emphasis on techniques needed.

Show and Tell

The two mediums of stage and film are mostly contrasted in terms of "show and tell." As a generalization of emphasis, the film mostly shows character and story elements and physical action that a stage play mostly tells through dialog.

The Stage

There is often one set with actors moving in a limited space, and the characters, plot, and themes are developed primarily through dialog, that makes it more of an auditory medium or "tell" to an audience.

The actors on-stage are real people moving and talking, and you identify with these characters on a conscious level in real time. As an audience member watching a full stage production, you can select and focus on a variety of different elements: the set, the characters speaking, the reaction, the costume, etc. But you are always at the same relative distance from the action on-stage. And, performances can change slightly each time the actors perform for a limited audience.

Film

Because visual images are such a large element in the story, most of the story is told through a visual medium or "show" to a camera. Film is more about showing the story of the characters and the plot visually through physical action in many locations that are appropriately described as "moving pictures."

The fragmented images that make up film move at a different pace than reality, and are more closely associated with the sub-conscious state or dreams. And sometimes — particularly in the case of commercials — the pictures are flashed images. The images may be larger than life as in motion pictures or relatively the same size as in TV. The camera shows people at different distances and frequently shows people at a much closer range than they would be seen in a theatre. After the final editing in film, the images are patched together and do not change. The camera is an audience of one that becomes many people — all seeing the same performance — when the film is shown.

Size of Performance

One often noted difference between stage acting and film acting is a matter of size. It is generally said that acting on-stage is bigger, and acting for the camera is smaller. That is, large performance vs. small performance. While that has some truth, it is also an oversimplification that is not totally accurate.

For Stage

As you all know by now, when performing in the theatre, the stage actor needs to project body movement, facial expression, voice and emotions to an audience that is sitting approximately twenty to seventy feet away from front to back, and perhaps thirty to fifty feet wide, depending on the size and shape of the audience area. The audience is at the same relative distance from the stage throughout the whole performance.

Since this generally requires a larger sized performance in body, voice and emotional intensity to be projected over a large area, the stage director often needs to say to a performer, "Louder!" "Can't hear!" or "Play it bigger!" The size of the performance and projection is somewhat less important in smaller, more intimate theatres. While both stage and film require an emotional intensity, the emotions for stage usually need to be larger or projected further and wider, because the size of and distance to the audience is greater.

For Film

Film presents a different problem for an actor. Instead of an audience being twenty to seventy feet away, the frequent practice of filming a scene calls for a variety of different camera positions at different distances, and therefore the audience views the action that way. This can mean the actor needs to make some change in the size of performance to accommodate the distance of the camera. For instance, a scene could start with a *master shot, establishing shot* or *long shot,* which might be thirty-five to sixty feet or more away in order to take in a large scene. This is like performing in a large theatre, but focused toward the camera.

Then, the camera moves into a fifteen to thirty-five foot range, perhaps like a small to midsize theatre, and films the same scene in a *medium shot.* As the camera moves closer, the performance needs to come down in size, and the performer needs to play it smaller, but still toward the single camera.

After that, the scene could be in a close-up with the camera just four to fourteen feet away focusing intimately on the actor. This could be from waist to head, shoulder and head, possibly over the shoulder of each performer or just the head or full face in the scene. Under these conditions the actor needs to adjust to the closer distance of the camera by projecting a smaller, more intimate performance with body, voice, thoughts and emotions. This means that "less is more" in facial expression, gesture, voice and emotional intensity or performing generally.

Acting for Film: Body, Voice, Thoughts and Emotions

Size and Speed of Movement

When the camera is at close range, the size of your physical movements needs to be smaller, slower, simpler, tighter and more controlled. Controlled, slower movements are important because, up close, fast movement can appear exaggerated or become a blur. With the camera at close range, it can pick up and record even the slightest movement or spontaneous gesture as well as character traits.

If your head fills the screen, then every involuntary facial expression, inner thought or movement is magnified tenfold. For motion picture screens, the head may be twenty feet high. And, in raising an eyebrow a quarter inch, it would go up about three inches on the huge screen.

The projection of body movement, facial expression and gestures are generally very intimate and narrowly focused and projected toward the camera lens. When the performance is "low key" and "intimate," then the relation to the other characters and the camera is intimate. Being intimate is being close, not only to the camera, but also to the other person.

Distance from Other Actors

In life ... and on the stage, people stand three to ten feet or more apart when talking to each other. But, on film this doesn't look natural. If you do this, you may not be in the same frame of the picture. So, if two people are playing a scene together and having a "normal conversation" they need to stand much closer than normal in order to be in the same picture. Actors on soap operas are about six to twelve inches apart in order to look natural and appear in the same frame together.

"Hitting the Marks"

The actors who move from one place to another may need to "hit the marks." That is, the performers arrive physically at a predetermined point or marks on the floor, so they'll be in the right place for the lights and camera.

"Matching the Action"

The "talent" also needs to "match the action." That is, when the same scene is filmed at different distances, they need to perform the same action in a long shot, a medium shot and a close-up. But in doing the same action, they will need to do it smaller as the camera moves closer.

Even if the camera is at the same distance and there are many "takes" of the scenes, there needs to be a consistency of performance so that the film's editor can cut to make the scene's flow of action believable.

"Line of Vision"

When looking at the person with whom you are playing the scene, look at the eye toward the camera. On-stage this applies to the audience. Once that is established, don't look at the other eye or lips. It is possible to look away, but when you look back, focus on the same eye that is toward the camera. And practice relaxing and keeping your blinking at a minimum.

Voice and Sound

The voice for film acting doesn't need to be as loud or project as far or diverse as voice projection for stage. Since "the audience" is the camera, which is often close, you can speak naturally and intimately in a conversational tone, as if talking to a friend.

At times, this low-key natural, almost "super real" low volume, low pitch delivery can almost become an intense whisper with controlled intensity. And when playing a character, it's generally advisable to speak slightly slower with more pauses and more detailed thoughts than onstage in order to help the editor when cutting the film. However, when filming commercials, you may need to talk faster to finish in a limited time.

Another factor to be considered is that your voice is recorded, and the sound engineer can make it louder or softer depending on the needs of sound. In fact, sometimes in filming, the visuals and the voices and the sound are not even recorded at the same time. It's possible to film some actors without even recording the dialog or sound.

Then, later, after the film is developed and edited, "voice-overs" are recorded to match the picture and the movement of the mouth. This might be done when actors are in noisy crowds or at a distance where filming and recording sound at the same time is difficult. This is also done in musical productions when the principal lead doesn't sing very well. Or, it is used in animated films and cartoons where there are no live actors. Or, a foreign language movie may be "dubbed" in English using new dialog in lip-syncing. Frequently, sound effects are also added later as is background music.

Thoughts and Listening

Film acting, or behaving for the camera is, to a large extent, about photographing the thoughts and reactions of actors. Remember, the eyes are the mirror of the soul and can show what the mind is thinking. While thinking before you speak and registering with thoughts about what you hear while you listen is important for playing all characters in all acting situations, it is crucial for film acting because film acting calls for simple, controlled, natural behavior and honesty of thoughts in short scenes.

It is tremendously important to be thinking at all times. Because the close camera is less forgiving than the stage, you need to take your time to listen, react and then speak. Stay focused on your character and the relationships in the scene in order to react

283

truthfully to the moment and project the performance to the camera. If you're honestly thinking and feeling the character, the camera will see it.

If you have few or no lines in a scene, think what you would say if you did speak. This may register even more strongly than if you have lines to say. (Review Chapter 8.)

Emotions

For close-ups in film it's important to convey inner turmoil, anguish and distress without doing a lot of acting, and reacting. At least, do not act in any usual large stage way, or it will be overdone.

In fact, acting for film is probably what you shouldn't do. If you try to show the emotion, the camera (audience) will see you trying to show it, and then the viewer won't believe you because you are acting instead of behaving naturally and thinking honestly. *In film ... as in life,* if you are not honest, or if you overact or try to "impress the lens," it will not believe you, trust you or like you.

Film directors who encounter stage actors frequently need to say to them: "Don't act," "Take it down," "Less is more," "Talk softly, but think hard," "Do nothing. There! — That's it!"

Inner thoughts of controlled emotions may be quietly expressed through looks and glances to show many nuances of character. You can show as much anger on film with the flicker of an eyebrow as you can on-stage by larger gestures and speaking loudly with great emotional intensity. The proper amount of emotion depends how intense the character is and the distance to the camera. If the emotion needs to be intense for the character but controlled for the camera, you can "put a cap" on the size of the emotion as you think the thoughts connected with the character and scene.

If you are playing a scene with someone who is emoting too much, it is wise not to play it bigger than the other actor, in order to outdo the other actor. But instead, it is usually better to play your part with less intensity, or underplay the scene in terms of size. And you mustn't watch yourself or listen to yourself perform or mug for the camera. Film acting calls for extreme and often simple honesty and truth.

Of course, it always depends on the story. An intense action-adventure film, Biblical movie or classic Greek or Shakespearean drama, in motion picture filming will probably call for a larger vocal, physical and emotional range than a smaller TV soap opera, kitchen drama or personal relation story.

Relating to the Camera and Direction

Acting or performing for a camera seems to call for a special, almost indefinable quality or *charisma*. The camera seems to love you, or it doesn't. And it doesn't necessarily have much to do with good looks or even good acting. But the audience almost instantly senses whether you have that quality or not. And while the camera seems to like some people better than others, most film actors have a respect for the camera lens. Some actors, in showing respect for the camera, have greeted or saluted the camera, and one actress was known to psychologically "make love to the lens."

Performing in front of the camera is frequently being yourself, which means the more you are like the character the less you have to act. That's why Hollywood does so much typecasting and often promotes a film with publicity that "So-and-so actor *is* The Character." This implies the actor is living the role truthfully.

In acting for the camera, the performance is projected to a camera lens as if you are sharing the performance with a personal friend. *As in life,* you don't need to act, perform or be something you're not for a friend. *For film ... as in life,* it is good to behave naturally and speak intimately with controlled intensity as you psychologically include or project your performance in the direction of the camera as if it is a friend. It can be helpful in projecting your performance to the camera by looking at the camera-side eye when playing a close scene with another actor.

Direction and Projection of Performance

To better understand how specific this focus of direction in film acting is, there is the story of one director — sitting near the camera lens — watching a skilled actor perform. The director said to the actor that he, the director, didn't feel anything while he was watching the actor perform the scene. But the actor assured the director he was playing the scene to the camera lens (which is the audience) and not to him.

And sure enough, when the director watched the *dailies* (the showing of the unedited film from the previous day), the actor's thoughts, emotions and performance were right there on film, even though they were felt no place else in the studio. (See "Including the Audience" in Chapter 8, and the section on "Thinking" in the Chapter 13.)

There have been occasions when some film company or a friend of a cast member have had the idea to film a live stage play — with film or a camcorder — while it is being performed in front of a live audience. The actors play their performances to the live audience, and the audience feels involved. But later, in viewing the film, nothing is felt because the camera was only recording a group of actors performing a play in front of an audience, at a distance. It looks almost nothing like a film usually looks because the performers were projecting to the audience — not the camera. The result is frequently a disappointment.

Memorizing, Rehearsal and Continuity
Stage Plays

The rehearsal for a full-length stage play is frequently on the set where the play is going to be performed or in a temporary rehearsal space. It is usually two to three hours a day, four to five days a week for a period of four to six weeks. In rehearsing a stage play during this period, the director and cast members work together to analyze and explore the play's themes, plot development, each character's traits and motivations. While they memorize their lines, block the action and create stage business, they slowly establish their relationships with other cast members in order to create a cohesive ensemble and develop a smooth continuity for the whole play.

The cast needs to memorize and retain lines for the whole play and be able to perform it without stopping. These scenes may be rehearsed out of sequence, but they are performed from the beginning of the story to the middle and to the end in a logical, continuous flow of character and plot development. This presentation builds in a natural, normal, continuous sequence to the conclusion over a two-hour period.

Stage actors spend more time rehearsing scenes and much less on technical aspects. Actors on-stage don't need to be concerned about hitting their marks, where the cameras are located or sound recording. Most actors are not miked (microphone on-stage or person), but instead use their own voices. Stage lighting is more general than specific since the actors are not being photographed.

Industrials, Commercials and Short Films

Depending on the nature of the filming: Industrials/Commercials, TV, documentary film, short film or feature film, and rehearsals for films are quite different than stage rehearsals.

The most likely involvement in film for students would be

industrials (which are in-house training films) or *commercials* (which are for commercial products or business). You are probably cast because you are "a type." You look a certain way or have a quality that is right for the director and are called *the talent*.

Acting for commercials or industrials not only may require line-perfect, ready-to-perform actors (from the beginning), but also have few or no rehearsals on a one-day shoot. *The shoot* is going to some location to do the filming. This takes place in one long eight to twelve hour day, even for a thirty second or one minute result.

In these situations, you may be given a short script in advance (a day or two before the "shoot") and be expected to have it memorized upon arrival. Or, you may be given the script on your arrival for the shoot and be expected to memorize it quickly. Or, you may be able to read it from a position off-camera. Since commercials need to fit a time slot, you may be asked to speed up your delivery to get the most commercial message in the least amount of time. In these cases, all the research and preparation are left up to the performer and does not encourage much character development or interpretation before filming begins.

Feature Length Films

In preparation for a full-length film the best directors might have a one- to four-week rehearsal period before filming begins. But many directors do not. This is due to time constraints or concerns about other aspects of pre-production that involve the script, the budget, shooting locations, etc. And there is the expectation that professional actors will prepare on their own and be ready to perform, line perfect, when the filming begins.

Once at the shoot, there is usually a lot of waiting around and getting ready to perform with only a small amount of rehearsal, if at all, because the director is then frequently busy on the set with all the technical aspects of the production. This involves preparation of the set, lights and microphones for recording sound and camera placement for the best angles. Lighting a scene for the actors, particularly in close-ups, is quite precise.

Still, actors need to be fresh and spontaneous and adaptable to possible changes in script and interpretation and totally focused on their lines at the right level of thought and emotion when the actual performing for the camera begins.

In order to conserve energy and stay focused while waiting, many skilled film performers like to stay alone, quiet and calm in order to achieve an inner stillness and stay focused. Since film acting calls for more subtlety, restraint and subtext, particularly during close-ups, performers need to stay relaxed physically, but focused mentally to be in control of the low but intense level of emotion. They think about their characters and run lines.

There are usually fewer lines to memorize because film is more of a visual medium, and the filming is in short, intense takes one scene at a time. Then, after the scene is filmed satisfactorily, there may be no reason to remember the lines. But, it's best to be ready to perform any part of the script at any time.

One advantage to film is that the scenes are not all done on the same day. Even after filming begins, the filming usually involves many short, interrupted scenes or segments of film that are called *takes*. And there are frequently many short or interrupted takes of the same scene, because there are needed changes in the lights, or camera angles, or sound recording, or actors "fluff their lines." So the same scene may be performed and filmed again and again from several different angles and distances in order to get it right.

It has been noted by a long-time director, as a generalized pattern, that many actors get their performances right on the first or second takes. But, if not, it's then about the seventh or eighth take. An explanation for this might be that if the characterization doesn't work right away, an actor can have a tendency to get self-conscious and have a need to use several more takes as a rehearsal time to become relaxed, confident, comfortable and involved in the character.

What becomes important is to get all the needed scenes "in the can," or recorded film in the canister, before the final "wrap" or the end of filming.

Filming Conditions
Shooting Sequence

One of the most difficult things to adjust to in filming is the practice of shooting out of sequence in order to accommodate a variety of situations and conditions of movie making. This may be done because of availability of locations, weather, availability of cast members, availability of film equipment, lights, camera, budget, script changes, deadlines and any number of other reasons.

Because of many of the reasons above, the filming sequence of a story may go from the breaking up of a romance, to the wedding reception, to the first meeting of the young couple, to a showdown between two guys over the girl, followed by a pre-wedding ceremony. When the scenes are not in sequence, it can be difficult for an actor to perform with the exact needed emotional level that each scene requires. Sometimes the schedule is changed at the last minute and calls upon surprised actors to be line perfect for scenes they haven't even studied or rehearsed. This situation requires not only a quick study of lines, but also a good memory for the emotional level and most probably conducting your own rehearsals.

Locations

Any number of factors may cause locations to change the shooting schedule. Sometimes there are problems in availability of locations that cause changes in the sequence of shooting. For instance, when filming on location, there could be a problem with permits to film in a neighborhood. Or, the owner of the property may not agree on some aspect of the arrangements. If a set is being built and decorated, it may not be finished and ready.

While some filming is done in a studio (like most TV), many of today's film stories take place in, and are filmed on location in, many different places. But the filming process is usually organized on the basis of grouping all like locations together rather than story continuity. This is done in order to minimize change in cast and crew and setting up and moving equipment such as lights, sound, and camera.

For example, the story sequence may go from apartment to park to office then back to the apartment and then the office again. But it makes good sense to film all the apartment scenes at one time and office scenes at one time, while the sound and lighting equipment is set up, even though the scenes take place in different parts of the story.

Weather

In terms of weather, it might be feasible to film all the outdoor scenes at one time because the sun is out, or when it's raining (when the scene calls for rain). And the outdoor scenes may be one, five, nine and twelve, and indoor scenes may be three, seven, ten and eleven.

While filming outdoors, the weather may suddenly change and the continuity of the scene is interrupted. And you need to move indoors. So, the filming priorities change. And this forces a change in location and cast members and involves moving equipment.

Availability of Properties, Costumes and Equipment

Props, such as old cars, airplanes or costumes from earlier periods or military uniforms and hardware may not be available at the times needed. This may also apply to rental of lights and cameras for a low budget production. Or there may be a rush to finish filming to return the props, costumes and equipment in order to avoid creating further expenses.

Availability of Cast Members

This also may change the sequence of shooting. Key people may not be available for certain scenes because of prior commitments or illness, which can make filming in certain locations at certain times with certain actors a logistical problem. This may also apply to technicians working the film.

Editing Process

The editing process is somewhat like the editing technique used in the cut-and-paste editing on a computer. The images or fragments are arranged (patched together) to give continuity and satisfying story sense to a film that has believable characters acting in a logical motivated sequence.

Because editing involves patching film fragments, and because the film editor can make it appear that several people are playing a scene together by "cutting" from one face to another, it's possible for a performer to be reading the script from some monitor with the other characters not even being there.

Filmmakers are always looking for perfect moments so they can patch the best scenes together in the editing process for the finished film. From the many takes of a scene, the director and/or film editor choose the best of several takes to use in the final film. Because of length, or final story sequence, an actor's best scenes may end up on the "cutting room floor."

The Director and Film Acting

On-stage, the best performance you can give is not recorded, except in the minds and memory of other cast members, the director and the audience. Of course, it's possible a critic may review the performance and try to capture the performance in words. However, most of the time when rehearsing for stage, you need to rely on the stage director to evaluate your performance.

This gives you the opportunity to keep working on your character through many rehearsals and during each performance for all the different audiences in an effort to get everything as right as possible.

But film is a director's media. And the same scene may be filmed many times from different angles with different interpretations. With the director's permission, it might be possible for you to keep the scenes fresh by making minor changes in each take if they fall within the structure of the scene.

If the production company shows the "dailies" — those scenes that were filmed the day before — then this allows you to watch and evaluate your acting for the camera. You only need to get the performance right once because it's on film, and it's permanently recorded. You don't need to do it again, unless, of course, the director has something else in mind, then the scene can be re-shot to make it better.

Comedy and Drama

Charlie Chaplin, voted the best film actor of the first half of the twentieth century, said, "Tragedy is looking at life in a close-up, and comedy is looking at life at a distance." In other words, we are emotionally involved in serious drama (such as tragedy and sentimental drama) and we back off from personal emotional involvement or view comedy from a distance. In film, cameras are often used this way.

For instance, for soap operas and some serious or dramatic movies that call for emotionally intense acting, the actors are focused on the interior lives of their characters. There are many close-ups with an emphasis on inner thoughts. The actors often deliver their lines slowly with many dramatic pauses. The partial sets are dimly lit and background music is frequently supplied by heavy organ music to increase the somber tones of the drama. Method acting training that approaches character inside/out seems to be quite well suited to this genre.

Sitcoms, or situation comedies on TV are often like filming a light comedy in a small theatre. There is usually one set — frequently a living room — that is brightly lit. We often view one or more characters from head to foot and at a distance — taking in a large portion of the room. A soundtrack of audience laughter helps set the scene. Improvisational training that puts more emphasis on working outside/in keeps actors open and free with a certain amount of detachment. It's as if the actor is watching from the

291

outside while performing and not personally and emotionally involved in any deep way.

Exercise and Discussion

Watch one or more TV soap operas and one or more sitcoms. Notice the difference between acting and filming for comedies and dramas. Notice and estimate how close the actors are from each other. Did they talk with an almost whispered intimacy in the serious dramas? Was there an intimacy of line delivery and use of thoughts to fill pauses in the dialog? What was the difference in the size of the performance: body movement, voice volume, emotional intensity in both soap opera and sitcoms?

Compare soap opera style acting and filming with sitcom style acting and filming. Watch and analyze how good actors perform for the camera. Notice how many TV performers move in a controlled way. What is needed of the actor to successfully act for each genre?

Exercise: Compare Stage Technique with Film Technique

1. *Choose a short scene.* This may be a new scene or one that you have already memorized and performed for stage. It can be:

    a. A cutting from a published play

    b. A scene from a scene in the textbook

    c. An original scene or improvisation

    d. Your choice: monolog, or dialog

2. *Perform for the class/audience.* With the class seated twelve feet or more from the stage, perform with all the acting skills needed for a stage play. Play out a scene for stage. If a camcorder is available, consider filming the "stage play." Observe and discuss and evaluate the scene you have filmed and what changes need to be made for film.

3. *Make all the acting changes necessary to act the same scene for film.* Rehearse the same scene and perform it for film focusing on the techniques that have been discussed in this chapter such as:

    a. Controlling voice and movement

    b. Playing the scene in a close approximation to others

    c. Being in the right place for camera and lights

    d. Being natural and honest in thought and emotion

    e. Projecting your performance to the camera lens

4. *Perform the scene again.*

    a. With a camcorder, film the newly rehearsed scene

    b. Or, if a camcorder is not available, have several people move very close, and choose one designated audience member to "be the camera"

5. *View the performance you have filmed.* Review the differences between the two scenes and evaluate the results and the difference in performing onstage and for the camera. Discuss and critique what else needs to be changed to make it successful for the different medium.

6. *Experiment until you find the optimum acting style for a camera.*

Discussion: As an audience member, compare the good features and bad, or advantages and disadvantages involved in the following drama experiences:

1. Live theatre
2. Motion pictures at public theatres
3. TV shows including sitcoms, soap operas, dramas, murder mysteries and sports on TV, TV movies (at home) or videos and DVDs (at home)

Discuss in terms of:

1. Type of audience each attracts and your favorites
2. Accessibility of viewing (location and times of performance)
3. Price of tickets for each
4. Quality of production (acting, directing, etc.)
5. Refreshments
6. Commercials and interruptions
7. How many hours per month you watch each
8. Value of each in terms of personal growth

Appendix

In an educational program there are times when people want to know what the goals and objectives of a drama program are. Some of these people might be a department chairman, principal, some representative from the schools' district office, a school board member, a parent or a national evaluation organization. The following goals and objectives have been helpful as both a guide in teaching and explanation of the program that are being taught. Many of the exercises in this textbook fulfill these goals and objectives.

Curriculum Objectives in Drama

Special Curriculum Objectives in the area of drama are:

1. To be able to use the body (movement) and voice (sound) to communicate effectively to others in both verbal and non-verbal ways, and to receive with sensitivity what others express.

2. To develop skills in analyzing the who (characters), the what (story or plot), and the where (place or setting) in an improvisation or play and translating this information into creative characterization.

3. To develop skills in portraying characters with a variety of physical and emotional traits.

4. To be able to inventively solve problems, real and imagined, working both individually and cooperatively in small groups.

5. To develop and increase an awareness and knowledge of other societies and cultures, both past and present, which make up the American heritage and translate these into creative characterizations in order to contribute better understanding to our changing culture.

6. To develop an understanding and appreciation of drama as an art form and a sense of aesthetic judgment about the quality of a presentation.

Comprehensive Objectives for Drama

Through the exploration of drama, the student will develop an understanding of drama as an art form and will recognize and understand the interrelationship of all learning (psycho-motor, cognitive, affective and social) in the development of the whole human being.

1. The student will have the opportunity to develop perceptual skills (psycho-motor: visual, auditory, tactile, kinesthetic, olfactory, gustatory) as tools for learning in all areas of the curriculum.

2. The student will have the opportunity to acquire cognitive skills (thinking styles and concepts) necessary to interpret and respond to drama.

3. The student will have the opportunity to develop ability in creativity and problem solving through identifying problems, exploring alternatives and evaluating solutions.

4. The student will have the opportunity to develop skills and to explore options leading to careers and livelihood in drama.

5. The student will have the opportunity to develop the skills and understanding necessary to enable her or him to participate in drama as an avocation throughout a lifetime.

6. The student will have the opportunity to develop a sense of self-confidence and personal worth through successful participation in drama.

7. The student will have the opportunity to develop the psycho-motor, cognitive and social skills necessary to deal successfully with others.

8. The student will have the opportunity to recognize the importance of divergent thinking and the value of unique expressions.

9. The student will have the opportunity to grow in ability to respond aesthetically.

10. The student will have the opportunity to develop an appreciation for the dramatic works of people from other societies and cultures and, through this, gain an understanding of and a respect for others.

Bibliography and Reading List

Adler, Stella. *The Technique of Acting*. New York: Bantam Books, 1990.

Barker, Clive. *Theatre Games*. New York: Drama Book Specialists, 1977.

Barkworth, Peter. *The Complete ABOUT ACTING*. London: Methuen Drama, 1991.

Barr, Tony and Kline, Eric Stephen. *Acting for the Camera*. Boston: Allyn and Bacon, 1982. New York: Harper "Personal Library," 1986.

Barton, Robert. *Acting: Onstage and Off*. New York: Holt, Rinehart and Winston, Inc., 1989.

Belt, Lynda and Stockley, Rebecca. *Improvisation Through Theatre Sports*. Seattle, Washington: Thespis Productions, 1991.

Benedetti, Jean. *Stanislavski and the Actor*. New York: Routledge, Theatre Arts Books, 1998.

Bernardi, Philip. *Improvisation Starters*. Crozet, Virginia: Betterway Publications, Inc., 1992.

Brook, Peter. *The Empty Space*. New York: Avon Books, 1995.

Chekhov, Michael and Gordon, Mel. *On the Technique of Acting*. New York: Harper Perennial, 1991.

Cranston, Jerneral. *Dramatic Imagination*. Eureka, California: Interface California Corporation, 1975.

Charlton, James. *Charades: The complete guide to American's favorite party game*. New York: Harper and Row, 1st ed. 1983.

Dean, Alexander and Carra, Lawrence. *Fundamentals of Play Directing*. Rev. ed. New York: Holt, Rinehart and Winston, Inc., 1989.

Esslin, Martin. *The Theatre of the Absurd*. New York: Doubleday and Co., Inc., Anchor Books, 1969.

Gassner, John. *Masters of the Drama*. New York: Random House, 1954.

Hagen, Uta with Frankel, Haskel. *Respect for Acting*. New York: MacMillan Publishing Co, Inc., 1973-1978.

Halpern, Charna; Close, Del and Johnson, Kim "Howard". *Truth in Comedy*. Colorado Springs, Colorado: Meriwether Publishing, Ltd., 1994.

Hamblin, Kay. *Mime: A Playbook of Silent Fantasy*. San Francisco, California: Headlands Press, Inc., 1978.

Hartnoll, Phyllis and Found, Peter. *The Concise Oxford Companion to the Theatre*. Oxford, England: Oxford University Press, 1992.

Hartnoll, Phyllis and Brater, Enoch. *The Theatre: A Concise History*. New York: Thames and Hudson, 1998.

Hodgson, John. *The Uses of Drama: Acting as a Social and Educational Force*. London: Eyre Methuen Ltd., 1977.

Hodgson, John and Richards, Ernest. *Improvisation*. London: Eyre

Methuen Ltd., 1974.

Johnstone, Keith. *IMPRO: Improvisation and the Theatre*. London: Eyre Methuen, Ltd., 1981.

Kelly, Elizabeth Y. *The Magic IF.* Baltimore, Maryland: National Educational Press, 1973.

Lee, Robert L. *Everything About Theatre!* Colorado Springs, Colorado: Meriwether Publishing, Ltd., 1996.

Lewis, Robert. *Method – or Madness?* Samuel French, Inc., 1958.

McKeon, Richard, ed. *Introduction to Aristotle*. New York: Random House: The Modern Library, 1947.

Mekler, Eva. *The New Generation of Acting Teachers*. New York: Harper and Row: Penguin Books, 1987.

Meisner, Sanford and Longwell, Dennis. *Sanford Meisner on Acting*. New York: Vintage Books: Division of Random House, 1987.

Nelms, Henning. *Play Production*. New York: Barnes and Noble: College Outline Series, 1967.

Shanker, Harry H. and Ommanney, Katherine Anne. *The Stage and the School*. Glencoe: McGraw-Hill Company, Inc., 9th ed., 2005.

Passoli, Robert. *A Book on the Open Theatre*. New York: The Bobbs-Merrill Company, Inc., 1970.

Redgrave, Michael, Sir. *The Actor's Ways and Means*. London: William Heinemann, Ltd., 1953, 1954. New York: Theatre Arts Books, 1961.

Spolin, Viola; Sills, Carol Bleakley and Sills, Paul. *Improvisation for the Theatre*. Evanston, Illinois: Northwestern University Press, 1963-1970. London: Pitman, 1977. London: Methuen Publishing, Ltd., Reissue: 1980.

Stanislavski, Constantin. *An Actor Prepares*. Trans. Elizabeth Reynolds Hapgood. New York: Theatre Arts Books, 1948. London: Methuen Publishing Ltd., reissue, 1980, 1988.

Stanislavski, Constantin. *Building a Character*. Trans. Elizabeth Reynolds Hapgood. London: Methuen Publishing, Ltd., reissue, 1979. New York: Theatre Arts Books, reprint ed. 1989.

Stanislavski, Constantin. *Creating a Role*. Trans. Elizabeth Reynolds Hapgood. Ed. Hermine I. Popper, 1989. New York: Theatre Arts Books, 1961. London: Methuen Publishing, Ltd., reissue, 1980.

Stanislavski, Constantin. *My Life in Art*. Trans. J. J. Robbins. New York: Theatre Arts Books, 1948, 2005. London: Methuen Publishing Ltd., reissue, 1980.

Sweet, Jeffrey, ed. *Something Wonderful Right Away*. New York: Avon Books, 1977.

Tanner, Fran Averett. *Basic Drama Projects*. Topeka, Kansas: Clark Publishing Company, 1972–1999.

About the Author

Most of Jack Frakes' adult life has been involved in playwriting and teaching and directing theatre. He began his theatre career early, acting in elementary school. He joined Mary MacMurtrie's Tucson Children's Theatre for a number of years and continued to act in a variety of productions through high school, college and, later, many community theatres. Mr. Frakes is a member of the Screen Actors Guild.

After graduating from the University of Arizona as a psychology major, he took courses in speech and drama at San Diego State University, followed by graduate work in theatre at Stanford University.

Of his fourteen years teaching high school drama Mr. Frakes says, "This was a very productive period in my life and an extremely rewarding experience. I was fortunate to have many bright and talented students from that era who still remain true and valued friends." He moved on to serve as the drama coordinator for the Tucson Unified School District, where he developed curriculum and conducted acting and directing workshops for teachers and students from kindergarten through high school. During this time he was actively involved in statewide Thespian conferences.

A move to the northern California bay area in the 1980s led to Mr. Frakes serving as artistic director of a community theatre in south San Francisco, where he directed numerous productions. In 2001 he returned to Tucson, where he currently lives with his wife.

A lifetime interest in playwriting has led Mr. Frakes to numerous original productions as well as publications of four one-act plays by Samuel French: *Final Dress Rehearsal, Once Upon a Playground, Sally and Sam,* and *The Spoofydoof's Funnybone.* He is a longtime member of the Dramatists' Guild of America and meets regularly with Old Pueblo Playwrights.